# mlr

## Marxist Left Review

**Number 23 – Summer 2022**

**Editor**
Omar Hassan

**Editorial Committee**
Mick Armstrong
Sandra Bloodworth
Omar Hassan
Louise O'Shea

**Reviews Editor**
Alexis Vassiley

© Social Research Institute

Published by Socialist Alternative
Melbourne, Februrary 2022

PO Box 4354
Melbourne University, VIC 3052

www.marxistleftreview.org

marxistleftreview@gmail.com

Contributions to *Marxist Left Review* are peer-reviewed

ISSN 1838-2932
rrp. $17

**Subediting and proofreading**
Tess Lee Ack
Diane Fieldes

**Layout and production**
Oscar Sterner

**Cover**
James Plested

Printed by IngramSpark

*Marxist Left Review* is a theoretical journal published twice-yearly by Socialist Alternative, a revolutionary organisation based in Australia.

We aim to engage with theoretical and political debates on the Australian and international left, making a rigorous yet accessible case for Marxist politics. We also seek to provide analysis of the social, political and economic dynamics shaping Australian capitalism.

Unless indicated otherwise all articles published reflect the views of the individual author(s).

We rely on our readers' support to continue publication. You can help by subscribing at *marxistleftreview.org*

# mlr
**Marxist Left Review**

## Number 23 – Summer 2022

continued on next page →

## REVIEWS

OMAR HASSAN

# Editorial: Morbid symptoms

**Omar Hassan** is an editor of *Marxist Left Review*. He has been active in anti-fascist and Palestine solidarity work, and has written extensively on the Middle East.

THE FINAL MONTHS OF 2021 WERE CELEBRATED by the ruling classes across the world, and particularly in Australia, as the beginning of the end of the pandemic. They insisted that society would be returning to normal, saved by the widespread availability of vaccines. Finally it would be possible to live with the virus at minimal human, social and economic cost.

Yet before the year was up, COVID had struck back, forcing the massive celebrations planned for the New Year to be scaled back. For most people, the stroke of midnight was met not with hope but with dread, driven by rightful concern for public health and inflation-driven drops in living standards.

Omicron is driving a wave of cases that is pushing case numbers to record heights the world over. The famed "mildness" of the variant has not prevented it from driving hospital admissions in many countries, and, in Australia at least, deaths, beyond the worst days of the pandemic so far. Even if this wave subsides, there is every reason to expect a new wave or variant down the track. In the absence of a globally coordinated campaign to suppress, if not eradicate, the virus, we remain trapped in a deadly game of Russian roulette, as politicians stake millions of our lives on the unpredictable outcomes of COVID's evolutionary imperatives.

Just as the roaring 1920s became synonymous with economic and cultural flamboyance, the 2020s are set to be defined by this seemingly endless pandemic. As a result, it looks set to be a decade in which the working class is subject to the most extreme forms of oppression, exploitation and death since the world wars of the early twentieth century.

The past two years have seen the virus cut a terrible swathe through humanity. At the time of writing, researchers at the *Economist* magazine – not known for its compassion for the world's poor – estimate that 19.8 million people have been killed by COVID.[1] The pandemic is therefore approaching the death toll of World War I. As in the killing fields of Europe, so it is in the hospitals today: risks are never distributed equally. The major casualties of this virus have been workers and the poor, those who are unable to isolate themselves from dangerous environments, or lack the means to access the full spectrum of care needed to avoid, or survive, a COVID infection.

This is commonly understood as a geographical and national division between the global North and South. Hence the widespread and righteous fury at the ongoing global vaccine apartheid that denies the global South access to lifesaving treatments. There are other examples of this divide; one of the most underreported is the criminal failure of wealthy countries to cancel the debt of the impoverished, which has prevented them from engaging in desperately needed social spending. This has resulted not just in unnecessary misery through the pandemic so far, but also condemns these countries to years of lower growth in its aftermath.

Yet the crisis belies a simplistic third worldist analysis. For instance, deaths per capita in the UK and Italy are substantially higher than in their traditional imperial stomping grounds in Nigeria and Ethiopia, even taking into consideration the discrepancies in testing and reporting. Though there are of course geopolitical dynamics, a comprehensive account of this disaster requires more serious analysis with class at its centre. It is frontline and essential workers – usually drawn disproportionately from oppressed groups – who have sacrificed the most to

---

1.    *The Economist* 2021.

keep society functioning. This holds true in New York and Melbourne as much as it does in Ankara and Rio de Janeiro. In particular, health workers have borne the brunt of the past two years, facing long hours and high casualty counts, with no end in sight. Little wonder that they are leaving the industry in record numbers.

The pandemic is far from the only example of capitalism's threat to human life. The spectacle of another failed international climate conference – in a year when Texas froze and Siberia burned – was a reminder of the runaway climate crisis. The plates of world imperialism continue to shift as the West attempts to contain China's rise, even at the risk of direct military confrontation. At the same time, US weakness – real or perceived – is encouraging Putin, Xi and other players to take increasingly bold risks, most dramatically in Ukraine. Meanwhile, inflation and economic instability threaten living standards in much of the world. This is compounded in poorer nations, where higher US interest rates will turn painfully high debt repayments into insurmountable ones. To top it all off, an emboldened far right is gaining influence in much of the advanced capitalist world, riding on a wave of violent campaigns against the limited public health measures that remain in place.

Given all this, it's not surprising that a sense of doom casts a pall over society.

It is clear now that this is a protracted, era-defining crisis. While early predictions of a new great depression – made by Marxist and bourgeois economists alike back in 2020 – may have been misplaced, there is no sign that the situation is being resolved. The incredibly rapid development of the new vaccines was heralded as a panacea twelve months ago, but they have revealed themselves to be inadequate. Social distancing, lockdowns and mask mandates have been abandoned or undermined by inconsistent application. The quasi-generous payments doled out in 2020 are history. There is no section of capital that is serious about using the crisis to launch a reforming project. There will be no building back better, as indicated by Biden's pathetic defeat at the hands of Joe Manchin and an increasingly self-confident Republican party. Beyond these contingent factors, his plans for a weak Keynesian turn were thwarted by a complacent and ill-disciplined bourgeoisie, who prefer to risk a second Trump term than pay marginally more tax.

For the left, the situation is made worse by the pacification of the historic social struggles that shook the world in 2019. Some reached their limits, as with Hong Kong and Lebanon. Others were tamed into gradualist channels, as in Chile, while others, such as Belarus and Kazakhstan, were simply violently suppressed. Crucially for the Western left, the wave of struggle around the climate – and to a lesser extent, women's rights – has been completely squashed by the pandemic. There have been no new issues filling the void of mass resistance so far. Despite COVID being a workplace health and safety issue second to none, few unions have taken the opportunity to organise in defence of their members against callous bosses and governments. While teachers in Chicago and the UK have demonstrated some of the possibilities, overall the workers' movement has been notable for its passivity in the face of this unprecedented crisis. Worse, some unions have made defending the small number of anti-vax reactionaries among them a priority. For these and other reasons, the workers' movement shows few signs of a sustained revival[2] even as labour shortages and rising inflation mean that objectively, the conditions for industrial action are favourable.

Here in Australia, the Morrison government is in a struggle for its very survival. It has been badly damaged by its failure to prepare for the disastrous reopening of society, which has resulted in Australia having suffered at times the worst rates of infection, hospitalisation and deaths in the world. Morrison appears as a man adrift, his front bench having deliberately exited stage right, leaving him to face the consequences of their policy choices. It is satisfying to see this cruel and heartless monster, who once awarded himself a boat-shaped trophy for his barbaric treatment of refugees, who brought a lump of coal to parliament as if it were a sacred religious icon, and who has flirted with the anti-vax far right, thrashing around so helplessly.

Yet the hard truth is that an Albanese Labor government offers workers nothing better. Federal Labor have said and done nothing

---

2.  Henwood 2022.

to differentiate themselves from the Coalition since 2019, adopting instead a small-target strategy. They have supported each and every one of the policies and plans that led to the COVID catastrophe we currently face. They also backed the government's reactionary tax cuts for the super wealthy, and abandoned the very limited and tepid social democratic reforms championed by their former leader, Bill Shorten. Their climate policy is a hollow shell, promising nothing and refusing to offer a plan to achieve it, for fear of alienating the coal and gas industry. The state Labor premiers, who for a time carried a marginally more sensible pandemic policy in the face of corporate opposition, have now overwhelmingly capitulated to the relentless drive to reopen the economy. While WA premier Mark McGowan has maintained the minimal measure of keeping his border with the ravaged eastern states closed, he joins other Labor premiers in having failed to invest in a hospital system that could not cope with the regular healthcare needs of the country, even without COVID. Given all this, and the failure of the Greens to make themselves a force of resistance to the major parties, it will be vital that as many people on the left as possible support the Victorian Socialists campaigns in upcoming federal and state elections.

The most dynamic factor in Australian politics has been the far right. Australia, the country that has been one of the safest through-out the pandemic, has perversely become, in the twisted perspective of the global anti-vax movement, a land of tyranny and dictatorship. Boosted by this international attention, existing far-right figures joined with new faces to mobilise enormous demonstrations on a regular basis. While some on the left were confused by their appropriation of democratic discourse, the violent attack the anti-vax movement launched on the headquarters of the traditionally militant construc-tion union in Melbourne served to clarify the stakes of the moment. In a context of the largest right-wing demonstrations since the depression of the 1930s, the Campaign Against Racism and Fascism has taken small but important steps to cohere resistance to this new threat.

Faced with a difficult situation characterised by escalating crises but an inadequate response from workers and the left, it is worth returning to fundamentals. Marx's historical writings repeatedly emphasise the significance of crises in the development of human society; they lead to ruptures, instability, they open up the possibility of radical transformations, from above and below, precisely because they are subjectively devastating and destabilising for those who live through them. There would have been a revolution in Russia regardless of World War I, but the catastrophic toll of the war made success more likely, by radicalising the tsarist army and the peasantry on which it was based. A similarly terrible experience drove German sailors to mutiny in 1918, inspiring a revolution that shook the foundations of capitalism in one of the world's most important countries. The Bengal famine spurred the Indian independence movement to new heights, while the horrors of the Great Depression led millions of workers to revolutionary conclusions. Reflecting on the defeat of the 1905 revolution in Russia, Leon Trotsky describes this contradictory relationship between crisis and progress in the following moving passage:

> The whole of history is an enormous machine in the service of our ideals. It works with barbarous slowness, with insensitive cruelty, but it works. We are sure of it. But when its omnivorous mechanism swallows up our life's blood for fuel, we feel like calling out to it with all the strength we still possess: "Faster! Do it faster!"[3]

The point here is not to make predictions about impending revolutionary struggle, nor to offer pat optimism in the face of a terrible situation. Rather, it is to say that the horrors of capitalism are, in a contradictory and painful way, engines for social change. Regardless of its short-term impact, the bitter experience of the pandemic for billions of workers is itself a social fact of central importance, and will likely have substantial political implications in the years to come. Some will conclude that capitalism is a failed system, others that it is merely radically unfair, and needs drastic reform. Some will not think in terms of capitalism at all, but simply burn with rage at the murderous incompetence of their government. Without predicting the pace of developments,

---

3.    Trotsky 1907, p.292.

these dynamics can lead to struggle and opportunities for the left as well as the right.

In the meantime, as Trotsky's quote implies, the left cannot sit back and watch the capitalist machine grind on, but must attempt to make itself a factor in the historical process, at whatever scale is possible at a particular juncture. As part of this approach of building resistance wherever possible, the project of rebuilding a specifically revolutionary current is vital. For surely now, after two years of this pandemic, it is clear that belief in a humane capitalism that protects the lives and wellbeing of its population is more utopian and fantastical than a determined struggle for the revolutionary overthrow of the entire barbaric mess.

## References

*The Economist* 2021, "The pandemic's true death toll". https://www.economist.com/graphic-detail/coronavirus-excess-deaths-estimates, accessed 24 January.

Henwood, Doug 2022, "No Strike Wave In 2021", *LBO News*, 17 January. lbo-news.com/2022/01/17/no-strike-wave-in-2021/

Trotsky, Leon 1907, *1905*. https://www.marxists.org/archive/trotsky/1907/1905/

PANOS PETROU

# Dark clouds over Europe: Facing the new far right

**Panos Petrou** is a member of the DEA (Internationalist Workers' Left) in Greece, and of the editorial boards of the *Workers' Left* paper and *Kokkino* (*Red*) journal.

THE RISE OF THE FAR RIGHT and/or authoritarian political forces in countries with some sort of parliamentary rule has been a global trend in the twenty-first century. This is especially the case during the turbulent period the world has entered since the financial crisis of 2007–08. So we have seen Trump in the US, Bolsonaro in Brazil, Modi in India and Duterte in the Philippines, to list just a few examples.

Yet Europe is probably the region most affected by this phenomenon. The far right's breakthrough from the margins to the mainstream has been the rule and not an exception, as similar developments have been observed in almost every European country.

Over the past few years, both Austria and Italy have been ruled by coalition governments with far-right parties as a strong component, that is, not a "junior partner" of a dominant ally. In France, Marine Le Pen has emerged as an established and resilient political player, one who contends for governmental power at provincial and national levels.

Most countries in Eastern Europe have traditionally had a dominant presence of various reactionary political currents. This continues to be the case.

Scandinavian countries, long considered the strongholds of

social-democratic politics and progressive rule, have not been exempt. Far-right parties such as the Sweden Democrats, Finns Party, Danish People's Party and the Progress Party etc have moved from the margins to constantly secure double-digit electoral scores, and have at times provided centre-right governments with the parliamentary support they need to survive. The same applies to central European countries that were traditionally considered bastions of liberal "tolerance", such as the rise of Geert Wilder's Freedom Party in the Netherlands.

It was also proven that even Southern European nations which have living memories of far-right military rule – Spain, Portugal, Greece – are not immune as initially believed. Greece witnessed the neo-Nazi Golden Dawn – a small paramilitary gang active since the 1980s – entering parliament in 2012. In Spain, Vox triumphantly entered the national parliament in 2019, just seven years after its formation, winning 10.25 and 15 percent in elections that year. Portuguese exceptionalism was dealt its first blow when the far-right Andre Ventura and his Chega party won 12 percent of the vote in the presidential elections of January 2021. Another famous "immunity" has been put to the test by the emergence of Alternative für Deutschland (AfD) in Germany, which has been increasingly normalised despite its fascist core.

To sum up, the rise of the far right has become the new normal across Europe. No one can rest complacently behind the false claim that "this can never happen here".

In order to understand the breadth and depth of this phenomenon, we should examine some common factors that lie behind it and some features that emerge as (more or less) common in the contemporary galaxy of far-right currents.

## Economic and political crisis

The global financial crisis of 2007–8 and its aftermath has been an obvious and important factor driving the growth of the far right. The weak recovery has generated a sense of social and economic insecurity, and in some cases, turmoil. Permanent unemployment or under-employment has become a persistent reality for some parts of the working class, and wages have been largely stagnant. The middle classes have been under various pressures, in some cases material decline but at the very least constant anxiety about their prospects. There is the temptation among parts of the big bourgeoisie to look for and experiment with alternative strategies for governance. Combined, these factors provide the far right an audience to appeal to. The widespread feeling of a "dead end" and the subsequent social exasperation can be translated by the far right in terms of "the nation's decline" that should be addressed by "restoring its former glory".

The political crisis is the second obvious factor that benefits the far right. While the financial crisis is the background and the fundamental reason for the political turmoil, we should examine the latter distinctly. The political crisis is a more resilient phenomenon, a result of many factors with its own dynamics that precede the financial crisis. The fortunes of traditional parties and political stability have not always been in *total* sync with the economic situation. In my organisation, Internationalist Workers' Left (DEA), we used the term *metastasis* to describe the political turmoil that emerged even after the first episodes of the economic crisis were relatively contained. The collapse or relative decline of the established parties that used to monopolise the political allegiances of the vast majority of the population for decades after World War Two has unleashed centrifugal forces creating an opening for smaller political parties. While certain far-right parties might have made some inroads among the working class, the far right has tended to benefit from crises in the traditional centre-right, which release social elements already inclined to support conservative ideas.

These global trends have been exaggerated and taken a unique form in Europe. In this region, the economic and the political crisis were translated into a crisis of "European integration", meaning the Eurozone and the European Union project. The handling of the crisis by Brussels took two forms. The weaker, harder hit countries of Southern Europe were offered bailouts – depicted perversely as a form of support – in exchange for harsh fiscal austerity. These measures were designed to protect private creditors from any losses by squeezing workers and the poor.

This strategy was commonly agreed to protect the core of

ruling-class interests in all countries involved. But the international agreements – referred to as memoranda – and the European mechanisms formed to oversee their implementation inflamed nationalist feelings across the board, as everyone tried to deflect public anger from local capitalists. In the North, the nationalist argument complained that "our tax money is spent so that the lazy people of the South maintain their care-free lifestyles". In the South, nationalists argued that "austerity is being imposed upon us by the vicious Northerners, who want to weaken and colonise our country". As things evolved, this way of shifting the blame spread almost everywhere – not just between North and South. French nationalist feeling targeted "German hegemony in the EU". British nationalism revolted against the EU, and so on.

We are living in an era of sharpening capitalist and imperialist competitions. The rise of right-wing "anti-globalism", in the form of a protectionist economic and political model, is an attempt to address the new situation. Trump has so far been the most vocal proponent of this shift. When he argued in the UN that "the future belongs to patriots"[1] he understood that he advocated a strategy that appeals to many political forces, reflecting the soul-searching among many ruling classes. In the European context, this protectionist spirit has become more prevalent among the far right for two reasons. Firstly, Europe has been the home of the most advanced globalist/integrationist project, in the form of the EU. Secondly, this project is facing the existential anxiety of lagging behind in international competition and losing its place in the hierarchy of world imperialism.

So, for emerging far-right forces, all vices and ills can be attributed to the bureaucrats in Brussels, and all salvation will be found by reclaiming national sovereignty. This was clearly on display from the Euro-sceptic wing of the Tory Party and Nigel Farage's UKIP during the Brexit referendum. But national priority has become a common banner for all the European far right. Sometimes there is a concession to geopolitical realities by arguing for a stronger Europe in the form of a refounded "free association of sovereign nations".

---

1.    In his address to the UN General Assembly in September 2019. See Borger 2019.

## Islamophobia

If these factors emerged in the post-crisis world situation, we must take into account factors that strengthened their prospects before that and continue to fuel them. First of all there is racism, specifically, Islamophobia. Anti-Muslim bigotry has probably been the sole feature that is common among all far-right forces in Europe. Some are more protectionist while others are more neoliberal. Some are fully reactionary, while others maintain a liberal facade when it comes to social issues. But they all hate Muslims.

The far right has been feeding on the mainstream, state-sponsored Islamophobia that prevailed in the Western world during the War on Terror. Building on over a century of Orientalist prejudices, paired with decades of negative stereotypes of Arabs as terrorists, the campaign to stigmatise Muslims has been a powerful tool. It has justified imperialist aggression beyond the borders, racism on the borders and authoritarianism within the borders. In this context the far right has found a very convenient scapegoat, and presented itself as the most determined to confront this new threat.

Some parts of the contemporary far right – especially in Northern Europe – have even presented themselves as gay-friendly and feminist, in order to claim they are defending supposedly European values against Islamist immigrants. While the emergence of "hipster Nazis" is an interesting development, it is unlikely to be the norm.

## A reactionary backlash

The far more common posture on the far right relies on a conservative backlash, twisting reality and arguing that it is the oppressed that are the major/existential threat to society. In this view, the rights of women Europeans, white people and men are being endangered by the arrival of immigrants, the hegemony of minorities and the assertiveness of women.

Some combine these and other issues in a conspiracy called "the Great Replacement". According to this theory, anti-sexist movements – challenging the traditional family and leading to a decline in native births – are in cahoots with anti-racist movements – asking for open borders and leading to more immigration – in order to replace "native" Europeans with Islamists. Some include progressive environmentalists in their targets, as they see their politics as threatening to national industries and/or causing sympathy to climate refugees.[2] Most blame a shadowy globalist elite led by George Soros for these menaces, but when they feel stronger or more confident, they show their true colours and target the left: the Marxist advocates behind these various causes.

A notorious Greek neoliberal/alt-right spokesperson recently argued that what bothers him in feminism is that "it tries to inflame confrontation...always with the support of the left. Now that class struggle is over, they [leftists] constantly create new types of conflicts in order to maintain the credibility of their left-wing narrative".[3]

Now this statement is wrong on many levels. Class struggle is not over, the left is not – at least should not be – looking for substitute movements, and struggles for women's rights should be understood as part of the broader class struggle. But the political messaging is clear: the New Right is targeting any social movement that has challenged the ruling class in some way, and provided opportunities for the left to grow and spread its anti-capitalist message. As soon as workplace militancy is on the rise, these "populists" will almost certainly oppose strikes and workers' organisations, as the far right always has.

## COVID

In addition to these existing factors, the pandemic added a new element to the far-right arsenal. In its early stages, many European far-right forces were prepared to treat the threat seriously. Few felt confident to oppose health measures as public fears of the pandemic peaked. Many voted for the first lockdowns or broader state of emergency powers. Instead they used the crisis as a means of whipping up hysteria towards their preferred enemies: some suggested it was a Chinese attempt to

---

2.   See Farand 2019 for an overview of the European far right's positions on climate. The AfD leader is quoted describing climate change as a "replacement religion of all left green world parties".
3.   Tzimeros 2022.

undermine the West, others saw it as a globalist virus to weaken the nation. For Vox in the Spanish state, it was the opportunity to bash the feminist strike that happened a few days before the first lockdown. But when in power, reactionaries adopted a denialist policy, as per Trump, Bolsonaro, Boris Johnson. Soon enough the European far right followed their lead. With Trump as a global loudspeaker, opposition to various health measures became a common policy for the vast majority of the European far right.

In the absence of serious research in this field, it is hard to elaborate on details and case studies, which vary depending on the concrete situation in each country. Some scattered and initial remarks follow.

In countries with an individualist right-wing libertarian tradition – the USA being the exemplar – opposition to all health measures as steps towards a communist dictatorship is the dominant theme of the far-right. The same can be said about fascist groups in most countries, with their typical disregard for life, their support for so-called natural selection, and their hostility to societies "going soft". These groups remained faithful to the historical motto of the Spanish Falangists: "Long Live Death!" Such groups have been responsible for the most violent and openly anti-health attacks during wider anti-lockdown or anti-vax protests, including attacks on vaccination centres and COVID clinics.

Other far-right parties have tended to prioritise opposition to specific measures, depending on their audience, local conditions and their own unique features. Some countries witnessed loud opposition to lockdowns but a relative silence on the vaccine, possibly reflecting the middle-class desire to "open up for business". Other countries had no noteworthy opposition to lockdowns but are facing protests against the vaccine. This is especially the case where conspiracy theories, obscurantism and religious fundamentalism form a sizeable part of the far-right ecosystem.

Finally, in countries where traditional themes of nationalism, racism and anticommunism provide them with better opportunities to build their forces, the far right have added opposition to this or that healthcare measure to its repertoire, but not as a top priority.

While it would be a stretch to say that all European far-right forces have made opposition to health measures their focus, it is the case that oppositional/denialist movements in every European country were marked by the active presence of far-right forces, either intervening into or leading them. These movements provided an opportunity for the far right to promote its narrative on the pandemic and its own distorted version of resistance to the elites. How sustained they will be, and how much lasting impact they will have on strengthening the far right into the future, remains to be seen.

## The current situation

Having explored the factors shaping their growth and development in recent times, I will try to assess their current state.

In electoral terms, the past couple of years have witnessed a halt to the previously rapid advance of the far right, but also an affirmation of their established presence. The 2019 elections to the European parliament provided the most recent evidence for this at a continent-wide level. In an electoral contest that is usually advantageous to them, the far right in most countries failed to rise to their expectations of an unstoppable march. But at the same time, they held their ground overall, maintaining the support they won in their initial breakthrough phase. They have now proven that they are here to stay, that their organisations express something deeper and more resilient than an accidental protest vote.

In terms of national elections, the most recent and typical example of this is Germany. The Alternative for Germany (AfD) entered the national parliament in 2017, winning third place and 12.6 percent of the vote. In September 2021, they won 10.3 percent and fell to fifth place. With certain exceptions, this failure to build on previous success has been the norm around Europe lately.

For now the centre has withstood the electoral pressure. This has taken different forms. In some cases, we've seen the resilience of the established centre-right or centre-left parties, depending on the country and whether they were not in government during the worst days of the crisis. Elsewhere we've seen the emergence of new forces that provide a shiny gloss to the neoliberal establishment – see Macron

– or the strengthening of smaller parties such as the Greens. The point is that the centre in the broader sense of the term, which includes parties that might not be traditional but are *politically* mainstream, has proven its ability to survive and adapt.

It is worth noting that the far right has faced the usual troubles associated with governance in the late neoliberal era. In Austria the Freedom Party won its best result for nearly 20 years in 2017, with 26 percent of the vote. It entered a coalition government as equals with the mainstream right-wing Austrian People's Party. This was undermined in mid-May 2019 as the Ibiza scandal emerged, when its leader was recorded soliciting funds from a Russian oligarch and suggesting that he intended to censor Austrian media for his own gain. The coalition collapsed and in the subsequent election the Freedom Party vote was reduced to (a still impressive) 16 percent. In Italy, in August of 2019, Mateo Salvini felt confident enough to bring down the coalition government with the Five Star Movement, hoping to win an election and form a pure far-right government. He was outmanoeuvred by Prime Minister Conte, who managed to avoid an election and form a new coalition government with the Five Star Movement and the centre-left Democratic Party (PD). The latest developments in France seem to suggest that Marine Le Pen might be paying the price of her relentless effort to appeal to the ruling class as a respectable and trustworthy party of government, leaving her far-right flank exposed to competition from Eric Zemmour.

It is not easy to explain this temporary halt. One could argue that the far right is lacking a clear economic project, trying to balance between accommodation to neoliberalism and promoting welfare chauvinism. They are similarly torn between expressing Euroscepticism and an acknowledgment of the irreversible – or at least, hard to reverse – nature of certain aspects of globalisation and Europeanisation. This hybrid that Henri Wilno has described as national liberalism[4] is hardly a coherent strategy that can win the trust of the majority of the ruling class at this stage. The headaches generated for the British ruling class by Brexit is the most dramatic example.

---

4.   Wilno 2019.

Another reason that could explain their failure to build the support needed to claim government is that the ruling class might consider them a liability in terms of guaranteeing social peace and overseeing politics as usual: A typical criticism of Trump, even from some of his supporters, was that he was stirring the hornet's nest with his brash and confrontational style of politics.

These factors combined would suggest that the far right is not the first choice for most ruling classes. They prefer to exhaust other options before promoting the populists to government. The far right is a valuable reserve, but still just a reserve. At least for now. It is worth noting that Steve Bannon, the Dark Prince of the far right internationally, has moved to Brussels to bring his expertise, connections and material support behind various far-right parties in Europe.

The main feature of the period is volatility and uncertainty. It would be naive to try to make predictions on the future course of events. Alarmists who predicted that the far right was on an unstoppable march to power have been proven wrong. But the same can happen to complacent and self-congratulatory assertions about the defeat of populism and the resilience of the centre, which prevail in liberal commentary at the moment.

This is one reason to avoid complacency. There is a second one, which is realising the magnitude of the problem that is the permanent establishment of the far right as a mainstream political force.

In 1999, when the far-right Freedom Party entered a coalition government in Austria, Europe was shocked. Chumbawamba circulated an edited version of their older anti-fascist song "Enough is Enough", which was played live in massive concerts in Austria and became an instant anthem all around Europe. Anti-fascists protested in many European countries. Governments felt obliged to talk about suspending ties with Austria. Twenty years later, many anti-fascists are relieved when far-right parties "only" receive low double-digit votes.

This established presence of the far right impacts far more than electoral results. The latter serve as a concrete manifestation of a deeper problem: the normalisation of far-right ideas. Fearing murder at the hands of his enemies, Mithridatis, the ancient King of Pontus, regularly injected himself with small doses of poison, so that his body become accustomed to the harmful substances. The term "Mithridatism" hails from this story, meaning the gradual accommodation and numbness towards normally harmful effects. This term describes accurately what has been happening in Europe when it comes to racism and far-right ideas in general.

Electoral scores of the far right reflect this situation and serve as part of a vicious circle: the centre applies reactionary policies that enable the growth of the far right, and then the strengthened far right pushes the centre to adopt even more of its ideas. What was once seen as a fringe concern is now legitimised, thus enabling the further growth of the far right on an even more extreme basis. The issues of racism and refugees are a clear example: things that would have been considered extremist years ago are now common sense in Fortress Europe. Intellectuals of the New Right in France and Italy have argued for this strategy since the 1970s. They understood that sticking to symbols of the discredited past was harmful to their cause, and urged the neofascists to focus "on the field of values, which are not related to politics in the traditional sense of the term, but have a direct impact on the existence or not of social consensus, which is governed by politics".[5] Jean-Marie Le Pen has been a disciple of this school and the phrase "Lepenisation of minds" emerged in French public discourse, in order to describe the reach of his ideas in French society, beyond those prepared to vote for him. As Pierre Milza had argued, "Gramsci's ideas were used for the triumph of his enemies",[6] referring to the ongoing war of position and struggle for hegemony by the New Right. It is this kind of war we have been facing over past years.

The rise of the far right is a complex phenomenon, with many variations, as the reactionaries adapt to concrete local situations. In the following part of this article, I shall address a few different cases which I know enough to elaborate on, cases that highlight the different forms the far right is taking, and which, taken altogether, can contribute to understanding the phenomenon in its totality.

---

5.   Alain de Benoist, "Orientations pour les années décisives", quoted in Milza 2002 (a study on the trajectory of the European far right after World War Two), p.326 of the Greek translation published in 2004.

6.   Milza 2002, p.324 of the Greek edition.

## Italy: from the racist-nationalist transformation of Lega to the rise of Fratelli D'Italia

Italy's Northern League has been around since the early 1990s. It never waged an open struggle for independence, but scapegoated southern Italians for being poor and lazy, arguing that greater autonomy would enable the richer North to avoid paying taxes to sustain the South. It enjoyed some level of support among the middle classes in northern Italy, displaying strong results in municipal/regional elections and occasionally serving as a junior partner to Silvio Berlusconi's national governments.

Under the leadership of Matteo Salvini the party shifted to take advantage of a series of developments. In particular, the crisis of Berlusconism in the aftermath of the global financial crisis unleashed centrifugal forces in the right-wing camp. The party has also taken strong stances around refugees and the debt crisis of Italian capitalism.

The party now abandoned its geographic reference point, rebranding itself simply as Lega. Salvini projected his party as the main national force on the right. Migrants replaced Southern Italians as the main scapegoat, and their narrative shifted from defending the northern middle class against the state to a nationalist defence of the Italian middle class against the European bureaucracy in Brussels. The Lega has made some inroads in parts of the working class and in parts of central and southern Italy. But it remains mostly a party of small and middle capitalists, based mainly in the North.

When it comes to the economy, its main message revolves around tax breaks for business. But more recently it has had some success in building a nationalist-racist coalition around opposition to the most globalised sectors of big capital, which Salvini associated with the stridently pro-EU centre-left party, and to migrants. When in power, opposition to the former was proven to be mostly demagogic, but Salvini, as Minister of Interior, overcompensated with rigorous activity against the latter. To cover for his typical neoliberal policies and agreements with the EU, he made a series of infamous decrees targeting migrants' rights and NGOs that engaged in rescue missions in the Mediterranean, but also restricted the right to protest and strike. He also cracked down hard on the social centres, occupied buildings that serve as the strongholds of Italian Autonomism. These spaces were among the last bastions of continuous left-wing activity in the aftermath of the retreat of the political left and the trade-union movement.[7]

After the fall of the first Conte government in August 2019, the Lega returned to opposition until February 2021, when it began providing parliamentary support to a national unity government. This new coalition brought together the full spectrum of Italian parliamentary politics behind the establishment's favourite Mario Draghi, the former head of the European Central Bank.

The only parliamentary party that is not part of this national unity is the Brothers of Italy (Fratelli d'Italia). This organisation is the latest in a series of mutations and rebrandings of the old MSI, the fascist current that emerged after the fall of Benito Mussolini. Concerningly, the Brothers are the most successful to date. Their growth was enabled by the toxic climate created by Salvini in government, and now they benefit from being the sole parliamentary opposition. In the polls, the Brothers have surpassed the Lega as the major force on the right, a trend that was confirmed during recent municipal elections. In Rome, their most popular council candidate was Rachele Mussolini, the granddaughter of the fascist dictator. The lack of any personal career and fame suggests that Rachele was elected entirely *because* of her family name, and not *despite* it.

Many analysts believe that a governmental coalition between the Lega and the Brothers is a very possible – if nightmarish – outcome of the next election. Even if this doesn't occur, Italy is now firmly established as a country where the traditional centre-right has been relegated to junior status in the right-wing camp. If the Brothers manage to overcome the Lega, after the Lega defeated Berlusconi, this will be an extremely disturbing sign of a steady radicalisation on the broad right.

---

7.  Most insights on the nature of the Lega, especially during its time in government, draw heavily from an interview with comrade Antonello Zeca during the Conference of Sinistra Anticapitalista in February 2019. It was published in the Greek Marxist journal *Kokkino* ("Red").

During the rise of Lega, the reactionary sentiment was mostly expressed by individual acts of racist violence.[8] The Lega itself was more or less "institutionalised" from the outset. While it held the occasional ritual rally to provide a vague sense of belonging to its supporters, it was always a party that primarily concerned itself with the routine tasks of local administration. The current context is quite different. In the context of the rise of the Brothers of Italy and the growing anti-vax protests against the Green Pass, the organised fascists of Forza Nuova have felt emboldened to escalate. They attacked the headquarters of the CGIL, the main trade union federation, in Rome – not in the shadows, but in broad daylight, as leaders of a 10,000-strong mob.[9] One hundred years after the destruction of Chambers of Labour by Mussolini's Blackshirts, this was a menacing reminder of the threat looming behind this constant radicalisation to the right.

## Spain: Vox and the reactionary backlash

The background to the sudden rise of Vox was accurately described by Miguel Urbán of Anticapitalistas, in the title of a relevant article: "Francoism never died".[10]

The transition from Franco's dictatorship to a parliamentary democracy from 1978 was a smooth process, controlled entirely by the ruling class. This was assisted by the compliance of both the Socialist and Communist parties. The Francoists remained powerful in the state machinery, which was never purged of fascist elements. Even the mainstream right-wing party, Partido Popular, has its roots in an alliance of Francoist organisations founded by former officials of the dictatorship.

The PP faced many tests during the global economic crisis. Strong social movements challenged its rule and the political system inherited from the transition, targeting the monarchy, austerity and the central-ist constitution of 1978. These challenges include the most massive

---

8.  In the most notorious incident typical of that time, Luca Traini wounded six Africans in a drive-by shooting in the city of Macerata. He was a former member and local candidate of the Lega.
9.  See Turigliatto 2021 for more on this incident.
10. Urbán 2019 is a very helpful article for understanding Vox.

and militant feminist movement in Europe, mobilising hundreds of thousands of women and organising successful "feminist strikes" every International Women's Day; a re-awakening of Catalan nationalism, with the emergence of a movement that pushed for a referendum about Catalan independence; a series of scandals that hurt many of its leading members and subsequent electoral losses.

This was the background to the formation of Vox. Francoist currents, which had remained for years in the big tent of the PP, felt that there was both the need and the potential to organise an independent political intervention.

Vox is probably the most typical example of the reactionary backlash driving far-right growth. It is possibly the most aggressively sexist party of the European far-right, being very vocal on its outright hostility to women's rights. It is not a coincidence that this is happening in the country with the most militant feminist movement.

In a similar vein, Vox can be described as a product of the constitutional crisis over Catalonia. Of course there is a consensus over the "integrity of Spain" among all national political forces. But with Spanish nationalism whipped into a frenzy against the autonomists, it was Vox that benefited most, blaming the Socialists and Podemos as traitors for their insistence on a negotiated solution, and targeting other right-wing forces for being unwilling to confront this supposed existential threat.

Vox also draws heavily from the medieval theme of the *reconquista,* when the pope sought to drive all Muslims out of the Iberian Peninsula. According to Vox, Spanish Christians must "reconquer" Spain from Muslim immigrants and refugees. The term was also popular among General Franco's forces, which fought to "reconquer" Spain from the scourge of godless communism. This fusion of bigotry and fascistic reaction was accelerated after the emergence of a coalition government of the Socialist Party (PSOE) and Unidas Podemos, which relied on parliamentary support from regional nationalist parties from Catalonia and the Basque Country. In Vox's narrative, this re-enactment of 1936 threatens the "Una, Grande Y Libre!" – One, Grand and Free – Spanish state. Autonomist forces threaten the unity of Spain; the "communists" of Podemos threaten its liberty, while PSOE is targeted for enabling them both.

## The Greek exception? The rise and fall Golden Dawn

Greece has been a rather unique case in the general trend of far-right growth. Generally we see in Europe the rise of far-right parties and right-wing populists who respect the rules of liberal regimes – or pretend to do so for now – somewhat separate to violent paramilitary formations which are smaller and more marginal. In Golden Dawn, we witnessed the rise of a group that enjoyed parliamentary representation and a mass following and also had an openly fascist ideology and violent militias in the streets.

While cautious, I tend to believe that the (foreseeable) future belongs to what we call "fascists in ties" as opposed to "fascists with boots". This has been the prevailing model, and it has paid off for the European far right. Having said that, Greece serves as a reminder that it would be naïve to argue that something more closely resembling historical fascism can't happen again.

There are many factors that help explain why Greece was the location of this terrible development. The scale of the crisis – both economic and political – was unmatched elsewhere in Europe. The modern history of the country, with a Civil War from 1946–49, a regime of White Terror during the 1950s and a military dictatorship from 1967 to 1974 offers recent experiences for the far right to draw on. Finally, the collapse of the respectable version of the far right – LAOS, Popular Orthodox Rally – after it joined a coalition government to help impose the dictates of the IMF and the EU are some parts of the answer.

But the most important factor was the level of class struggle. It is no coincidence that Golden Dawn escalated its activities, and found increased support among parts of the media and the Greek state, in early 2009. In December of 2008, the police murder of 15-year-old Alexis Grigoropoulos led to a youth uprising that shook the ruling class and challenged the ability of the police to control the streets. Such was the turmoil that some mainstream government officials were openly contemplating deploying the army to restore order. The rebellion eventually lost its steam, but with Greek capitalism about to face the devastating economic crisis, it was widely understood that December's revolt was a glimpse of one potential future. The extreme militarisation of the Greek police accelerated in the aftermath the protests, as well as a vicious political and ideological counterattack against protest movements in general. It was a multidimensional campaign that has been described as "anti-rebellion politics", a form of pre-emptive counter-revolution.

The promotion of Golden Dawn was part of this strategy. During the chaotic scenes of December 2008, no-one paid much attention to the early reports about groups of citizens taking the law into their own hands to protect property. These stories, depicted positively in the media, were simply the prelude. From 2010 to 2012–13, widespread resistance to austerity shook Greece. There were dozens of 24-hour general strikes, and some of them 48-hour, a myriad of militant sectoral struggles and movements of civil disobedience, a two-month-long occupation of public squares inspired by Tahrir in Egypt and the *Indignados* in Spain, massive protests encircling parliament for hours in the face of unprecedented police violence. It was in this heaving political situation that SYRIZA, a small coalition of reformist, centrist and revolutionary forces, was catapulted from a minor party that received 3–5 percent of the vote, to contending for governmental power.

During the same period, Golden Dawn benefited from growing support from a range of organisations.

The police had a long history of active collaboration with the far right, which reached new heights during the "dark biennial" of 2011–13. In this period Golden Dawn conducted numerous attacks on the left and immigrants in broad daylight, at the same time as around 50 percent of the riot police voted for the neo-Nazis.[11]

As a powerful institution in Greek society, the Orthodox Church has lent meaningful support to Golden Dawn. Many high-ranking priests displayed public support for the "good lads in black", a reference to the black uniform T-shirts used by Golden Dawn thugs. Bishops met GD leaders and attended openings of new local headquarters of the party to bless them. They found a common cause when GD violently shut down Terrence McNally's play *Corpus Christi*, which was condemned by the Church as blasphemous.[12]

---

11. Makris 2012.
12. Siegel and Targonski-O'Brien 2017. This rather mild report mentions just a few examples of public displays of support by certain bishops. In a country where it is

A section of the most notorious and aggressive capitalists, including those involved in organised crime and the shipowners of the Port of Piraeus, provided support to Golden Dawn in this period. Their most important collaboration involved a serious attempt to try and break the Communist-led unions on the docks, while a range of smaller capitalists also provided material support to GD's efforts to create its own structures of welfare; but only for Greeks.

Overall then, Golden Dawn was either tolerated or actively supported, as a valuable reserve for a ruling class that felt threatened during those tumultuous years of class struggle.

In Greek mythology, when someone commits the sin of *hubris*, the gods mess with their mind, causing *tisis*, a blinding self-confidence that leads them to commit even more arrogant acts. This eventually leads to *nemesis*, a severe punishment that brings their humbling downfall. This could be a summary of the trajectory of Golden Dawn.

In September 2013, the dog tried to escape its leash and started to bite uncontrollably. A Golden Dawn battalion viciously attacked Communist Party unionists who were putting up posters in disputed territory in Piraeus. It was a serious escalation that risked an open war with the CP, a party that remains organisationally strong in the area, and with an established presence in mainstream politics.

Soon after, Golden Dawn physically attacked a number of centre-right politicians at a nationalist forum organised each year to pay tribute to those executed by partisans for collaborating with the Nazi occupation. Given its significance to right-wing mythology, it was a big step for Golden Dawn to try and intervene in this aggressive way to claim hegemony over the broad right.

To top off this month of violent aggression, Golden Dawn thugs murdered anti-fascist rapper Pavlos Fyssas on the night of 17 September. He died standing defiantly, protecting his friends from a Nazi squadron, remaining true to his rhyme, "there is no way I will be afraid".

This slogan became the battle-cry for many tens of thousands of protesters marching outside Golden Dawn headquarters in big cities and small towns all around Greece. Thirty such protests were organised

---

an open secret that many priests use their Sunday sermons for political propaganda, such instances were only the tip of the iceberg.

immediately after the murder, with 100 taking place over the next couple of weeks. These demonstrations involved thousands of people, well beyond those who usually engage in anti-fascist activity.

This anti-fascist revolt and the widespread popular anger forced the government's hand. The minister of the interior, a man who had earlier sought to sue *The Guardian* for revealing police torture against arrested anti-fascists, suddenly "discovered" dozens of cases of Golden Dawn crimes that had been collecting dust in his drawers for years.

Golden Dawn had overplayed its hand, at a time that the Greek ruling class had not reached the point of enabling some sort of "fascist solution". But it was the massive fightback that made it clear to the ruling class that escalated neo-Nazi violence would cause more problems than it would solve. The existence of a vibrant anti-fascist movement, a strong left and the broader context of strong working-class resistance meant that Golden Dawn's ambitions were a political liability.

The outcome of the subsequent trial against Golden Dawn – and their prospects in general – was not a given. Initially the left understood the pressing of charges against GD as a half-hearted concession to the anti-fascist revolt. We expected that the trial would end in a compromise between the state and the Nazis, possibly sacrificing some leading members but allowing Golden Dawn to continue its activities.

But in the end, the result was far better than we had dared to hope for. All members of the leadership and the parliamentary group of the party were found guilty of being members of a criminal organisation, while party leader Nikos Michaloliakos and his senior henchmen were found guilty of directing a criminal organisation. In three separate cases that were examined in parallel with and as part of the big trial, the verdict was also against GD members of the squadrons that killed Pavlos (murder), attacked Egyptian fishermen (attempted murder) and CP unionists (inflicting serious injuries). Sentences ranging from five to 13 years, depending on the charges –as there was a bunch of other offences for each, like illegal possession of arms etc – were imposed on 57 GD members, with the maximum sentences being for the top leadership (except for the thug who killed Pavlos, who received a life sentence).

The significance of the verdict was that GD was declared a

criminal organisation as a whole, bearing full responsibility for the crimes committed by its squadrons. This left no room to present the crimes committed during all these years as isolated incidents – separate from the party's true nature – or to shift all the blame onto the expendable thugs at the lower echelons.

This outcome was determined by social struggle and political developments in Greece over the years of the trial. This is not meant to minimise the efforts of the leftist lawyers who ran the trial. Far from it, their legal intervention and their detailed legal and political work over five to six years were proven important during many stages of the trial. "Without the existence of the Civil Action, there would be no case at all!", argued a defender of the neo-Nazis. Indeed, the state prosecutor initially proposed the acquittal of all Golden Dawn members of all charges, and never stopped displaying her sympathy for them. One can only imagine a trial with Nazi defence lawyers on one side and this so-called prosecutor on the other! But the Civil Action lawyers, being seasoned left-wing activists, always acknowledged the importance of a mass movement in determining the final outcome.

Anti-fascist mobilisation never ceased, with the annual anniversary of Pavlos' murder becoming an extremely important date for any activist's calendar. Golden Dawn was proven weak when it lost the confidence that the state will always be there to protect it. Forced to withdraw their gangs from the streets, under pressure from both the trial and the anti-fascist movement, Golden Dawn organisationally disintegrated, while their most high-profile electoral allies jumped the sinking ship. This is all the more remarkable given that the political situation provided them with opportunities – mass rallies against Macedonia, rising tensions with Turkey, growing numbers of refugees.

In the summer of 2019, they were finally kicked out of parliament and a series of splits followed. New Democracy has rallied the right-wing vote around it and won the full confidence of the ruling class. Meanwhile a new far-right party, "Greek Solution", entered parliament, declaring its distance from the most fascist practices of Golden Dawn. So, when the time came for the verdict, the fascists were politically expendable. To be crystal clear on the order of things: the party was defeated before the judgement; the decision reflected the success of the political movement to isolate and smash them.

The lesson from Golden Dawn is that it can be a fatal mistake to focus exclusively on the machinations from above, which can lead to being passive, a posture which underestimates the intervention of the masses in shaping the terrain. The day of the verdict was a final reminder – and what a reminder! – of who were the ones who beat the Nazis. On 7 October, a day we shall never forget, many tens of thousands of people rallied outside the court.[13] They were there to celebrate, in anticipation of a victory they rightfully understood as their own making, or to explode in case the Nazis were left off the hook.

Kostas Plevris, the elder patriarch of Greek National-Socialism, who was recruited as a lawyer by one of the GD leaders in the final stages of the trial, summed up the mood of the day: "On my way to this courtroom, I felt like I was entering a People's Court during the French Revolution".

## A different animal: "Orbánisation" in Hungary

In addition to the electoral rise of far-right parties or the activity of more openly neofascist formations, we should mention another development, which is qualitatively different but part of the trend: The radicalisation of established right-wing parties. This process has been named Orbánisation, after Hungarian Prime Minister Viktor Orbán.

His party, Fidesz, has gradually moved to the right. During the 1990s it evolved from liberalism to conservatism, leaving the Alliance of Free Democrats, which brings together parties like the German FDP or the British Liberal Democrats, to join the European People's Party, the alliance of the centre-right. Since winning office in 2010 the party has continued its evolution further to the right. It has adopted a series of reactionary policies against the Roma, LGBTQ people, non-Christian immigrants and the homeless. It has sought to extend the party's control over branches of the state and the media, engaged in occasional – actual and staged – conflicts with Brussels, and targeted

---

13. For an account of that day and the trial, see Petrou 2020.

George Soros in public propaganda that veers dangerously close to explicit anti-Semitism. On the economic front it has engaged in a limited shift from the economic orthodoxies, deploying some interventionist economic policies, certain aspects of paternalist protection, forcing electricity companies to charge less and paying them the difference. At the same time, they've dismantled workers' rights while making life insufferable for the unemployed. Fidesz's leaders don't shy away from openly describing the regime they have been trying to build as a "Christian illiberal democracy".[14]

Victor Orbán has presided over the most extreme version of this general trend within the mainstream right. It is telling that the European People's Party felt embarrassed enough by this ally that it suspended Fidesz and then changed the rules of its parliamentary group to allow the expulsion of a party's entire delegation. Fidesz has since left the parliamentary group and begun consolidating its ties with the far right.

In this sense, we should be precise about the uses and abuses of the term Orbánisation. It can be applied to describe an observable tendency of the radicalisation of the centre-right, which in certain conditions could lead to the Hungarian outcome, but this is not a predetermined process. Its results depend on a range of factors, most important being the political situation and the class struggle. Overuse of the term, in a way that identifies certain right-wing parties with Fidesz and Orbán, is usually a tendency among the centre-left. To strengthen the pull of lesser-evilism even as social-democracy moves to the right themselves, it is necessary to present their centre-right adversaries as constantly on the cusp of outright fascism.

Having said that, elements of the "Orbánisation" tendency can be found among many parties of the centre-right. The British Tories under Boris Johnson and after the implementation of his nationalist-racist version of Brexit is a case that should be monitored. In German Christian-Democracy there has been an emergence of a more hard-right current, especially among its Bavarian affiliate the Christian Social Union. Merkel has been under fire in her party for enabling the

---

14.  Reuters staff 2018. For the far-right reasoning behind this theme by an Orbánist source, see Kovács 2019.

entry of certain numbers of refugees during the Syrian refugee crisis of 2015–16. Of course, Merkel's motive for allowing a greater number of asylum seekers was a cynical calculation of how much imported labor was needed by German business. But this was considered too generous by many Christian Democrats, who blamed Merkel's pro-immigrant stance for the rise of AfD. With the Merkel era over and the party in opposition after a substantial electoral decline, it is worth monitoring the debates that will inevitably emerge about the party's future direction.

One of the most advanced cases is that of Partido Popular in Spain. We have already mentioned the reactionary roots of this party and the significance of its political discourse for the emergent Vox. To make a long story short, the PP is shaping its tactics in opposing the centre-left government, always trying to outcompete Vox, and, before that, the populist nationalists of Ciudadanos. The latest and most flagrant example of this course is the rise of Isabel Ayuso. She won the Madrid regional elections by combining anti-lockdown rhetoric with virulent anti-communism and a toxic Trumpian mix of politics.[15] Her campaign started with the slogan "Socialism or Freedom" which soon evolved to "Communism or Ayuso". Ayuso is now considered a potential contender for the national leadership of PP, and has become famous for repeating the argument that "If they call you a fascist, you should know that you stand on the right side of history".[16]

## The Greek government

Similar trends emerged in New Democracy in Greece, which has a similar history to that of the Spanish PP. As well, both parties possess sizeable monarchist, far-right, reactionary and ardently anti-communist currents within their organisations.

However, there are some differences. The Greek junta was brought down by the historical uprising of November 1973, which played a big part in bringing down the military junta, and the subsequent

---

15. On the political importance of these elections see Garí 2021.
16. A left-wing European MP, Kateřina Konečná, tweeted a declaration condemning the statement on TV. https://twitter.com/konecna_k/status/1383028690473381889. See laSexta 2021 for a Spanish report and video on the incident.

governments were plagued by high level of class struggle and left-wing militancy. So while the Spanish "Transition" is a synonym for the lasting power of the far right and the demand for a break with its institutions is a slogan of the anti-capitalist left, the Greek term, *Metapolitefsi*, is a synonym for working-class militancy and the prevalence of left-wing ideas and the demand for a "break" with it is a right-wing slogan.

In this different post-dictatorship background, the Greek right was forced to actively rein in its reactionary currents and appear to be more serious about transforming into a modern liberal-democratic party. But we should not forget that New Democracy was founded as a re-incarnation of National Radical Union (ERE), the party that oversaw the brutal "White Terror" of the 1950s. For many of its leaders, members and supporters, New Democracy is still understood as the party of the right-wing victors of the Greek Civil War.

So there has always been an affinity between ND and the Greek far right. Sometimes the far-right fraction gets the upper hand in the party, sometimes it is forced to accommodate a more centrist leadership, sometimes far-rightists try to operate independently, other times they choose to return back to the fold of the mothership.

Since 2015, New Democracy has been led by Kyriakos Mitsotakis, who is considered a neoliberal centrist. But they found it difficult to oppose SYRIZA's economic austerity – which they voted for alongside the SYRIZA leadership in a blow to the now expunged SYRIZA left. Instead ND drew on classic themes of conservatism, spending four years inflaming nationalism, racism and law and order. SYRIZA's policies were not particularly progressive on these issues, but it was easier to create a sense of differentiation. ND accused the government of failing to halt immigration and of being unable to deal with crime because of an anti-police prejudice in SYRIZA's ranks. Crucially, they attacked the SYRIZA government's deal to recognise the former Republic of Macedonia as Northern Macedonia. Despite it being celebrated as a victory by many Greek capitalists, enabling NATO to integrate this country into its defence agreements, New Democracy denounced it as high treason. Amid these specific policies, there was a steady barrage of propaganda riffing on traditional conservative fears of communism and the left.

Since coming to power in 2019, Mitsotakis has ruled in ways that correspond to the conservative feelings his party whipped up while in opposition. He has sought to maintain support from far-right voters and keep the organised political far-right current of the party happy. This convergence of an avowed centrist with far-right elements has a more strategic reasoning than mere electoralism or cynical management of internal party politics. The neoliberals embarked on a project to "finish off *Metapolitefsi*", requiring both a full-scale material attack on working-class conditions as well as an aggressive political attack on left-wing ideas.[17] This anti-left revanchist campaign is the point of strategic convergence between the centre and the far-right.

This process is reflected in the fate of the former main far-right party of Greece, LAOS. After its collapse during the financial crisis, most of the top lieutenants jumped to New Democracy, where they now hold ministries. This situation led the former LAOS leader to joke that his party is in power but he is not part of it. One of those former LAOS leaders, Interior Minister Makis Voridis, is one of the most sophisticated representatives of the Greek far right. Before evolving into a strategist, he spent his youth in fascist formations and was notorious for wielding an axe in street fights with anarchists during the 1980s.

So, when a fascist group attacked leftist protesters this autumn, a cartoonist brilliantly summed up the situation. He drew a couple of armed young fascists talking:

> "Are you sure what we are about to do is safe? I mean, some of the guys that did such stuff are now in jail."
>
> "Don't worry, some other guys who did such stuff are now in government."

As previously mentioned, it would be wrong to draw from these facts that the far right is in power, or that Mitsotakis is identical to Orbán. It is probably the most dangerous government we have faced since 1974, it has a strong far-right current which dictates part of the governmental

---

17.  For more on the right-wing revanchist project after 2015, see Petrou 2021.

agenda, but it is not a far-right government. A serious assessment of our enemies is the precondition for developing tactics and strategies to fight them.

The experience of Greece shows that far-right policies and ideas are becoming mainstream not simply due to the radicalisation of the right-wing of traditional conservatism, but also because of their cynical adoption by the political centre as a whole.

## Centrist adaption to the far-right agenda

The rise of the far right has led to a growing awareness of the danger it poses, even among mainstream politicians. There are many problems with anti-fascist arguments used by establishment parties, generally, though not exclusively, of the centre-left. Firstly, they are usually characterised by exaggerated alarmism, constantly screaming "Fascism!" in order to herd together voters who seek stability. Secondly, such arguments tend to be paired with purely electoral action. If the centrist alarmists were right about an imminent fascist threat to democracy, they could not be defeated by a simple vote. Thirdly, this sort of centrist anti-fascism tends to rely on a defence of the capitalist status quo. This is obviously not the historical task of a left that is worthy of the name, and in any case is not an effective tactic for rallying opposition to insurgent far right forces.

But the most important critique of centrist arguments against fascism is that they cannot address their own role in making the far right a despicable threat. Denmark is the most typical example of a trend that can be seen to varying extents across Europe. There, a social-democratic government is overseeing one of the most inhumane versions of institutional racism. And it is highly vocal about it. Most mainstream commentators admit that the social democrats are implementing the program of the far right.

The Italian PD, long discredited for implementing austerity, has gambled on posing as the anti-fascist opposition to the Lega. They have improved their standings as a result. They also benefited from the healthy anti-fascist mood that emerged with the mass "Sardine" protests during Lega's governmental alliance with the Five Star Movement. Despite the sizeable demonstrations, the movement's vague messaging that avoided any concrete political/social questions other than hatred for Salvini made it easily co-optable.

After the outmanoeuvring of Salvini by his former allies in the Five Star Movement, the PD returned to government in a new coalition that presented itself as a democratic alternative to the far right. Yet after eighteen months in power, the notorious "Salvini decrees" were still in place, and initiatives that aimed to save refugee lives in the Mediterranean continued to be harassed by the Italian Navy. Then, when Mario Draghi formed a government of national unity in 2021, the PD proved the limits of its anti-fascism by once again collaborating with the Lega.

## The disturbing situation in France

Tariq Ali popularised the term "extreme centre" to describe the convergence of centre-left and centre-right and their adaption of radical pro-capitalist policies. President Emmanuel Macron is arguably the living embodiment of the neoliberal centre. He declares himself "neither left nor right". He built a new party from scratch, drawing in politicians from both the Socialist and Republicans on the promise to re-establish a stable centre ground for capitalist politics. He is a Europeanist and a liberal, and has experience in the public sector – as an advisor to governments – as well as being a former businessman. He managed to win the presidency on the basis of widespread disgust with his opponent, the far-right Marine Le Pen.

Yet despite the promise of liberal restoration, under Macron, French politics has moved substantially to the right. France has spent a big part of Macron's tenure under a state of emergency that grants extra powers to the army and police. Terrorist attacks have been opportunistically used to curtail democratic rights, including at times the right to public protest. The scale of repression Macron unleashed against the Yellow Vest movement of 2019 was unprecedented in the contemporary European context. When such events take place in countries that are not allies of the West, they are condemned as authoritarian and undemocratic. Yet in this case, Brussels and the wider EU were silent as thousands were arrested and injured, with many losing an eye or a leg after vicious attacks by the French riot police.

Islamophobia has been a constant feature of successive French governments, but under Macron it has risen to new, extreme levels.[18] The biggest outrage was the state-enforced dissolution of the Collective Against Islamophobia. It is a rather mainstream organisation that works with local and international institutions to provide legal support to Muslim victims of discrimination. It was banned for supposedly collaborating with terrorists, but the only "proof" given was the fact that it had rightly described some government policies as Islamophobic.[19]

This was part of a reactionary assault on leftist and anti-racist activists and ideas, especially on the campuses. Macron even coined the phrase "Islamo-leftism", a concept dangerously similar to the far right's stalking-horse of "Judeo-Bolshevism" in the interwar years. Darmanin, the notoriously reactionary minister of the interior, occasionally criticises Marine Le Pen from an even more hard-right point of view on these issues.

It is in this context that the French far right is becoming more and more audacious. A notorious hard-right journal had Jean-Luc Mélenchon on its cover, under the provocative headline "The Islamo-collaborators", while Communist party offices have also been tagged with graffiti calling them collaborators. It is a shocking appropriation and reversal of the term, which was traditionally used to describe and shame the Vichy regime of World War Two, and those on the right who were sympathetic to the Nazis.

In this context, it is no wonder that a number of retired army generals felt confident to publish an open letter warning of the looming threat of a civil war, and implied the need for a military coup. Though extreme, their arguments were merely an exaggerated version of the mainstream discourse in French politics. If the government was not up to the task of confronting the enemy, the generals expressed their confidence that "colleagues in active duty" shared their feelings and would take action to ensure the homeland was safe.

Back in 2017, between the first and the second round of the French presidential elections, some walls of Paris were covered with a slogan: "Macron 2017 = Le Pen 2022". From a purely electoral perspective, it is

18.  For a more detailed account see Mullen 2020.
19.  Cossé 2021.

too early to say whether it was right or wrong. But the political dynamics suggested by the slogan have been vindicated. Given the nature of the Macron government, it is no surprise that Marine Le Pen and a number of other far-right figures have been legitimised as serious contenders for the presidency.

This is an important part in explaining the contradictory nature of the so-called detoxification of the French far right, set in train by Marine Le Pen. It is true that the National Front/National Rally seems to have made a few steps away from its fascist past towards mainstream politics. But it is also true that mainstream politics have moved closer to the positions of the old National Front. One could say that liberal democracy and Marine Le Pen have met halfway. This simplistic picture doesn't conclude the debate on the nature of the National Rally, but serves to illustrate the broader trend.

Stathis Kouvelakis recently described a "double banalisation of Le Pen's discourse": she speaks "like everyone else", after having led "everyone else" to speak like her. The latest worrisome development in France is the rise of Eric Zemmour. A journalist with extreme far-right views, he has become popular in the political climate created by Macron. His rise reflects the fact that many far-right nationalists are unhappy with Le Pen's detoxification strategy. This approach "seriously undermines her ability to channel the anger and various resentments that she had earlier managed to crystallise". Kouvelakis quotes Zemmour himself:

> There is no longer any difference today between her discourse and that of Emmanuel Macron... Marine Le Pen speaks like Emmanuel Macron, Emmanuel Macron speaks like Marine Le Pen, they are already in the second round, since no one is supposed to exist apart from that second round [matchup], and it is clear that voters are refusing to be forced into this choice.[20]

Zemmour is building support by being more extreme – or more honest – about his agenda. He propagates the Great Replacement

---

20.  All quotes from Kouvelakis 2021.

conspiracy and is open about his enemies. In a public meeting he described France's education system as "infiltrated by Marxism, anti-racism and LGBT ideologies". Zemmour wants to force parents to give their children "French names", banning alternatives like Mohammed. He is even harsher than Le Pen in his opposition to migrants, arguing not only for closed borders, but for mass deportations. His best-selling book attributed France's decline to so-called "feminine" values, denouncing women's rights as an "emasculation" of society. It is telling that he won the implicit endorsement of Jean-Marie Le Pen, the veteran fascist who has been alienated by his daughter's approach to politics. Jean-Marie has argued that Zemmour is saying "all the things I always said", but his Jewish origins help protect from accusations of being a Nazi. On this score, Zemmour has even argued that Jews were protected by the French state during World War Two, whitewashing the Vichy regime that sent thousands of French Jews, unionists and leftists to death camps in Germany.

It is not yet clear whether Zemmour is simply winning over parts of Le Pen's support or if he is bringing in new forces to the far-right camp. But no matter what the electoral outcome, those who actually face the threat of the far right and are willing to actually confront it, are now facing a new enemy. This further radicalisation of the far right, similar to Fratelli d'Italia challenging the hegemonic role of the Lega, is a worrisome trend. A youth movement, called Generation Zemmour, was recently founded. Its name is an open acknowledgment of the connection with *Generation Identitaire,* the neo-fascist group that was officially dissolved a few months ago. In reality, it has probably been rebranded, this time around a recognised leader who enjoys some level of popular support.

## Confronting the new far right

This vast experience amassed from different countries and different examples help us sketch the rough outlines of our response.

• The far right is trying to win over positions and build its strength; it has already managed to establish itself and the political/social situation will continue "feeding" it or at least providing it with opportunities. Confronting this kind of enemy is not a question of an intense but brief campaign that could smash them in a manner of months, as could be the case with marginal extremist groups in the past. We should organise for a protracted struggle.

• Mobilising on the streets is essential. Tactics may vary, depending on the exact situation, the balance of forces, the nature of the each threat (eg fascist or not). But controlling the streets in the broader sense of the phrase, meaning building mass movements, holding protests, doing the work of local organising – all kinds of extra-parliamentary activity are vital. Such activity can stop the growth of the "traditional" fascists, confront efforts to build new, broader racist "movements" and prevent the electoral support of the far-right parties from translating into something more menacing, with deep social roots, extra-parliamentary organising and so on.

• Waging an ideological/political battle should accompany this task. Now, this is something Marxists always strive to do in all their interventions in any struggle. But in the context where there is an overall drift to the right, fighting to reverse this trend, confronting far-right ideas in general (and not just the party that explicitly advocates them), winning people's minds over to solidarity against hate, building and raising arguments against racism, sexism, nationalism and authoritarianism is very important. To put it differently, resting on the laurels of anti-Nazi feelings that prevailed in the decades after World War Two is not enough to rally mass support in the fight against this new, different, enemy.

• Social struggles that can help build (or at least offer glimpses of) an alternative are a necessity in our fight against capitalist exploitation and systemic injustice, but are not irrelevant to the fight against the far right. Such struggles were the "fuel" that in some cases enabled the emergence of left-wing challenges to the centre in the recent past. In the past few years in France, Marine Le Pen, constantly a protagonist in public life and political debates, felt irrelevant twice. The first time was during the Yellow Vests protests. The far-right tried to intervene in this movement, but as soon as it took an anti-police, anti-repression character, Le Pen was forced to keep a distance, torn between the need to appeal to cross-class anger against Macron and the need to remain on the side of the police, a bastion of support for the French far right.

The second time was the inspiring strike movement against Macron's pension reform, this time a class movement by unionised workers. Le Pen found herself torn between maintaining her anti-neoliberal demagogic posturing and not alienating employers and her traditional middle-class supporters.[21]

These broad "guidelines" lead to a conclusion, making another feature of anti-fascist activity very clear: that a serious confrontation with the far right is necessarily combined with a confrontation with the state (institutional racism, police brutality etc) and the bourgeois political forces. It is not simply a matter of not counting on them as reliable allies. In order to be up to the tasks described above, activists should be conscious about challenging the system that constantly enables the rise of such vicious forces.

## A few strategic constants

We are facing a multi-faceted threat and there is a wide variety of enemies that fall under the broad category of the far right. Each case should be analysed and dealt with accordingly, taking into account the specific national context. There are ongoing debates about the nature of Le Pen's National Rally in France, and much analysis needs to be done to classify and organise against both the Lega and the Fratelli. Similarly, there are big tactical differences involved in confronting and defeating Golden Dawn squads versus fighting against a right-wing government with reactionary politics.

But a couple of strategic constants remain valid, undisputed starting points before moving on to elaborate our tactics.

One obvious error is to ignore the threat posed by the far right. The Stalinist idea of "social-fascism" and its attendant ultra-leftism are not popular among serious parts of the left in any country. But simplistic arguments about "everyone being the same" can resign activists to passivity and indifference to a growing threat. These arguments are found everywhere, as are tendencies that seek to downplay the threat. The right-wing drift of mainstream politics can make these arguments more compelling, as in the case of Macron. But it is dangerous to

---

21.  John Mullen has made that insightful point in many articles about FN/RN. In Mullen 2021 he expands on the strengths and weaknesses of RN.

gamble on the possibility that far-right governments will be no worse than their bourgeois counterparts. My argument is not about electoral choices; the problem mostly begins if the attitude of "a plague on both your houses" translates to the refusal to engage in the specific fight against the far right during the many hundreds of days other than election day.

In the European context, an even more dangerous version of passively downplaying the threat seems to emerge among fractions of the left. Hostility to globalisation, the EU and the liberal centre leading to some sort of implicit "understanding" of the rise of the far right. Especially among some of those with a Stalinist background, a historic refusal to engage with anti-racist, anti-sexist, anti-nationalist struggles is sometimes attributed to these issues being part of the so called "globalist liberal" agenda. This position plays an identical though inverse function as the dominance of identity politics and Europeanism among other parts of the left. In the latter case, the left is hegemonised by the liberal wings of the establishment, while in the former it accommodates to the politics of the far right.

The most worrisome version of this trend is the argument in favour of listening to the legitimate concerns of the far-right base. This is inevitably paired with a push for the left to try and win over people from the far right by capitulating to parts of their agenda. This became a major point of tension in the Dutch Socialist Party, combined with an electoralist calculation to avoid the unpopular demands of the anti-racist or environment movement.[22] Mélenchon's France Insoumise has been tormented by similar debates among its ranks, mostly around issues of Islamophobia and French nationalism, and in Greece we are definitely no strangers to such ideas among leftists.

The most typical example of this trend is the circle around Sahra Wagenknecht in Germany and Die Linke. From her origins on the left of the party, Wagenknecht has ended up criticising her party for being in favour of open borders and trying to out-green the Greens. These are all supposedly examples of losing touch with normal workers. Her conclusion is that Die Linke should take up the racist legitimate

---

22.  De Jong 2021.

concerns of workers to prevent them from being radicalised towards the AfD.[23] Describing these reactionary arguments as based on a "class perspective" cannot hide the fact that it is a capitulation to chauvinism and nationalist protectionism.

The second pitfall is probably more prevalent. It is a resurrection of Popular Frontism, which involves seeking to build alliances with discredited mainstream figures as a strategy for fighting the right.

Journalist Paul Mason was one of the earliest to revive the term as a positive program for political action during the Brexit debates in the UK. On the one hand, Mason glowingly referenced the Popular Fronts in Spain and France, limiting his vision to 1936 and the early victories of the governmental coalitions. The tragic defeats that followed, and the rise of far-right governments in both cases, were conveniently written out of his narrative.[24] Yet even then, Mason's preferred policy of an electoral alliance between the contemporary Labour Party and the Liberal Democrats – with a slightly improved trade deal with the European Union as the main platform – makes the earlier versions seem revolutionary by comparison.[25] The same caricatured arguments emerged in 2020 when leftists were urged to vote for Biden to avoid the re-election of Donald Trump.

Caricature or not, in the face of more or less serious threats, the logic of Popular Frontism has re-emerged in a number of countries across Europe. It does so under the slogan of rallying behind the status quo – be it the EU or the liberal centre – as a bulwark against far-right populists. The call usually comes from the centre-left, who are generally in a better position to play the anti-fascist card than the centre-right. But there are cases of politicians of the centre-right trying to claim anti-fascist credentials or pose as the last line of defence against the far-right. Some leading members of New Democracy claim anti-fascist credentials for providing a mainstream electoral alternative to parts of the GD electorate, while Xavier Bertrand had announced his intention

---

23. Such arguments can be found in most articles published by *Jacobin* after Die Linke's bad election result. See Marx21 2021 for a response to these ideas.
24. Bloodworth 2019.
25. For a reply, both on the failures of the historical Popular Front and on the politics of the "contemporary" proposal by Mason, see Clark 2019.

to run in the Republicans' primaries in France by invoking his victories over the RN candidates in the regional elections of 2015 and last June.[26]

The strategy we should counterpose to those two dangers is also known from the past, the United Front, as advocated by Trotsky in his writings against Nazism. Of course this is easier said than done in the contemporary world, with the working-class movement in a very different situation than it was in interwar Europe. The task is to extract the essential reasoning of the strategy: trying to mobilise the broadest forces possible, uniting them in action, maintaining working-class independence from the bourgeoisie and its parties, maintaining freedom to criticise and independence from reformist allies. To be translated into tactics this logic must then be applied to a concrete analysis of a concrete context.

Another strategic constant in our fight against the far right, not irrelevant to the logic of the United Front, is the need to combine struggles and social movements. Our activity should not be confined to a very narrow sense of anti-fascism, involving direct confrontations with far-right hooligans. Confronting racist policies, supporting migrants and refugees, building a movement that fights under the banner of class solidarity against racist hate, are also important in building the left and pulling the rug from under the far right's feet. Of course the same applies to LGBTQ rights, women's struggles, fighting against nationalist warmongering, but for now, and in most countries, racism and Islamophobia remain the main banner of the far right. Fighting against the far right should not be the exclusive work of committed anti-fascists, but a common cause for the mass movements of the oppressed, the working class and all the potential victims of far-right policies.

## Returning to the Greek experience

I will conclude with some additional examples of the experience in Greece that illustrate some of these points.

In early October 2021, on the anniversary of the conviction of Golden Dawn, a series of fascist attacks on leftist activists sounded the alarm. They were organised by marginal and violent groups that were

---

26. "History will relate that twice here in the territory of Hauts-de-France the Front National has been stopped and we have pushed them back." Quoted in Mallet 2021.

overshadowed and semi-absorbed by Golden Dawn in the past. It is too soon to tell whether it is the beginning of an organised campaign. The point is that massive protests were organised in the following days and there was public outcry against the re-emergence of fascist violence. Especially in Thessaloniki, the epicentre of recent fascist activity, a thousands-strong march was organised with participation ranging from the Communist Party to anarchist groups.

This kind of reflex was not always a given. The absence of such responses was a factor that enabled Golden Dawn to grow in the first place. Too many on the left only started paying attention after GD entered parliament. In the case of the Communist Party, it took another year to seriously upgrade its anti-fascist activity. Until then, the best organised working-class party in Greece was mostly absent, content to argue that fascism will be vanquished when we deal with capitalism.

Perhaps it is not too hopeful to say that recent experiences have developed a stronger immune response by most parts of the left and among broader parts of the population. Compared to the rise of GD or the mass electoral support for far-right parties around Europe, the threat by these new groups is minimal, for now. But the massive response was an important and positive sign.

Faced with criticism for harbouring the far right and enabling these attacks, New Democracy played on its anti-fascist credentials, since they were in power both when charges were pressed against GD in 2013 and during the final verdict in 2020. It is a sick joke for ND to claim credit for the victory against Golden Dawn. But such an argument is in line with the concept of "The Wall of Democracy" put up as a headline in a progressive newspaper back in October 2020, featuring anti-Nazi comments by the leaders of all the parliamentary parties, including Mitsotakis and former Prime Minister Antonis Samaras, a leader of the far-right current of New Democracy.

An actual, material wall was being built during the same period, with the blessings of most parliamentary parties. A wall in Evros, on the Greco-Turkish border, where extremely militarised tactics are constantly employed against refugees dismissed as tools in the hands of Recep Tayyip Erdoğan, who are thus treated as invaders. During a flare-up on the border in March 2020, the army was deployed. The mainstream media and most parties cheered their repression of unarmed, hungry and desperate refugees as if they were facing an invading army. In this climate, impromptu militias emerged, willing to supplement the military's efforts to defend the border. This is what the "Wall of Democracy" looks like.

This example highlights the importance of confronting the state and government, as part and parcel of the fight against the far right. During the past few years, Golden Dawn was unable to utilise the opportunities presented to it. But the activation of the "social" far right (in the form of army veterans' associations, local churches, racist "citizen committees") was rising and falling in tandem with mainstream politics. During 2015–16, hundreds of thousands of refugees arrived in Greece and a magnificent and inspiring wave of popular solidarity welcomed them and helped them in their journey, while racists went silent. When the borders closed and the EU-Greece-Turkey agreement was signed (stipulating that no more border crossings are allowed), the governmental and mass media propaganda started portraying the refugees as a "problem". As soon as that happened, racists felt confident enough to start organising against accepting them in their towns or villages.

The same applies with nationalism, especially in the midst of escalating tension with Turkey in the eastern Mediterranean. Another recent example illustrates how state policies can encourage the far right even as the same governmental forces can use the threat of the far right to strengthen its popular support.

The fascist attacks in Thessaloniki happened as a new military agreement with France was being voted through in parliament. Nationalist fervour prevailed in the mass media. Any dissent to the expenditure was dismissed as naïve at best or treasonous at worst. One New Democracy MP quoted a far-right leader of a historical nationalist Greek-Cypriot organisation that fought to unite Cyprus with Greece: "We faced the British, the Turks and the Communists. And our biggest problem were the Communists". It was widely understood as a signal of sympathy to the fascists that the previous day violently attacked leftist students.

Nikos Dendias, the foreign minister, intervened to reprimand his party's MP and he was lauded as taking a progressive and anti-fascist stand. But it is interesting to note what he said. Dendias criticised his colleague's comments as unnecessarily divisive at a time that Greece needed to unite against the national threat coming from Turkey – actually promoting a nationalist warmongering argument. When he was called by the opposition to denounce the MP's smooth co-existence with Golden Dawn members in a ceremony that commemorates the nationalist-monarchist victory in the Civil War, he did it with ease, describing sharing any space with GD as unacceptable. But he skilfully dodged the question of many centre-right politicians attending such reactionary events, "winking" to his far-right audience: "I don't know who attends those contemporary events about the battle of Vitsi. I do know that my father was present at the battle of Vitsi".

Dendias was the minister of the interior when charges against GD were pressed and he is trying to build a democratic reputation. Suffice to say that during his time in the ministry of the interior, he launched the Orwellian campaign of "Xenios Zeus" – ancient God of Hospitality – to clear the streets of Athens of immigrants, and that during his time anti-fascists were tortured by police.

As I finish this article, news has emerged about the police murdering Nikos Sabanis, an 18-year-old Roma boy. He died after a car chase ended with seven cops opening fire on an unarmed and non-threatening group of three youths, shooting 38 bullets. One was murdered, another sent to hospital. In Greece, Roma lives don't matter. While the police were forced to start an investigation, Adonis Georgiadis, a government minister and deputy to the prime minister, rushed to proclaim on Twitter that the officers "did a great job". The minister in charge of the police rushed to meet the murderers as they were held in custody, and later expressed his gratitude for their release. His measures to address the issue consisted of more police, after the mass media turned reality upside down and presented the affair as a case of mass lawlessness.

Meanwhile, during a joint press conference with the prime minister of the Netherlands in November 2021, a Dutch journalist had the courage, all too lacking among her Greek colleagues, to publicly confront Mitsotakis on the crime of refugee boats being turned back in the Aegean Sea. The prime minister lashed out against her, and the next day the Greek media portrayed the affair as a moment of national pride.

The important fact is that in both those revolting incidents, the government's vitriolic messaging enjoyed the support of a sizeable part of its base. So, both the social and the political material for a far-right rebirth are present. If and when the centre-right party enters a crisis, especially if this is accelerated by the handling of national questions, this galaxy of forces on its right could find both an opening and potential allies among forces that currently roost inside the big tent.

After the end of the Golden Dawn trial, two extreme reactions emerged, an over-optimistic and an over-pessimistic one. The first triumphantly argued that the threat of the far right was over, while the second bitterly argued that nothing changed. We argued instead that we should celebrate the victory, and pay attention to the qualitative differences between reactionaries and conservatives voting for a right-wing party, attending rallies of a far-right party, or joining a fascist fighting battalion. But we must also keep in mind that a far-right social base always exists – they live among us. Constant features of capitalism, like institutional racism and nationalist warmongering, will continue feeding this current in society.

We will have to constantly face them, at times achieving some victories and winning some breathing space, only to have to fight them yet again. At the end of the day, when not used as a justification for passivity, the argument remains: to get rid of the far right once and for all, we will have to get rid of capitalism.

## References

Bloodworth, Sandra 2019, "From revolutionary possibility to fascist defeat: The French Popular Front of 1936–38", *Marxist Left Review*, 19, Summer. https://marxistleftreview.org/articles/from-revolutionary-possibility-to-fascist-defeat-the-french-popular-front-of-1936–38/

Borger, Julian 2019, "Donald Trump denounces 'globalism' in nationalist address to UN", *The Guardian*, 25 September. https://www.theguardian.com/us-news/2019/sep/24/donald-trump-un-address-denounces-globalism

Clark, Nick 2019, "Paul Mason's 'popular front' of failures is not the way to beat the right", *Socialist Worker* (UK), 19 August. https://socialistworker.co.uk/art/48799/Paul+Masons+popular+front+of+failures+is+not+the+way+to+beat+the+right

Cossé, Eva 2021, "French Court Confirms Dissolution of Anti-Discrimination Group", *Human Rights Watch*, 27 September. https://www.hrw.org/news/2021/09/27/french-court-confirms-dissolution-anti-discrimination-group

De Jong, Alex 2021, "Why the Dutch Socialist Party Is in Crisis", *International Viewpoint*, 19 January. https://internationalviewpoint.org/spip.php?article7004

Farand, Chloe 2019, "Denial and Dampening Ambition: Where do Europe's Right-Wing Populist Parties Stand on Climate Change?", *DeSmog*, 16 May. https://www.desmog.com/2019/05/16/right-wing-populist-parties-climate-science-denial-european-parliament-elections/

Garí, Manuel 2021, "May 4 in Madrid: A defeated left (a chronicle of urgency)", *International Socialism Project*, 9 May. https://internationalsocialism.net/may-4-in-madrid-a-defeated-left-a-chronicle-of-urgency/

Kovács, Zoltán 2019, "PM Orbán at Tusványos: 'The essence of illiberal democracy is the protection of Christian liberty'", *About Hungary* blog, 27 July. https://abouthungary.hu/blog/pm-Orbán-at-tusvanyos-the-essence-of-illiberal-democracy-is-the-protection-of-christian-liberty

Kouvelakis, Stathis 2021, "The Zemmour moment", *International Viewpoint*, 26 October. https://internationalviewpoint.org/spip.php?article7367

laSexta 2021, "Ayuso: 'Cuando te llaman fascista estás en el lado bueno de la historia'", *laSexta*, 21 May. https://www.lasexta.com/noticias/nacional/ayuso-cuando-llaman-fascista-estas-lado-bueno-historia_20210315604f3537ad0f4b0001e59d0f.html

Makris, A 2012, "More Than Half of Police Officers Voted For Neo-nazi Party", *Greek Reporter*, 11 May. https://greekreporter.com/2012/05/11/more-than-half-of-police-officers-voted-for-neo-nazi-party/

Mallet, Victor 2021, "Resurgent old parties of right and left triumph in France vote", *Financial Times*, 28 June. https://www.ft.com/content/6c184774-0b53-4f69-b171-6f8fa72e96d1

Marx21, 2021, "Die Linke: seven theses on the way forward. After the German election debacle", *Tempest*, 1 October. https://www.tempestmag.org/2021/10/die-linke-seven-theses-on-the-way-forward/

Milza, Pierre 2002, *L'Europe en chemise noire: Les extrêmes droites européennes de 1945 à aujourd'hui*, Fayard.

Mullen, John 2020, "Murder, McCarthyism and Islamophobia in France", *Red Flag*, 23 October. https://redflag.org.au/node/7425

Mullen, John 2021, "How dangerous is Marine Le Pen?", *Red Flag*, 6 May. https://redflag.org.au/article/how-dangerous-marine-le-pen

Petrou, Panos 2020, "Goodnight Golden Dawn", *Red Flag*, 10 October. https://redflag.org.au/index.php/node/7404

Petrou, Panos 2021, "Broad response to the neoliberal authoritarianism of the right-wing government", *International Viewpoint*, 26 March. https://internationalviewpoint.org/spip.php?article7084

Reuters staff 2018, "Hungarian PM sees shift to illiberal Christian democracy in 2019 European vote", *Reuters*, 28 July. https://www.reuters.com/article/us-hungary-Orban-idUSKBN1KI0BK

Siegel, Zachary and Marie Targonski-O'Brien 2017, "When Golden Dawn and the Greek Orthodox Church align", *The Groundtruth Project*, 24 May. https://thegroundtruthproject.org/golden-dawn-and-greek-orthodox-church-unite/

Turigliatto, Franco 2021, "Build the response to the fascist attack and the policies of the bosses", *International Viewpoint*, 17 October. https://internationalviewpoint.org/spip.php?article7352

Tzimeros, Thanos 2022, "Gynecology and gynecoparasitism", *The President*, 15 April. https://www.thepresident.gr/2021/04/15/gynaikoktonia-kai-gynaikoparasitismos-grafei-o-thanos-tzimeros/

Urbán, Miguel 2019, "Franco never left", *Jacobin*, 1 May. https://jacobinmag.com/2019/01/spain-vox-partido-popular-far-right-franco

Wilno, Henri 2019, "The coming crisis and the rise of 'national liberalism'", *International Viewpoint*, 8 November. https://internationalviewpoint.org/spip.php?article6281

TOM BRAMBLE

# AUKUS and the US alliance: Australian imperialism in the Indo-Pacific

**Tom Bramble** has published widely on political economy and the labour movement and is a regular contributor to *Marxist Left Review*. His recent books include *Labor's Conflict: Big Business, Workers and the Politics of Class* (with Rick Kuhn), *Introducing Marxism: A Theory of Social Change*, and *The Fight for Workers' Power: Revolution and Counter-Revolution in the 20th Century* (with Mick Armstrong).

AUSTRALIA IS PLAYING A LEADING ROLE in the growing imperialist competition in the Indo-Pacific. The Morrison government, with the full support of the Labor Opposition, is backing the United States in its contest with China for supremacy in the region. This is consistent with Australia's longstanding record as a junior partner of US imperialism. In this article, I will outline the various ways in which the Australian government is inserting itself into US attempts to halt China's growing challenge to US hegemony. In doing so, Australia is making military conflict in the region more likely, with potentially devastating consequences. The left must oppose Australia's involvement in the US-led war drive. At the same time, socialists must not give ground to the idea that China is in any way a lesser evil or supportable. Our main enemy remains our own ruling class, but the military adventurism of both the major imperialist camps, China as well as the US and its allies, must be opposed.

## Australia's spring offensive

The spring of 2021 saw a series of announcements that indicate Australia's growing military aggression in the Indo-Pacific. The first episode in what could be called Australia's Spring Offensive was the announcement on 16 September of the tripartite AUKUS pact, joining

Australia together with the United States and Britain in a new military alliance. While the three countries have been military partners in many wars in the past century and have regularly conducted joint exercises in peacetime, AUKUS is a step up from the status quo. Certainly, that is the intention of its architects, with a top US official describing the pact as "a fundamental decision that binds decisively Australia to the United States and Great Britain for generations"[1] or, in Scott Morrison's words, "a forever partnership".[2] This new pact, supposedly put together to defend democracy against autocrats, was stitched together and announced as a fait accompli to the publics of the three countries without even a parliamentary vote.

AUKUS is an aggressive alliance designed to maintain US imperialist domination of the Indo-Pacific region. Australia's decision to scrap the French diesel-powered submarine fleet in favour of an American-British nuclear-powered fleet is a significant step in this regard. The sole basis for this decision is to equip Australia with a submarine fleet capable of joining the US in a war far from its shores. Even more than diesel submarines, nuclear-propelled submarines are a purely offensive weapon. They can remain underwater for months, reducing the chance of detection, and can travel much longer distances without refuelling. These two factors make them perfect for engaging in operations in the South China Sea or close to Taiwan. True to its record as an imperialist party, the ALP welcomed AUKUS and the new submarine contract.

The significance of the AUKUS announcement goes beyond the new submarines, which will not be able to undertake missions for at least two or three decades. More important in any coming conflict were the other measures announced the following day at the annual meeting of Australian and US defence and foreign ministers in Washington, known as AUSMIN.[3] These included the development, through the AUKUS partnership, of "deeper integration and security-related science, technology, industrial bases and supply chains, as well as deeper cooperation on a range of defense and security capabilities". The latter will involve the rotational deployment of US aircraft of all

---

1. Borger and Sabbagh 2021.
2. Tillett 2021.
3. Source for the detail in this paragraph: AUSMIN 2021.

types in Australia, including B1 bombers, increased use of Australian ports by the US Navy and more joint exercises on land. The Northern Territory and Western Australia will be the focus of this increased military activity.

The NT has seen an increasing US presence in recent years and is becoming a staging point for military personnel, logistics and resources. The US already stations 2,500 Marines on rotation through what is effectively a US base outside Darwin and conducts regular exercises with the Australian Army. The US has announced about $2 billion in funding for future defence projects across the NT, including construction of giant fuel storage tanks on Darwin's RAAF base, enabling the US to conduct more military flights to and from the Territory. The Australian government is supporting this US commitment with more than $700 million in infrastructure upgrades across the NT's defence bases as part of a planned $8 billion military spending program over 10 years in the Territory.[4] It is likely that the US Navy will also seek access to the HMAS Stirling base in Perth for its nuclear ships and submarines, while the US will supply the Australian Navy with long-range Tomahawk cruise missiles. US chargé d'affaires in Australia, Michael Goldman, told the ABC that the rotation of US military forces was likely to be "only getting bigger, more integrated, more ambitious and better in the future".[5]

Other joint US-Australian initiatives discussed at AUSMIN included the creation of a "Guided Weapons and Explosive Ordnance Enterprise" in Australia along with hypersonic weapons and electromagnetic warfare research and production. Australian ministers acknowledged US certification of Australian-made TNT explosives as an alternative source of supply to the US military and welcomed the US Department of Defense's decision to commission Australian company Lynas to build a factory in Texas to boost production of rare earths, for which China otherwise holds a monopoly.[6] The decision in December by the Australian Defence Force to ditch its entire fleet of European-designed Taipan helicopters, replacing them with new Black Hawks and Seahawks imported from the United States at a cost of billions

---

4.   Mackay 2021.
5.   Mackay 2021.
6.   Lynas 2021.

of dollars, is another indication of Australia's desire to integrate its hardware with that of the US to facilitate future military operations.[7]

Just a few days after the AUSMIN meeting, the first in-person meeting of leaders of the Quadrilateral Security Pact (the Quad) took place in Washington, the third element of Canberra's Spring Offensive. This brought together US president Joe Biden and the prime ministers of Australia, India and Japan. The Quad has been many years in the making, but with Quad partners all experiencing growing tensions with China, it is now a strategic priority for the four nations.[8]

Although the Quad's communiques promise cooperation on vaccine manufacture and distribution, international education and climate action, its main, if unstated, purpose is to coordinate nations to fight China in the name of advancing "a free and open Indo-Pacific". To this end, the Quad members will cooperate on cyber security, new technology and secure supply chains. Joint military exercises are also a priority. Since 2014, the navies of Japan, India and the US have conducted annual exercises, and in 2020 Australia joined the trio in the Bay of Bengal and the Arabian Sea.[9] If China attacks or blockades Taiwan, the Quad could coordinate military assets, including land-based anti-ship missiles and other strike capabilities that could hit China.

With the Quad now formalised, there is already talk of who else might join it, and of other regional groupings of small numbers of countries, so-called "minilateralism", that might come together to form an overarching web of alliances in Asia to challenge China. In 2019 the Philippines joined Japan, India and the US in so-called freedom of navigation operations in the South China Sea, while South Korea has held military exercises with Australia, Japan and the US. In 2020, Canada joined Quad members in anti-submarine exercises. Another option open to the Quad is sharing military intelligence with the "Five Eyes" intelligence partnership.[10] The confirmation in December of a $1 billion deal with South Korean company Hanwha to build 30 self-propelled howitzers and 15 armoured ammunition resupply

---

7. Greene 2021.
8. Rudd 2021; Jaishankar and Madan 2021.
9. Kaushik 2021.
10. The "Five Eyes" comprises the US, Britain, Canada, Australia and New Zealand.

vehicles for the army in Geelong is another indication of Australia's growing military ties with Asian allies.[11]

The Quad is not yet Asia's NATO. It is still a relatively untested alliance. Japan has little recent overseas military experience. India's main military rival is not China but Pakistan, and the country has traditionally looked to Russia, rather than the US, for military supplies. Japan also has a history of fractious relations with South Korea rooted in Japan's imperialist past. But regardless of such weaknesses, these alliances between major industrial powers are far stronger than anything China possesses.

The fourth element of the Morrison government's Spring Offensive was its very public commitment to joining the US in the event of war with China over Taiwan. For years, the US has maintained what it calls "strategic ambiguity", refusing to say whether it would go to war with China if China attacked Taiwan. Australia followed this protocol. The Biden presidency has now cast doubt on this principle, making ambiguous statements, and the Morrison government is keen to encourage a shift to a more openly belligerent stance.[12] In October, former prime minister Tony Abbott visited Taiwan in a supposedly private trip and told his audience of Taiwanese and other Asian leaders that Australia must throw its weight behind Taiwan.[13] Serving Australian ministers have become equally forthright. After the AUSMIN talks, Australia's ministers described Taiwan as a "leading democracy" and a "critical partner" and in November Defence Minister Peter Dutton told *The Australian* newspaper that it "would be inconceivable that we wouldn't support the US in an action if the US chose to take that action".[14]

While the dominant position on the Australian left is that Australia joins the US in wars because its political leaders are too weak to stand up to US bullying, the AUKUS pact is in large part the work of the Morrison government. The government recognised in 2020 that the planned fleet of diesel submarines was incapable of undertaking

---

11. Greene and Dziedzic 2021.
12. Sanger 2021.
13. Hurst 2021a.
14. Bramston 2021.

the kind of Australian missions required for a war with China.[15] It approached and won the support of the British government, the only nation to enjoy access to American nuclear propulsion technology, and together they approached the new Biden administration to add Australia to this very exclusive club. Australia is quite capable of stirring up imperialist tensions without in any way being pushed into doing so by the US.

None of this has anything to do with defending Australia, if that is understood to mean the people of Australia, which is how politicians usually try to promote military spending. These moves aim to boost Australian power and protect US domination of the region. As Australia's ambassador to the US, Arthur Sinodinos, put it in November 2021, referring to the nuclear submarines:

> We want to be able to, in these deteriorating strategic circumstances, be able to project our power further up, rather than taking an approach that all our defence has to be a defence of the mainland. This is about how we project power, and therefore how we are able to shape the security environment in which we operate in the Indo-Pacific.[16]

Canberra's Spring Offensive emerges out of several years of heightened Australian antagonism towards China. Successive Defence White Papers (2009, 2013, 2016) have identified China as the chief threat to Australia's imperialist interests in the Asia-Pacific. Coalition governments have steadily lifted military spending since 2013 and in the 2021 federal Budget, the Morrison government forecast that military expenditure in 2023–24 will be 27 percent higher than in 2018–19.[17] Acquisition of nuclear submarines will push the bill still higher.

Gone are many of the diplomatic niceties that once prevailed. In 2014, Chinese president Xi Jinping became one of the few state leaders afforded the privilege of speaking to a joint sitting of the Australian parliament. Six months later, when the text of the new free trade

---

15. Knott 2021; Parker et al 2021.
16. Cranston 2021.
17. Hawkins 2021.

agreement between the two countries was finalised, Abbott described it as a "milestone in bilateral relations" and congratulated the two negotiating teams who had drafted it:

> What you have collectively done is history making for both our countries, it will change our countries for the better, it will change our region for the better...change our world for the better.[18]

This language has been relegated to the history books. In 2017, Abbott's successor Malcolm Turnbull introduced foreign influence legislation, measures targeting supposed "fifth columnists" among Australia's Chinese community, and tighter regulation of Chinese investments in Australia. At a time when Britain was celebrating its growing ties with China, including handing Huawei responsibility for rolling out 5G, Australia led the charge to exclude the Chinese company from Western telecommunication networks. In recent years, Australia has played a leading diplomatic role, hypocritically denouncing human rights abuses in Xinjiang and Tibet as well as China's crackdown on democracy in Hong Kong. In 2020, the Morrison government called for an independent inquiry into the origins of COVID, hoping to embarrass the CCP. Even decisions the Coalition government once defended, including leasing the port of Darwin to the Chinese company Landbridge, it is now looking to overturn under pressure from the US and the Australian national security agencies. The "serious" Nine print media and ABC have been cheerleaders for this turn in Australia's foreign policy. There are still occasionally faint echoes of "not being forced to choose between the US and China" in speeches by government ministers, but the AUKUS announcement was definitive: Australia has chosen, staking out a role as one of China's leading antagonists.

China of course is not a passive victim of all this: imperialism is nothing if not a contest. China is just as keen to push the US out of what it regards as its sphere of influence in Asia as the US is to preserve its dominance. For several years, China has been steadily expanding its

---

18.  Conifer 2015.

military presence in the South China Sea, including building air strips on atolls. It has dramatically increased spending on aerial, naval and space weaponry. It has imposed direct rule on Hong Kong in all but name. It has increased its intimidation of Taiwan, including dozens of flights by the PLA Air Force into what Taiwan claims as its air defence zone. And it appears equally willing to spar with Australia. In response to the Australian call for an inquiry into the origins of COVID in 2020, China imposed restrictions on imports of Australian coal, followed by meat, cotton, wool, barley, timber, copper, sugar, lobster and wine. It then issued a list of 14 demands on the Australian government, demanding it back off its aggressive measures or suffer continued Chinese sanction. Soon after, it imposed restrictions on official meetings and communication with government ministers and expelled the last remaining Australian journalists. These actions demonstrate that what is taking place cannot be reduced to Western bullying of an oppressed nation, but is a contest between imperial rivals. While the US and its allies, including Australia, enjoy a series of advantages, China remains an active and aggressive protagonist in the overall system of competition

## Labor's response

The Morrison government's more aggressive posture towards China has been fully backed by the ALP. Within 24 hours of the announcement of AUKUS and the submarine deal last September, the Opposition announced its support for them both:

> Labor looks forward to strengthened cooperation with our close allies, through the AUKUS partnership announced today.

> This affirms what Labor has been calling for; deeper partnerships with allied and aligned nations, to build a region which is stable, prosperous and respectful of sovereignty.[19]

Except for the Maritime Union and the Electrical Trades Union, no unions criticised the announcement, neither the tens of billions that

19.  Albanese et al 2021.

will be added to the military budget nor the military threat that the submarines represent to the people of the Indo-Pacific.

The only time the Labor Opposition criticised the Morrison government was when it over-reached established protocols. And so when Dutton stated that Australia would back Taiwan, contradicting "strategic ambiguity", Labor's foreign affairs spokesperson Penny Wong accused the minister of playing dangerous "political games" and "amping up war". Dutton's statement was, Wong argued, "wildly out of step with the strategy long adopted by Australia and our principal ally".[20] If and when the US shifts strategy towards Taiwan, it is very likely Labor will follow suit, and if the US does go to war with China over Taiwan, Labor will be at America's side.

It is not just federal Labor that has failed to criticise the Morrison government's aggressive militarism. Labor state premiers vie with their Coalition colleagues in promoting their states as defence manufacturing hubs. The Palaszczuk government in Queensland boasts of partnering with German company Rheinmetall to produce military vehicles and with Boeing to manufacture drones, backed by millions of dollars in subsidies.[21] The Andrews government promotes the arms industry in Victoria, stating that it is the home of hundreds of companies supplying the Australian armed forces with land, sea and air weapons systems.[22]

Labor's stance should come as no surprise. Labor has a longstanding record backing Australian and US militarism. The party was in power during both world wars, as well as the 1991 Gulf War. It supported the war and occupation of Afghanistan, the occupation of Iraq and Australia's regular armed deployments in Pacific islands. Successive Labor governments have safeguarded the Pine Gap spy station and welcomed visits by US nuclear warships.

Support for the US alliance is an item of faith in the US parliamentary caucus. The ALP takes pride in the fact that the first steps towards what became ANZUS were taken by the governments of John Curtin and Ben Chifley, and every Labor leader pays homage to it. In

20. Wong 2021.
21. Walker 2021.
22. Victoria State Government.

March 2011, for example, then prime minister Julia Gillard addressed a joint sitting of the US Congress, in which she told those assembled:

> In both our countries, real mates talk straight. We mean what we say. You have an ally in Australia. An ally for war and peace. An ally for hardship and prosperity. An ally for the sixty years past and Australia is an ally for all the years to come.[23]

Now that the stakes are being raised in competition with China, no Labor figure wants to be seen to be critical either of the US alliance or of the growing preparations for war with China. This was obvious in November 2021 in the responses to a National Press Club speech by former leader Paul Keating attacking Dutton's commitment to join the US in defence of Taiwan.[24] Keating argued that Australia had nothing to gain from doing so. It would be not only militarily foolhardy but financially disastrous going to war with the country's leading trade partner. Keating argued that rather than raising military tensions with China, Australia should try to suppress them. He argued that the nuclear submarines would reduce Australia's military autonomy because the propulsion units would be controlled by US technicians and would as a result "simply be part of the United States force directed by the United States".[25] He attacked the mainstream media for its hypocrisy, highlighting China's human rights abuses while ignoring that of the US and its Asian allies.

In some respects, there was nothing exceptional about Keating's speech: it was not a socialist or internationalist response to Dutton's comments. It epitomised what had until recent years been a widespread opinion in ruling class circles, that Australian capitalism had more to gain by creating space for China's rise in the region than by treating it as a threat. But while Keating's comments might once have been regarded as a legitimate contribution to a debate, they were now regarded as anathema by most of the political establishment. Dutton said that Keating was "out of control and damaging our country" and

---

23.  Gillard 2011.
24.  Dziedzic 2021
25.  Hurst 2021b.

called him "Grand Appeaser Comrade Keating".[26] Mainstream media commentators such as Chris Uhlmann and Peter Hartcher, along with Australian Strategic Policy Institute council member and Macquarie University academic Lavina Lee, attacked Keating as well.

But Keating was also attacked by federal Labor. While Dutton tried to implicate Albanese in Keating's statements, accusing the Labor leader of "backing in the Chinese government", Labor's deputy leader Richard Marles said that while Keating is "entitled to his view…Labor have made it completely clear the challenges that China represents".[27] Marles is right – the ALP has worked in lockstep with the Liberals over the question of China. There is nothing to suggest that if Labor wins office at the coming federal election it will be anything other than an enthusiastic supporter of the US in its efforts to contain China's power in the region.

## Junior partner of US imperialism

Australia's increasingly aggressive posture towards China runs parallel to that of the US itself. As I outlined in an article in the last issue of the *Marxist Left Review*,[28] the earlier approach based on "engagement", in which the US believed that it could contain China's rise within a broader framework of US hegemony in the Indo-Pacific, was abandoned by the Trump administration and replaced by a framework premised on "strategic competition". The Biden administration has only amplified this foreign policy shift. The US is now openly confronting China's rising power in the Indo-Pacific on a range of fronts: military, economic, diplomatic and political. Biden is increasing the military budget Trump bequeathed him. His foreign policy, spearheaded by noted China hawks, is pitched as a battle between the "democratic world" led by the United States and the "autocracies" led by China and Russia. Competition with China is also a big consideration in the administration's domestic agenda, with tens of billions of dollars devoted to investment in strategic industries. The administration has continued Trump's attempts to block China's access to military-related industries and US technological

26. Dutton 2021.
27. Ransley 2021.
28. Bramble 2021.

know-how. Biden is pitching rebuilding America's ailing infrastructure and patching over the yawning economic and racial inequalities in the US as winning the "competition with China for the 21st century".[29] Other than the modest social spending involved in Biden's financial packages, this agenda is backed to the hilt by the Republican party who rightly see in much of it a continuation of Trump's agenda.

The main difference between the Biden administration and Trump's is that the Democratic president spent much of his first year in office smoothing over diplomatic relations that were sabotaged by his predecessor. This presents the Australian ruling class with opportunities. One of its main objectives since the nineteenth century has been to secure first Britain's and now America's military engagement in the Asia Pacific. From the 1880s, when the Victorian government urged Britain to occupy the New Hebrides (now Vanuatu), through the 1960s when the Menzies government dragged the US deeper into the Vietnam conflict, to the 1980s when the Hawke government spearheaded the creation of the Asia-Pacific Economic Co-operation forum, anchoring the US in the region, the Australian ruling class has done its best to keep its chief imperialist patron embedded in the Indo-Pacific.

The Australian ruling class sees the involvement of a friendly great power in the Indo-Pacific as the best guarantee of its own interests. Chief among these interests is the security of the sea approaches to the island continent on which are carried critical trade and military supplies to and from Europe, the Middle East, East Asia and the United States. In addition, Australian capitalists have long regarded the country's neighbours, in particular PNG and the Pacific Island states, as Australia's backyard, with Australian companies dominating their economies and extracting profits. Looking to a great power to secure these sea lanes and prevent nationalist threats to its investments has been one of Australian imperialism's main priorities. Only when the imperialist big brother could no longer perform these duties, as occurred in early 1942 when British Prime Minister Winston Churchill tried to divert the Seventh Australian Expeditionary Force, then returning from the Middle East to Australia, to the Burmese theatre, leaving

---

29. Cheng 2021.

Australia and its colony PNG defenceless against Japanese attack, did Australia turn to the US instead. Prime Minister John Curtin's call on the US to stand with Australia as a matter of its own self-interest captures an important element of the relationship to this day:

> Australia is the last bastion between the west coast of America and the Japanese. If Australia goes, the Americas are wide open.[30]

The US's victory in the Pacific War contributed significantly to Australia's fortunes as an imperialist force in the post-war decades. It has benefited not just from the US Seventh Fleet patrolling the region, preventing any rival from threatening the security of Australia's maritime approaches, but also from the US-dominated architecture of economics and finance, the so-called rules-based liberal international economic order. The alliance with the US provides Australian imperialism access to the latest military hardware, shared intelligence networks and diplomatic backing from the world's most powerful state. Without this military umbrella and outside this financial architecture, the Australian ruling class would be much weaker. What is more, Australia gets US protection on the cheap. Australian military self-reliance would involve a military budget several times larger than what it currently spends.

Some left and liberal critics of AUKUS argue that it locks Australia into US military planning and renders the country a subordinate power.[31] But integration into US imperialist plans in the Indo-Pacific *enhances* Australia's clout with the United States and augments its capacities as a regional player. Without US backing, Australian imperialism would not be stronger, nor would it spend less on the military. To be self-sufficient within a capitalist framework, Australia would need to triple or quadruple its military spending and probably acquire nuclear weapons. As well, without the guarantee provided by the US Seventh Fleet, Australia would probably feel the need to involve itself in *more* regional conflicts to protect its vital interests and establish a credible presence.

30. National Museum of Australia 2021.
31. See for example Anti-Bases Coalition 2021.

Growing rivalry with China over the past decade has created a debate within the ranks of the ruling class, one wing of which argues that, to preserve good relations with its biggest trading partner, Australia must forge a path more independent of the US.[32] But, even if we were to focus only on the economic question, the continuing alliance with the US still pays Australian capitalism significant dividends. It is true that Australia earns eight times as much foreign exchange from merchandise exports (iron ore, coal, gold etc) to China as it does from exports to the US and twice as much from services exports (international education, tourism etc), but the US underwrites the basic framework of trade, investment and finance which underpins Australia's relations with the world. New York is one of the world's two main financial centres and the US dollar is the de facto world currency for international trade, investment and central banks. America's IT industry and IT protocols dominate the world. Its aerospace industry, universities, entertainment industry and other sectors are the default for most countries. The US is still the world's preeminent place to do business: one quarter of the global stock of foreign direct investment (FDI) is invested in the US, five times as much as is invested in China.[33] As for Australia, while trade with China is more valuable than with the US, the latter is a far more significant investor in Australia, accounting for one quarter of total overseas investment in the country, as compared to China's 2 percent share. Even adding Hong Kong investment only takes the Chinese figure to 5.5 percent.[34]

Australia appears thus far at least to be able to have its cake and eat it, trading barbs with Beijing and even becoming the target of substantial trade bans, while at the same time running a record trade surplus with China.[35] China's imposition of trade bans may even have worked to Australia's advantage: Australian coal producers have been able to find

32. See John Menadue's website "Pearls and Irritations", which runs regular contributions by retired ambassadors and foreign affairs and defence department bureaucrats criticising Australia's aggressive policy towards China and what they regard as excessive deference to the US and associated "loss of sovereignty": www.johnmenadue.com. Bramble 2011 provides an early review of this debate.
33. Department of Foreign Affairs and Trade 2020.
34. Department of Foreign Affairs and Trade 2020.
35. Hartcher 2021.

markets elsewhere following China's ban, but Chinese steel producers must now make do with more expensive, poorer quality metallurgical coal from other sources.[36]

If we consider the military balance of power, alongside questions of economics, the reasons for Australian imperialism's continued strong support for the US become even more clear cut. Abandoning military ties with the US would involve an extraordinary transition cost in military hardware and software. Australia and the US militaries have a long, shared history, having fought together in every major war since 1900. Australian weapons systems are designed for interoperability with those of the US. The US is an unrivalled military power globally with a wide network of allies, giving it the opportunity to protect Australian interests in the Indo-Pacific if the two allies come to blows with China. By contrast, China would be in no position to defend these interests from a US attack if Australia opted for China as its imperial patron. And unlike Britain in 1942, the US shows no signs of walking away from its military relationship with Australia; far from it, relations are only growing tighter.

The Australian ruling class's desire to keep first Britain and now the US strong and engaged in Asia explains why Australia has backed imperialist wars since the nineteenth century, which in most cases have had nothing to do with the security of the mainland. Sometimes, this has involved the dispatch of substantial forces, as with the world wars; at other times Australian support has involved quite modest deployments, as with the 1991 Gulf War and the invasions and occupation of Afghanistan and Iraq. Australia's biggest contribution to America's military power in recent decades, however, has not been soldiers, sailors, ships or submarines but surveillance – the jointly-run spy and communication bases in Australia, most importantly those at Pine Gap outside Alice Springs and North West Cape at Exmouth. Without the information gathered by these spy bases, the US Navy and Air Force in the Middle East and Indo-Pacific would be operating blind. The Australian ruling class hopes that by offering the US these kinds of assets, the US will come to its assistance if Australian

---

36. Bartholomeusz 2021.

imperialist interests are ever threatened, something it believes will deter any would-be aggressor.

## Australia and the "China threat"

These are the considerations that help to explain the recent intensification of Australia's imperialist tub thumping in the Indo-Pacific. If a strong US presence in the region is vital to Australia's imperialist interests, China is a clear and growing threat to US interests and therefore to Australian imperialism. The Australian ruling class sees an opportunity to reinforce America's attachment to the region, including Australia itself.

Biden's inauguration as president came as a welcome change for much of the Australian ruling class. Trump's erratic foreign policy had raised alarm in Canberra. His decision on his inauguration to abandon the Trans-Pacific Partnership (TPP), which was meant to lock in a US-centred economic bloc in Asia, sparked particular concern, as did his attacks on the World Trade Organization and imposition of tariffs on many US allies. These appeared to weaken the US's commitment to the imperialist order from which Australian capitalism has long benefited. The Australian foreign policy community was also worried by Trump's personal relations with the Russian and Chinese leaders and his tendency to take in good faith North Korean president Kim Jong-un's promises to denuclearise his country.

Biden, by contrast, is a known quantity. As vice president to Obama for eight years, Biden had a track record pursuing policies that suited Australia's needs. His emphasis as president on taking on China and rebuilding alliances as part of that process was what the Australian government wanted to hear; the adults were back in charge. And Biden's decision to commit to AUKUS comes with none of the political overheads such an agreement would have carried in Australia had Trump been the US signatory.

This does not mean that the Morrison government and Biden administration are completely in harmony. The Morrison government's reluctance to take even performative steps to tackle global warming jars with the White House, which has mastered the art of talking climate-friendly policies while doing the opposite. The Biden administration has kept Trump's tariffs and taken no steps to rebuild the World Trade Organization nor to join the Comprehensive and Progressive Agreement for Trans-Pacific Partnership (the re-badged TPP following US withdrawal), areas that Australia as a trade-dependent nation is keen to see action on and where China sees opportunities to promote its claims to regional leadership. And the Morrison government, along with America's European and Asian allies, was shocked at the collapse of the US presence in Afghanistan and the Taliban's rapid advance on Kabul in August 2021 and, apparently, annoyed that it had not been forewarned. Mitigating this shock, however, was its understanding that America's exit was part of a retreat (in the Middle East), the better to advance (in Asia), something that the US now promises with its AUKUS and AUSMIN commitments.

Such developments help explain why Australia has in recent years become one of the most belligerent powers towards China. In part, this is because China's growing ambitions in the Indo-Pacific threaten Australia's informal empire in PNG, East Timor and the Pacific Island states, its trade routes and, potentially, its influence in Indonesia, a critical player to Australia's north. But more broadly, Australia sees itself playing a leadership role urging those concerned by China's rise (in particular, Japan, Taiwan, South Korea, Singapore, Britain and now India) to stand together to challenge China. In this way it both advances its profile as an imperialist power and proves its value as one of the US's most important allies in the region. Australia can offer the US support from the strongest military in south-east Asia, with far greater capability to project force beyond its borders than any of its near neighbours. Strategically, Australia can also offer the US basing facilities beyond the reach of all but a few of China's long-range missiles, thereby providing the US with the ability to reduce its reliance on bases in Guam and Japan. An Australia with a fleet of nuclear-powered submarines will make it even more of an asset to the US, even if these submarines will only make a modest contribution to the overall US war effort.[37]

This is the context in which we can understand Morrison's talk of the "forever partnership" between Australia and the US. In contrast

---

37. The US currently has 68 nuclear submarines and is building more. Australia is committed to only eight, the first of which will be operational no earlier than 2040.

to the portrayal of Australia in the accounts of many liberals, the Australian ship of state is not a forlorn life raft, tossed about randomly on the stormy seas of great power rivalries. It is itself an active participant in the imperialist competition which characterises international relations under developed capitalism, using its substantial power to defend the interests of the Australian ruling class. Socialists need to stand firmly against Australian imperialism and oppose the US alliance, including the presence of American armed forces and military facilities such as Pine Gap and North West Cape. We must oppose the drive to war with China and imperialist measures that fall short of war, including restrictions on trade (tariffs, quotas, bans), financial and economic sanctions. As tensions with China rise, we can expect increasing demonisation of Chinese Australians and Chinese students; racism must be actively fought to prevent the ruling class undermining opposition to Australian militarism. Finally, we must reject any idea that China is in any way to be preferred to the United States in the contest for power in the Indo Pacific. China too oppresses and exploits people in the region and wider world.

## References

Albanese, Anthony, Penny Wong and Brendan O'Connor 2021, "AUKUS Partnership; Media Statement", 16 September. https://anthonyalbanese.com.au/media-centre/aukus-partnership-statement

Anti-Bases Coalition 2021, "The nuclear subs and the Australia-UK-US (AUKUS) security pact fact sheet", 28 September. https://socialistproject.ca/2021/09/dangerous-turn-arms-race-in-the-pacific/

AUSMIN 2021, "The Australia-US Ministerial Consultations Joint Statement: An Unbreakable Alliance for Peace and Prosperity", 17 September. www.foreignminister.gov.au/minister/marise-payne/media-release/australia-us-ministerial-consultations-joint-statement-unbreakable-alliance-peace-and-prosperity

Bartholomeusz, Stephen 2021, "China's ban on Australian coal has an expensive sting in the tail", *Sydney Morning Herald*, 7 September. www.smh.com.au/business/markets/china-s-ban-on-australian-coal-has-an-expensive-sting-in-its-tail-20210907-p58pij.html

Borger, Julian and Dan Sabbagh, "US, UK and Australia forge military alliance to counter China", *The Guardian*, 16 September 2021. www.theguardian.com/australia-news/2021/sep/15/australia-nuclear-powered-submarines-us-uk-security-partnership-aukus

Bramble, Tom 2011, "Australian imperialism and the rise of China", *Marxist Left Review*, 3, Spring. https://marxistleftreview.org/articles/australian-imperialism-and-the-rise-of-china/

Bramble, Tom 2021, "The Biden administration's plan for US imperialism", *Marxist Left Review*, 22, Winter. https://marxistleftreview.org/articles/bidens-plan-for-the-us-empire/

Bramston, Troy 2021. "Defending Taiwan against Beijing is a must, says Peter Dutton", *The Australian*, 12 November. https://www.theaustralian.com.au/nation/defence/defending-taiwan-against-beijing-is-a-must-says-peter-dutton/news-story/ef9dd7fd56515afbdc90021760d1d344

Cheng, Evelyn 2021, "Biden calls for the U.S. to become more competitive against a 'deadly earnest' China", CNBC, 29 April. https://www.cnbc.com/2021/04/29/biden-calls-for-us-to-become-more-competitive-against-china.html

Conifer, Dan 2015, "Australia and China sign 'history making' free trade agreement after a decade of negotiations", *ABC News*, 17 June. www.abc.net.au/news/2015–06-17/australia-and-china-sign-free-trade-agreement/6552940?nw=0&r=HtmlFragment

Cranston, Matthew 2021, "AUKUS about 'projecting power' north, says Sinodinos", *Australian Financial Review*, 10 November. https://www.afr.com/policy/foreign-affairs/aukus-about-projecting-power-north-says-sinodinos-20211109-p597cr

Department of Foreign Affairs and Trade 2020, *Foreign Investment Statistics*. www.dfat.gov.au/trade/resources/investment-statistics/statistics-on-who-invests-in-australia

Dutton, Peter 2021, Twitter, 10 November. https://twitter.com/PeterDutton_MP/status/1458289955789099009?s=20

Dziedzic, Stephen 2021, "Paul Keating plays down prospect of Chinese military invasion of Taiwan, urges Australia not to be drawn into conflict", *ABC News*, 10 November. www.abc.net.au/news/2021–11-10/paul-keating-plays-down-china-invasion-taiwan/100610102

Gillard, Julia 2011, "Julia Gillard's speech to Congress", 10 March. www.smh.com.au/world/julia-gillards-speech-to-congress-20110310–1boee.html

Greene, Andrew 2021, "Australia dumps troubled European-designed Taipan helicopters for US Black Hawks and Seahawks", *ABC News*, 10 December. www.abc.net.au/news/2021–12-10/australia-dumps-troubled-mrh-90-taipan-helicopters/100688550

Greene, Andrew and Stephen Dziedzic 2021, "Historic billion-dollar defence contract with South Korea amid rising regional tensions", *ABC News*, 13 December. www.abc.net.au/news/2021–12-13/australia-and-south-korea-billion-dollar-defence-contract/100694638

Hartcher, Peter 2021, "How Australia has shaped up to Xi's aggression", *Sydney Morning Herald*, 12 October. www.smh.com.au/world/asia/how-australia-has-shaped-up-to-xi-s-aggression-20211011-p58yw8.html

Hawkins, Phillip 2021, "Australian Government Expenditure". www.aph.gov.au/About_Parliament/Parliamentary_Departments/Parliamentary_Library/pubs/rp/BudgetReview202021/AustralianGovernmentExpenditure

Hurst, Daniel 2021a, "Mr Abbott goes to Taiwan: an unofficial message of Australian solidarity?", *The Guardian*, 16 October. www.theguardian.com/australia-news/2021/oct/16/mr-abbott-goes-to-taiwan-an-unofficial-message-of-australian-solidarity

Hurst, Daniel 2021b, "'Throwing toothpicks at the mountain': Paul Keating says Aukus submarines plan will have no impact on China", *The Guardian*, 10 November. https://www.theguardian.com/australia-news/2021/nov/10/throwing-toothpicks-at-the-mountain-paul-keating-says-aukus-submarines-plan-will-have-no-impact-on-china

Jaishankar, Dhruva and Tanvi Madan 2021, "How the Quad can Match the Hype: It's the best hope for balancing China in the Indo-Pacific", *Foreign Affairs*, 15 April. https://www.foreignaffairs.com/articles/united-states/2021–04-15/how-quad-can-match-hype

Kaushik, Krishn 2021, "Explained: the Malabar Exercise of Quad nations, and why it matters to India", *The Indian Express*, 31 August. https://indianexpress.com/article/explained/malabar-exercise-of-quad-nations-why-it-matters-to-india-7472058/

Knott, Matthew 2021, "In AUKUS pact, Australia grasps central role in great geopolitical struggle of the era", *Sydney Morning Herald*, 16 September. www.smh.com.au/world/north-america/australia-grasps-central-role-in-great-geopolitical-struggle-of-the-era-20210916-p58s2j.html

Lynas 2021, "Lynas signs contract to build U.S. light rare earths separation facility", https://lynasrareearths.com/wp-content/uploads/2021/01/210122-LRE-Separation-Facility-2167273.pdf

Mackay, Melissa 2021, "Marking 10 years in Darwin, top US diplomat signals bigger US marine deployments in Top End", *ABC News*, 10 October. www.abc.net.au/news/2021–10-10/ten-years-us-marines-top-end/100523120

National Museum of Australia 2021, "Curtin brings home troops", updated 31 August. www.nma.gov.au/defining-moments/resources/curtin-brings-home-troops

Parker, George, Sebastian Payne, Anthony Klan, Katrina Manson, Anna Gross and Victor Mallet 2021, "Aukus: How transatlantic allies turned on each other over China's Indo-Pacific threat", *Financial Times*, 25 September. www.ft.com/content/06f95e54–732e-4508-bc92-c3752904ba67

Ransley, Ellen 2021, "Labor 'does not share' Paul Keating's view on China after former PMs national address", *The Australian*, 12 November. www.theaustralian.com.au/breaking-news/labor-does-not-share-paul-keatings-view-on-china-after-former-pms-national-address/news-story/412c98a94a3bf06b1ce454e6cb9096fd

Rudd, Kevin 2021, "Why the Quad alarms China: Its Success Poses a Major Threat to Beijing's Ambitions", *Foreign Affairs*, 6 August. https://www.foreignaffairs.com/articles/united-states/2021–08-06/why-quad-alarms-china

Sanger, David 2021, "Biden Said the U.S. Would Protect Taiwan. But It's Not That Clear-Cut", *New York Times*, 10 November, www.nytimes.com/2021/10/22/us/politics/biden-taiwan-defense-china.html

Tillett, Matthew 2021, "PM hails new subs deal as 'forever partnership'", *Australian Financial Review*, 16 September. https://www.afr.com/politics/federal/pm-hails-new-subs-deal-as-forever-partnership-20210916-p58s3t

Victoria State Government, "Defence Excellence". www.defence.vic.gov.au

Walker, Damien 2021, "In defence of Queensland", *The Australian*, 1 June. www.theaustralian.com.au/special-reports/in-defence-of-queensland/news-story/e65e1341385cefeb92e20e183f5eb919

Wong, Penny 2021, "Expanding Australia's Power and Influence: Speech to the National Security College – Australian National University", 23 November. www.pennywong.com.au/media-hub/speeches/expanding-australia-s-power-and-influence-speech-to-the-national-security-college-australian-national-university-canberra-23–11-2021/

ROBERT NARAI

# "Until the end of the world": Myanmar's unfinished revolution

**Robert Narai** is a socialist activist in Melbourne who has written extensively about Myanmar for *Red Flag*.

*History is written with our blood*

*Revolution!*

*Those who lost their lives in the fight for democracy*

*Our country is a land built with martyrs*

*We will not be satisfied until the end of the world*

　　　　　– "Kabar Ma Kyay Bu" ("Until the end of the world")[1]

THIS ARTICLE IS A PRELIMINARY ACCOUNT of an unfinished revolution. It is an attempt to explore the implications of the great wave of strikes and demonstrations unleashed in response to Senior General Min Aung Hlaing's coup and the consequences of the armed conflict that has engulfed large parts of the country.[2]

---

1.　This song was written by Naing Myanmar during the 1988 uprising and has since been central to resistance against military rule.

2.　This article would not be possible without countless hours of conversations with revolutionaries on the ground in Myanmar. Many of the insights in this article are based on interviews I have conducted with them throughout the course of 2021, parts of which have appeared in *Red Flag*. For security reasons real names cannot be used, but I would particularly like to thank Me Me Myint, Ko Ko Zaw, Thar Yar Than, Ma Su Su Wai, Phyo Moe Lwin, Z, James, Katie, Kelvin, Min Khaing Khant, Soe San, U Toke Gyi, Mena, Saw Khu Zon, Ohn Nyo, Nyi Thuta and Aung Kaung Sett. Their revolutionary spirit has been a constant source of inspiration. My correspondence

There are two senses in which this revolution remains unfinished: that the forces opposed to the junta are far from exhausted (although the path many are now heading down is a much different one from that which was opened up by the February uprising); and that the material concerns motivating the initial uprising cannot be solved unless the revolutionary process "grows over" into an assault on the entire Burmese ruling class.[3]

The social forces and aspirations unleashed in the initial uprising are encapsulated in this account of the 22 February general strike by a seafarer in Yangon:

> There are delegations of workers everywhere: seafarers like me, but also nurses, engineers, factory workers, teachers, bank staff, civil servants, students. The nurses and civil servants are the true heroes of democracy since they are the ones who started the CDM [civil disobedience movement]. But now everyone joins CDM. Even now the construction workers are leaving the sites in downtown Yangon to join as the crowds gather and grow bigger. Everyone claps and cheers and sings when they see the sight of the railway workers marching in their columns. Everyone in the city knows that ALL the railway workers have been doing CDM... That day, it felt like every factory, every workplace, every township in Yangon was represented...
>
> People were no longer the same. Something had changed inside them; something had changed in their souls... Complete strangers behave as if they have known each other their entire lives. Everyone is making speeches everywhere. Every street corner is turned into its own parliament. Students from Yangon

with Stephen Campbell has also provided me with many insights. Omar Hassan's comments on an earlier draft have also been central to the finished piece.

3.    I use the terms Burma/Burmese and Myanmar interchangeably for the country and those who inhabit it. The former, which dates back to the last dynasty before colonial rule, derives from the majority ethnic group, the Burmans; the latter, a literary form, first appears in 12th century inscriptions. In 1989, the country's official name was changed to Myanmar by the ruling junta, with corresponding revisions for cities and ethnic groups. For more on the complex ethnic and linguistic connotations of the names see Callahan 2009a.

University with their degrees and knowledge are debating politics with factory workers on street corners. But they do so as equals, as if everyone's opinion truly matters and is respected...

There is also the great reckoning with our past sins, such as what happened to the Rohingya and other ethnic groups that have been persecuted by the military... If history is to remember me for anything it is that I am sorry I did not stand up for the Rohingya when they were expelled from our country and murdered in their tens of thousands... The revolution must deliver justice for these people and cleanse our country of these past sins that have been committed in our names.

However, there is one thing I remember very vividly that day. Something that I will never forget until the day I die. It was the sight of these day labourers arriving in downtown Yangon. These workers are very, very poor... If they stop work, they may not be able to eat the next day. But groups of them have put in all their savings and hired vans... And they drive into Yangon from the poor townships with revolutionary songs blasting from the van's windows. People are hanging out of the vans shouting that everyone must join the revolution. And when I see them there in the streets of Yangon, I think to myself: how brave and heroic these people are! These people who have nothing, who suffer so much. If they can do it, anyone can!

And all of us are chanting: "WE WANT DEMOCRACY! THE REVOLUTION MUST WIN!"[4]

The following will sketch the trajectory of the revolutionary process since February to help frame the challenges for the forces opposed to Min Aung Hlaing's junta. I will make a series of points: that the working class was the engine of revolutionary struggle during the early months of the uprising and drew behind them other oppressed strata (small farmers and ethnic minorities); that the Burmese ruling class is not simply the generals in power and their conglomerate companies

---

4.   Lwin 2021.

but a broader patchwork that includes Burmese state capital, "cronies" and regional capitalists; that the wing of the ruling class that was overthrown in the February coup is using the armed struggle against the junta to transform the revolutionary process into a form of capitalist restoration from above; that the inability of the February and March strike wave to topple the regime was due to the absence of a political leadership that could extend the strike movement into broader sections of the working class, transform the movement into a fight for control over production and promote widespread mutinies within the armed forces; and that the key task for revolutionaries in Myanmar today must be to begin laying the foundations for a revolutionary Marxist organisation that can cohere the most advanced workers into a fighting force capable of leading the mass of workers and drawing behind them the broader masses (small farmers and ethnic minorities) in a revolution that overturns not just military rule but the entire Burmese ruling class.

## From civil disobedience to armed struggle

Strikes and demonstrations engulfed Myanmar after the Tatmadaw arrested State Counsellor Aung San Suu Kyi and overthrew the newly elected National League for Democracy (NLD) government on 1 February 2021, installing Senior General Min Aung Hlaing at the head of the State Administration Council (SAC).

Beginning with small acts of defiance, such as the banging of pots and pans in central Yangon – a household tradition in Myanmar to ward off "evil spirits" – the call for a civil disobedience movement (CDM) against the SAC launched by health workers and civil servants, followed by demonstrations by garment workers in downtown Yangon on 6 February, acted as the social detonator for a countrywide movement opposed to the junta. Strikes paralysed whole swathes of industry while masses of people took to the streets in almost every corner of the country, culminating in the 22 February general strike that saw more than one million people march across Myanmar and many millions more participate in work stoppages.

In response, the Tatmadaw unleashed a fury of violence – including tear gas, water cannons, telecommunications and electricity shutdowns, curfews and mass arrests – in efforts to intimidate protest-ers and detain strike leaders. According to the Assistance Association for Political Prisoners, more than 2,100 people had been arrested and more than 200 killed by early March.

The scale of repression affected the resistance to the junta, with the large street demonstrations and open-air assemblies predominant in the early weeks of the uprising replaced with intense street fight-ing, while in rural areas ethnic armed organisations (EAOs) began protecting demonstrators from security forces and carrying out attacks on military bases. In working-class districts protesters and striking workers built barricades out of garbage bins, carts, tyres and barbed wire, and major roads in the cities were permanently blockaded. In scenes reminiscent of Hong Kong's 2019 uprising, protesters equipped themselves with hard hats, gas masks and makeshift shields to protect themselves during street fighting.

Meanwhile, the Committee Representing the Pyidaungsu Hluttaw (CRPH) – a group of parliamentarians largely drawn from the NLD – announced the formation of a National Unity Government (NUG). The NUG published a charter to rewrite the country's constitution, which promised to enshrine rights for all ethnic minorities, including the stateless Rohingya, and establish a Federal Union Army based on the pre-existing EAOs.

The revolutionary process reached a new turning point on 8 March when a coalition of trade unions launched an indefinite general strike aimed at toppling the junta. Ahead of the general strike, some of the largest demonstrations since 22 February were held across the country, including mass sit-ins that defied night-time curfews and mass meetings of garment workers in the industrial districts of Yangon. According to the Confederation of Trade Unions Myanmar (CTUM), large parts of the economy were completely paralysed by the general strike, including banks, shipyards, transport, railways, major factories, large-scale farms, oil refineries, mines, hospitals, schools and shopping centres. Importantly, all energy extraction had reportedly ceased, and the country's fuel and energy reserves were dwindling.

The response of the Tatmadaw was to mobilise the armed

forces at its command to crush the mass movement in a wave of counter-revolutionary terror: mass evictions of state-sector workers from government-provided housing were combined with massacres throughout the country. One incident, known as the Battle of Hlaing Tharyar, involved a four-day showdown of workers and students against the armed forces, which claimed the lives of at least 60 demonstrators in a working-class district of Yangon.

Since then, the countryside has become the key site of confrontation. Tens of thousands of youth and workers from the cities have sought safety in the ethnic-controlled borderlands, undergone guerrilla training and formed a number of armed groups under the banner of "People's Defence Forces" (PDFs). These groups now clash with the Tatmadaw in parts of Chin, Shan, Karen and Kachin states, across the Sagaing region and throughout the Irrawaddy Delta. Urban resistance continues in the more limited form of targeted assassinations of military personnel and their informants, while daily flash-mob demonstrations continue in major cities and townships. It is estimated that as many as 4,000 soldiers and police have been killed by PDFs, while a reported 8,000 have defected to the opposition (2,000 soldiers and 6,000 police).[5]

Meanwhile, the economic fallout from the coup has inflicted devastating blows to workers' living standards, with an estimated 1.2 million jobs lost in the first half of 2021 and predictions that almost half the population will be living below the poverty line in 2022.[6] This has been combined with a catastrophic third wave of COVID-19, beginning in late May, which has claimed the lives of at least 16,000 people.[7] Similarly, the official death toll of those killed by security forces since the coup currently stands at more than 1,400 and over 8,000 have been arrested. The consequences of these catastrophic blows on the working class and poor on their willingness to continue resisting Min Aung Hlaing's regime is unclear.

What is clear is that since the defeat of the extended general strike,

---

5.   The Irrawaddy 2021; Blazevic 2021.
6.   International Labour Organization 2021; UNDP 2021. For an account of the height of the third wave of COVID-19 in Myanmar see Narai 2021c.
7.   World Health Organisation 2021.

the NUG has been able to assert itself as the de facto political leadership of the anti-coup forces. It has promoted intervention by regional powers, sanctions on military-controlled businesses and the increasing militarisation of the struggle. In early September, the NUG officially declared a "people's revolutionary war" against Min Aung Hlaing's regime. But the declaration of war simply formalised what had been the political situation on the ground for several months, with tens of thousands already under arms fighting the regime. At the time of writing, significant parts of the countryside where resistance forces predominate (Chin, Shan, Karen, Kachin states and the Sagaing region) are being transformed into smouldering ruins by the Tatmadaw's counter-insurgency campaign, while bomb blasts and targeted assassinations of military personnel are an almost permanent feature of Myanmar's urban landscape.

## The engine of the revolution

The present impasse stands in stark contrast to the hopes and dreams of February. And the figures who now assert themselves as the de facto political leadership of the democratic forces – the NUG – could not be more removed from the workers, students, urban and rural poor and ethnic minorities who led the mass struggle against the coup in the early months of the uprising. Indeed, the initial source of strength of the uprising was not only its ability to mobilise in the streets, but in the workplaces as well.

Is Myanmar's working class capable of leading a revolution against Min Aung Hlaing's regime? Marxists argue that the working class has a special ability to challenge the ruling class because it creates all the wealth in society and performs the labour that is necessary for society to function. In Myanmar, this picture has been complicated by decades of dictatorship, war, and the combined and uneven forms through which the country has been integrated into international circuits of capital accumulation. The result has been widespread land dispossession in rural areas which has underpinned a low wage informal sector (84 percent of the workforce) in rapidly expanding urban centres.[8]

---

8.   Harkins et al, 2021.

It has produced a working class that is combined and uneven in character. Workers and the poor are the majority, but those in formal employment are in a minority. Most workers still retain a connection to the countryside through employment in the agrarian sector or ownership over small plots of land under constant threat of dispossession. Finally, militarised conflict in the borderlands has entrenched ethnic divisions that have pitted the Bamar-majority centre against the ethnic minorities in the periphery (30 to 40 percent of the population who occupy some 60 percent of Myanmar's total land area). Nevertheless, there are points in Myanmar's economy where concentrations of workers are endowed with immense potential power, such as the energy, extractive, export and transport sectors, and over the basic necessities of life that neither the civilian administrations nor the previous dictatorships have been able to provide for the majority of people.

The trajectory of working-class mobilisation throughout February and March also illustrates that it is possible to build unity in collective action between the employed and unemployed, between those in the "formal" sector (with higher wages or levels of education and professional status) and those who are marginalised and socially excluded, and between the Bamar centre and the ethnic periphery that have historically been pitted against each other. It is also significant that those sections of the working class that have the highest concentrations of women (nurses and garment workers) played a central role in leading other workers in struggle, breaking down sexist stereotypes that see women as passive and subordinate.

The unifying feature of these combined and uneven forms of consciousness was a defence of democracy that went beyond a simple reinstatement of the elected government; it was an attempt to defend, and sometimes extend, the material interests of the working class alongside those of the urban and rural poor against the incursions of direct military rule.

Healthcare workers provided the initial spark of resistance. They had borne the brunt of Myanmar's woefully inadequate healthcare system during the pandemic. "The hospitals were already completely overrun by COVID-19 before the coup", explained one striking nurse from Yangon Workers' Hospital. "We knew that this situation will get much, much worse under another military dictatorship."[9]

White-collar workers in the state sector soon followed: teachers pledged to keep the schools closed as long as the junta remained in power; workers in the civil service paralysed entire sections of the state bureaucracy. Overall an estimated three-quarters of civil servants were out on strike during February, including an estimated 60 percent of state electricity workers.[10] They were joined by workers in the banking and financial sector, with the entire private banking sector shut down by mid-February.

Industrial workers in the energy and resources sector in Nyaungdon (west of Yangon) and Singu-Chauk (central Myanmar), were some of the first to join the call for strikes on 5 February. Hundreds of workers at the military-owned Kyisintaung copper mine soon followed, alongside farm workers in the nearby city of Minbu, who play an important role in producing the agricultural products that feed the domestic population.

Garment workers from Yangon's industrial zones were crucial to swelling the initial demonstrations on 6 February that then spread throughout the entire country. These workers perform the labour that underpins Myanmar's largest export sector and can seriously disrupt the flow of profits to the ruling class. It is not surprising that garment workers had been at the forefront of union organising for more than a decade, which endowed them with a confidence and militancy that proved decisive during the early resistance to the coup. Indeed, it was the widespread reports of mass meetings of garment workers, the video footage of hundreds of women staging sit-ins while banging pots and pans in the lunchrooms, and the sight of women workers marching to demonstrations in downtown Yangon that played a crucial role in giving confidence to other sections of the working class to strike.

After these garment workers had temporarily usurped the power of capital over labour, the reverberations of their strikes were felt back in the factories. "Many workers return to the factories and must fight the factory managers to prevent victimisation for participating in the

---

9.  Myint 2021. For more on the impact of COVID-19 and Myanmar's healthcare system see Narai 2021c.
10. Paddock 2021.

strikes", explained one garment worker from Hlaing Tharyar. "This was leading to more and more workplace protests and strikes against the victimisation. The strikes were like the spinning wheel on our sewing machines – round and round they go."[11]

This spinning wheel propelled workers in the logistics sector into taking strike action. Railway workers participated in the 6 February demonstrations in downtown Yangon, going on to shut down the entire rail networks of both the commercial capital and Mandalay throughout the following week. They were joined by Yangon's truckdrivers, about 90 percent of whom were on strike by mid-February. The action taken by the drivers, many of whom link up with Yangon's major ports, propelled seafarers and shipyard workers into the strikes. Importantly, workers at Yangon's two major ports – the Thilawa and Yangon terminals – who handle 90 percent of maritime cargo and 70 percent of the country's total trade flows were some of the first to stop work. By late February there were widespread reports of shipping containers piling up in terminals. A striking seafarer from Yangon later explained: "One section of workers stops and all the wheels stop turning".[12]

The general strikes of 8, 15 and 22 February brought all these incipient elements of class power together into what one train driver described as the "engine" of revolutionary struggle.[13] By this he meant the process whereby each general strike drew greater numbers of workers into centralised actions, before dispersing them back into their workplaces and out of which new battles were born.[14] These battles included the garment workers mentioned earlier or the 6 February demonstrations that propelled railway workers into the movement. It was these displays of workers' power that led wider elements of "the people" into the struggle against Min Aung Hlaing's regime: the urban poor, small farmers and sections of the ethnic minorities, including the persecuted Rohingya languishing in the refugee camps in Bangladesh.[15]

---

11. Wai 2021.
12. Lwin 2021.
13. Zaw 2021. The 8, 15 and 22 general strikes were largely "spontaneous actions" called by CDM and supported by the various trade unions.
14. In the revolutionary Marxist tradition, this process has been called "the mass strike".
15. A number of protests pledging support for the uprising against the military took place in the refugee camps in Bangladesh over the course of February and March.

In the aftermath of each of these general strikes the regime tried to ramp up the level of repression in an effort to paralyse the movement. Initially the repression had a profoundly radicalising effect and drew increasing numbers into the fight. But as it increased and turned deadly, only the most militant would dare hit the streets, engaging in barricade-building and street fighting to sustain the broader strike wave. A librarian from Yangon who had joined one of the hundreds of street fighting groups across the country in early March explained: "We know that we can be arrested or killed by live rounds when the police and soldiers shoot at us – but we have to defend our comrades".[16]

After a temporary lull in the size of street mobilisations it was in the lead up to the 8 March general strike that some of the largest demonstrations since 22 February were held. This is because of the sense of collective power and confidence that striking workers can endow broad sections of the population with. These actions included sit-in protests that defied the regime's night-time curfews and martial law, alongside mass meetings of garment workers throughout Yangon's industrial districts that urged all working-class and poor people to rally behind the indefinite shut-down of the economy until the regime had been overthrown.

A Yangon bank worker painted a picture of the country at the height of the extended general strike in mid March:

> The hospitals are all closed; government buildings too. Money cannot be moved around like normal because all the banks are shut. The shipyards are at a standstill. The train drivers will not go back to work and the military does not know how to operate [the trains]. None of the shops are open and people say the workers on the big farms are refusing to work. All the factories are closed; and even if they were open there is very little fuel or raw materials to power them since the oil workers are on strike. The country has ground to a complete standstill – without workers, the world stops moving.[17]

---

16. Narai 2021a.
17. Z 2021.

It was the threat that this extended general strike posed to the entire ruling class that led to the counter-revolutionary terror that followed. Mass evictions of railway workers, nurses, civil servants and bank workers were combined with the carnage in Hlaing Tharyar and the bloodbaths that took place elsewhere across the country. The seemingly indiscriminate nature of the violence had the sole purpose of paralysing the engine of mass struggle and crushing the social soul at the heart of the revolutionary process. Carlos Sardiña Galache provided an apt depiction of the terror when he wrote in late March: "Such brutality can be seen as the desperation of a cornered beast unleashing its fury in all directions".[18]

## Two Burmas

Any understanding of the Burmese ruling class and the character of its state must begin with the patterns of combined and uneven development established under British colonial rule, which integrated the region into the global capitalist system and demarcated the country into two administrative zones of accumulation: a lowland centre structured around rice paddy production in the Irrawaddy Delta and oil drilling in the central plains; and a borderland periphery structured around mining and forestry. The British developed racialised "ethnic" categories based on geographical region, language and customary practices, with those living in the lowland centre (Bamar, Mon and Rakhine) placed under direct British rule and excluded from participation in the colonial state, while those in the borderland peripheries (Kachin, Shan, Chin, Karenni) given some degree of self-administration in return for the plundering of their natural resources. As a consequence, the concentration of ownership and control over the means of production in a handful of British firms hindered the development of an indigenous bourgeoisie, while the solidification of ethnic identities made it harder for a unified national independence movement to emerge.[19]

---

18.   Galache 2021. For more on the terror see Narai 2021b.
19.   Cady 1958. Galache 2020 provides an accessible overview of the diverse indigenous peoples who inhabited this region prior to British rule and the various conflicts that predated colonisation. Importantly, it refutes the dominant idea in much official

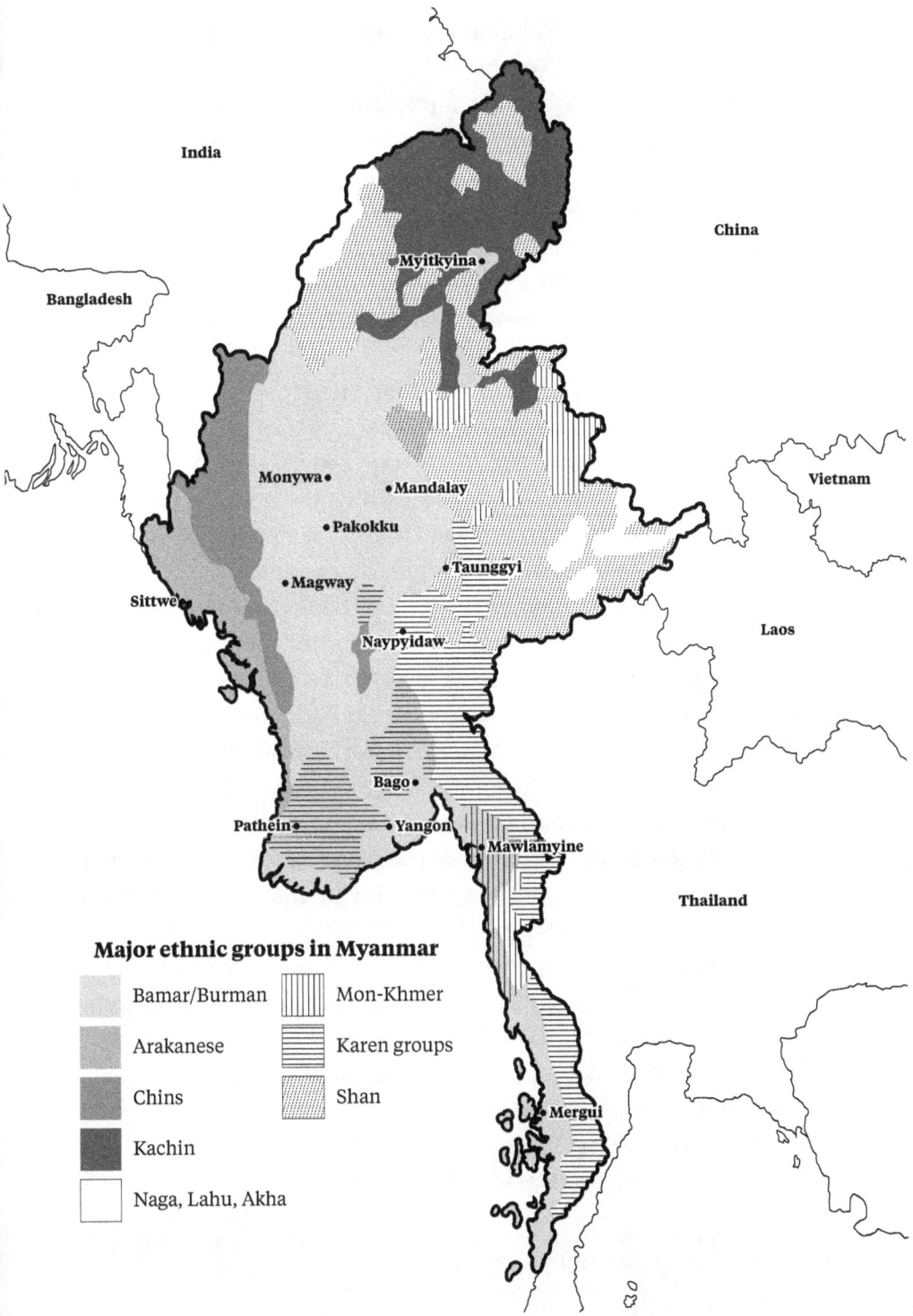

## Major ethnic groups in Myanmar

- Bamar/Burman
- Arakanese
- Chins
- Kachin
- Naga, Lahu, Akha
- Mon-Khmer
- Karen groups
- Shan

The struggle against colonial rule and the Japanese occupation during the Second World War helped consolidate these "two Burmas" by demarcating the nationalist forces who collaborated with the British and US (Kachin, Karen, Chin, Arakan Muslims) and those who collaborated with the Japanese (Bamar, Arakan Buddhists). Since gaining independence from British rule in 1947, the Burmese state and its ruling class have been shaped by the conflicts between the Bamar centre and ethnic minority periphery, which has helped obscure the deeper struggle for control over the land and the labour that inhabits these "two Burmas."

U Nu's post-independence governments tried to solve the problems of uneven development through a state capitalist regime that nationalised large swathes of industry and substituted the state bureaucracy for a weak domestic bourgeoisie. Meanwhile, the attempt to build a centralised lowland state and impose it upon the periphery plunged the country into civil war and the rapid expansion of the Tatmadaw. The central state was confronted not only with the Communist Party of Burma, but an array of ethnic armies all seeking independence. Adding further complexity, these forces were joined by the remnants of the Chinese nationalist Kuomintang armies that had retreated across the border after being defeated by Mao's People's Liberation Army.[20]

In a pattern repeated in much of the post-colonial world, the military emerged as the dominant wing of the ruling class. This process was exacerbated by the intensity of the ongoing armed conflicts in both the centre and the periphery, which coincided with the phase of rapid industrial development. Frontline officers became state administrators in a rapidly growing army that took on an expanded array of state functions. Through the Defence Services Institute the officer corps became the largest bloc of capitalists in the country, with interests in banking, manufacturing, construction, real estate, hotels, mining, agriculture, transport, entertainment, media, and a monopoly over import and export licenses. The Tatmadaw took advantage of ongoing crises in U Nu's regime and was temporarily handed power in

---

Burmese historiography that projects a pre-established harmony and fixed ethnic identities onto pre-colonial history.

20.   For a detailed account of this period see Callahan 2004.

a 1958 "caretaker government", before carrying out a definitive coup d'état under the leadership of General Ne Win (Tatmadaw commander-in-chief) in March 1962.

Ne Win's regime tried to solve the problems of uneven development by radicalising the state capitalist project under the banner of the "Burmese Way to Socialism". All remaining industries were nationalised, foreign and private capital confiscated and driven from the country, and through the export of oil the regime sought to build an advanced manufacturing base centred on heavy industry. The counter-insurgency campaigns against the left and ethnic armies continued throughout this period. Formal political power was eventually handed to the Burmese Socialist Programme Party (BSPP) in the early 1970s, perfecting the model of one-party Stalinist dictatorships seen elsewhere, with Ne Win preserved as head of state.

Yet by the 1980s the BSPP project was floundering, struggling to manage inflation and a sharp decline in oil prices. The structural adjustment programmes that sought to deal with these issues led to a wave of strikes and demonstrations throughout 1987 and 1988. Ne Win was forced to resign as head of state, but that did little to quell unrest. The movement culminated in a nationwide general strike in August 1988, including army mutinies and the widespread formation of township strike committees. The absence of a revolutionary leadership allowed Aung San Suu Kyi (daughter of Aung San, the military leader who led the independence struggle against colonial rule) and a section of former military officers grouped under the banner of the National League for Democracy, to channel a semi-insurrectionary movement into a tepid fight for free and fair elections. The Tatmadaw were eventually able to regain control of the situation, with a group of younger officers and generals seizing power in a coup and installing themselves at the head of the State Law and Order Council (SLORC). In the counter-revolutionary terror that followed, thousands of civilians were massacred and protest leaders cremated alive, while those who escaped such a fate, such as Suu Kyi, were thrown into jail or put under house arrest. The BSPP regime was dissolved, trade unions were outlawed, and the 1990 election results (which the NLD won in a landslide) were overturned. General Than Shwe and those grouped around him came to consolidate themselves within the SLORC, which they later renamed the State Peace and Development Council in the mid-1990s.[21]

## Burmese capitalism in the neoliberal era

Than Shwe's dictatorship oversaw the neoliberal transformation of Burma, now renamed Myanmar. His regime opened up the economy to foreign investment and gained access to large swathes of land and natural resources through ceasefire agreements with ethnic minority leaders. In doing so, the military leadership built an accumulation model structured around extractive industries in the borderlands and periphery – gas, rare earth minerals, precious stones, timber – that then laid the basis for the development of garment manufacturing, construction and finance in the lowland centre. That transformation has given the Burmese ruling class a number of distinct features that have persisted to this day:

### 1. The Tatmadaw plays a dominant role within both the state and the capitalist class.

In the absence of a strong domestic bourgeoisie a section of the officer corps transformed themselves from the managers of capital on behalf of the state into owners who now controlled the means of production. Than Shwe's regime established two military-owned conglomerates: Union of Myanmar Economic Holdings Company Limited (UMEHL), with interests in banking, trade, tourism and precious stones, and Myanmar Economic Corporation (MEC), with interests in heavy industry, mining and energy. As the regime opened up Myanmar's economy to overseas markets, UMEHL and MEC were able to absorb large parts of foreign direct investment.

At the same time, the Tatmadaw has carried out a massive expansion of its own ranks, devoting nearly half the state budget to the security sector. This included placing the riot police under its direct command, acquiring a range of advanced military hardware,

---

21. General Saw Maung, who many believe wished to hand power to the NLD in the 1990 elections, was overthrown in a palace coup in 1992 by Than Shwe's group. For an account of these struggles see Myint-U 2019, especially chapters 2 and 3.

and increasing the military's total numbers from 180,000 in the late 1980s to an estimated 400,000 today. Meanwhile, former military officers continue to populate large sections of the state bureaucracy's upper ranks.

The Tatmadaw's monopoly over the means of violence and sections of the state bureaucracy is enshrined in the 2008 constitution, with a quarter of seats in both houses of the parliament reserved for military appointees. This ensures that it can block any constitutional amendment, alongside control over the ministries of defence and home affairs.

## 2. Burmese state capital continues to play a dominant role in the economy through the natural resource SEEs (state-owned economic enterprises).

Another consequence of having a weak domestic bourgeoise was that privatisations were initially resisted until the Tatmadaw had secured its position within the capitalist class through its own conglomerates, which they achieved in an alliance with Burmese state capital, selling certain state assets to themselves while retaining state monopolies in key sectors. The largest SEEs are centred on the highly profitable extractive industries, including fossil fuels, minerals, timber and pearls.

The Myanmar Oil and Gas Enterprise's (MOGE) project in the Andaman Sea, the Yadana gas fields, is illustrative of this process. In 1994, MOGE signed a memorandum of understanding to supply Thailand with natural gas.[22] Chevron and Total then entered a joint venture to build and operate the pipeline. The Tatmadaw assisted by clearing a route through the Tenasserim and committed itself to protecting the project against attacks from armed ethnic groups. Today, more than $US460 million in rent is generated for the Burmese state each year, with significant profits going to both Chevron and Total. This arrangement is a mutually beneficial relationship for both the Burmese ruling class and its foreign partners.

Meanwhile, Burma generates an estimated $US31 billion in jade sales to China each year – with Kachin state alone producing

---

22. Half of Thailand's natural gas imports come from joint operations with the MOGE in the Andaman Sea.

70 percent of the world's jade supply. Similarly, an estimated half of China's rare earth feedstock is supplied by Burmese state-run mines. The majority of these profits go unreported and are siphoned into specially designated "other accounts" held by state officials and military personnel.[23]

The ongoing dominance of Burmese state capital within the ruling class means that while the SEEs employ just 145,000 people in a population of 54 million, they generate around approximately half of state revenues and receive half the state budget. Their central economic and political position allows them to exert an enormous influence over the broader direction of capital accumulation, including through their ability to dispense licenses and contracts in return for rents and profit shares.

To the extent that a private bourgeoisie has emerged in the neoliberal era, they have been reliant on nepotistic relations with the Tatmadaw. They have been a vital source of capital, contracts and access to international networks in China, Hong Kong, Thailand, Japan and Singapore. These "cronies" made fortunes exporting timber, rare gems, minerals and agricultural commodities, providing them with the capital to form construction firms that would capitalise on increased government infrastructure spending and a boom in private real estate. When privatisations of state assets finally did take place, the main beneficiaries were the conglomerates that these capitalists now controlled. Today, these cronies and their conglomerates are believed to comprise just 5 percent of firms but – alongside the military-controlled conglomerates and Burmese state capital – control the majority of the country's wealth.[24]

### 3. The persistence of the national question.

The attempt to build a modern nation-state that unifies the centre and the periphery has been a constant theme of Burma's modern history. It finds its expression in the ruling ideology of the "national races". While no single legal text fully captures this ruling ideology, the BSPP's 1982 Citizenship Laws helped codify Myanmar's ethnic divisions into 135

23. Bauer et al 2018.
24. Jones 2014.

"national races", all of whom were part of a greater historical kingdom known as Burma that lived harmoniously until the arrival of the British. The important exception to this historical mythmaking is the Rohingya Muslim population of Rakhine state, who continue to be considered illegal aliens from Bangladesh and part of the calamities inaugurated by British rule. The different groups that make up the "national races" approach the ideology in different ways and interpretations are politically contested within each group. For Bamar ethno-nationalists, it establishes a beneficial hierarchy that places them at the top, while for Kachin nationalism it involves freeing its members from the constraints imposed by the central Burmese state. By contrast, Rakhine nationalism hinges on the recovery of an imagined past as an independent and powerful kingdom.[25]

The patchwork of ceasefire agreements signed between Than Shwe's regime and a number of ethnic minority leaders has left political and economic power in the borderlands divided among a bewildering array of actors, including the central government, various armed groups, militias working with the government, ethnic warlords and networks of local and regional capital. Each of these groups is in a perpetual competition with the others for territory and resources.[26]

The result has been forms of primitive accumulation that Kevin Woods terms "ceasefire capitalism": in the mountainous borderlands, ethnic minority populations have been pushed into camps for the internally displaced to clear land for extractive projects, in particular forestry and mining; in the lowland Irrawaddy Delta and central plains, forms of indebtedness continue to force small farmers off the land into urban areas, while former rice paddy growing regions have been cleared to establish large-scale agribusiness such as inland fisheries and palm oil plantations. Despite most land in Myanmar being inhabited by small farmers and ethnic minorities, the Vacant, Fallow and

---

25. Galache 2020, Chapter 9 and Conclusion.
26. The first ceasefires were signed with the groups that emerged from the remnants of the Communist Party of Burma: the United Wa State Army and the Kokang Democratic Army (later renamed the Myanmar National Democratic Alliance Army). In return for access to natural resources in the border areas, the central lowland regime allowed them to control their own self-administered areas in northern Shan State, through which they built their own semi-independent states.

Virgin Lands Management Law passed in 2012 makes that land owner-less unless forms of legal certification can be provided, most of which does not exist. The impact of the law is illustrated by the fact that an estimated 45 million acres of land qualifies as vacant, fallow or virgin, of which 82 percent is in ethnic minority states.[27]

Meanwhile, the "national races" ideology has justified the ethnic cleansing of the Rohingya. This has taken many forms, from the denial of citizenship and statehood to the stoking of ethnic tensions, culminating in the Tatmadaw's 2017 campaign of forced transfers that included military rape, murder and the torching of homes. An estimated 30,000 Rohingya were murdered, more than 40,000 disappeared (presumed dead), and over 700,000 expelled into Bangladesh.[28] These atrocities have also produced attempts by ethno-nationalist militias to establish an independent Rohingya state, though their prospects are limited.

## "Discipline flourishing democracy"

The period of "discipline flourishing democracy" (the power-sharing agreement between the Tatmadaw and elected civilian leaders enshrined in the 2008 constitution) promised to usher in a new era of freedom and prosperity for workers and the poor. It was celebrated by the bourgeois media as an important step toward a more democratic society. In truth, the reforms were carefully designed by Than Shwe and the ruling generals to relinquish part of their power while maintaining a dominant and leading role for themselves in the country's political and economic landscape. It was also a manoeuvre through which many of the Western sanctions on the regime would be lifted and open up the country's capitalist class to widened opportunities for capital accumulation.

During the 1990s, Than Shwe's regime created a proto-party body, the Union Solidarity Development Association (USDA) to help build local patronage networks and a base of support for the regime. By 2009, the USDA claimed some 25 million members, including state-sector workers (a mandatory requirement), prominent and

27. Woods 2017.
28. The best account of this history is found in Galache 2020.

emerging capitalists, teachers and students. The USDA was then transformed into the USDP to contest the 2010 elections, which it won in a landslide – largely due to the fact the NLD refused to contest them – with former general U Thein Sein becoming the first "democratically elected" leader of the country in over 50 years. From 2011 to 2015, Thein Sein's USDP government introduced many of the liberal-democratic reforms often associated with liberal or social-democratic parties, such as the legalisation of trade unions, alongside increases in health and education spending.

The dominant political party during "discipline flourishing democracy" was of course Aung San Suu Kyi's National League for Democracy. The NLD is a liberal-bourgeois party; its founding members and leading personnel – Suu Kyi, former military officers, lawyers, journalists, intellectuals, doctors and other middle-class professionals – are all thoroughly committed to the rule of capital. Despite claiming more than one million members, most are drawn from the urban and rural middle classes and have no ability to influence the decision-making or policies of the NLD leadership. Meanwhile, Suu Kyi's ongoing association with the struggle against the previous junta and the country's founding "national father" (Aung San) provides the NLD with its popular and nationalist appeal.

The liberal-bourgeois character of Suu Kyi and the NLD explains why they were willing to compromise with the Tatmadaw and accept the parameters of the 2008 constitution. This meant providing legitimacy to the power-sharing agreement with the military, as well as supporting and adopting most of the USDP's policies and courting many of the country's "cronies". It also explains the NLD's terrible treatment of ethnic minorities, most notably their enthusiastic support for the Tatmadaw's campaign of ethnic cleansing against the Rohingya, alongside their use of repression against workers and small farmers in the lowland Bamar centre. Despite this, Suu Kyi and the NLD have remained extremely popular electorally – largely due to the absence of a credible alternative to their left grounded in the workers' movement and rural poor – winning both the 2015 and 2020 elections in a landslide before being overthrown in the February coup.

Why did Min Aung Hlaing decide to seize power? Four "enabling conditions" stand out:

### 1. Ongoing dependency on East and South East Asian capital.

Despite the lifting of sanctions, "discipline flourishing democracy" did not lead to a significant increase in FDI from Western capital, and the fallout from the Rohingya genocide had a particularly negative impact on investment. Instead, the key drivers of capital accumulation continued to be Singapore, China and Thailand. Meanwhile, the economic fallout from COVID-19 has only exacerbated this dependency on sections of the Asia region, in particular China.

### 2. Splits in the ruling class.

In government, Suu Kyi and the NLD have tried to weaken the grip of the officer corps and Burmese state capital over the direction of capital accumulation through stricter regulation of state operations and finances, attempts to privatise a number of "underperforming" SEEs, and transferring control over arms of the state bureaucracy away from the Tatmadaw. Significantly, a number of "cronies" have expressed support for the economic reforms and the moderate elements in the USDP are not opposed to them either.

### 3. Crisis in the military-proxy party.

Although the USDP still enjoys support among capitalists active in heavy industries, resource extraction, large and medium-scale agribusiness, soldiers and their families, alongside the most reaction-ary sections of the Buddhist clergy, together these forces do not provide a wide enough base of support to present the USDP as a viable electoral vehicle. In recent years, the USDP has been riven by splits and controversies. Many members left to form minor parties, and some even joined the NLD. Meanwhile, moderate USDP leaders have recently changed their candidate rules so that they no longer favour retired military officers. The 2020 election results also dashed Ming Aung Hlaing's aspirations to transition from military to civilian leader: despite the Tatmadaw's control over 25 percent of seats in both houses of parliament, the USDP's abysmal results would not be enough to appoint Min Aung Hlaing prime minister.

### 4. Ongoing armed conflicts against ethnic minorities.

Despite significant hype among the liberal establishment, Suu Kyi and the NLD did little to advance the ceasefire agreements of the previous military regime. Meanwhile, the war in Rakhine state between the Tatmadaw and the Arakan Army, an ethno-nationalist militia complicit in the atrocities committed against the Rohingya, aggravated tensions between the officer corps and the NLD. Despite the Arakan Army and the Tatmadaw brokering an informal ceasefire agreement and calling for the 2020 elections to take place in the Rakhine state, the NLD-appointed electoral commission cancelled them, as well as elections in a number of other minority areas. The conflict in Arakan – both Suu Kyi's unwillingness to acquiesce to the Tatmadaw and legitimate grievances over voter suppression – created a window of opportunity through which the most hardened section of the officer corps could reassert their dominance. The hard right in the USDP pursued claims of voter fraud against the NLD; while these were rejected by the electoral commission, they created the justification for the February coup.

Instead of marking a definitive rupture with the politics of "discipline flourishing democracy" – a framework established by the military leadership to ensure their ongoing political and economic dominance over the country – Min Aung Hlaing's coup is an attempt to reconfigure the arrangement. His regime represents a distinct constellation of class forces that have been unable to present a popular political alternative to Suu Kyi and the NLD. This includes the leading personnel of the Tatmadaw, the military-controlled conglomerates, Burmese state capital, the cronies who are willing to remain subservient to state patronage networks, the most reactionary sections of the Buddhist clergy and the hard right in the USDP.

Min Aung Hlaing's regime has sought to strengthen the most crony aspects of state patronage networks through its recently announced Myanmar Economic Recovery Plan (MERP). The MERP is a carbon copy of a similar plan proposed by the NLD prior to the coup, including major tax breaks for the rich and big business, with a few tweaks in the interests of the state capitalists. Meanwhile, the new government has put forward plans for new oil and gas refineries, an expansion of palm oil plantations, plus a number of infrastructure upgrades in Naypyidaw. The contracts will be awarded in corrupt public-partnerships that resemble those that built Than Shwe's regime throughout the 1990s and 2000s.

Despite being somewhat disgruntled by the coup, the key regional players involved in capital accumulation in the country – China, Thailand and Singapore – have shown no signs of withdrawing from the huge infrastructure projects they have spent decades building. There is little to suggest that the economic sanctions targeting the regime will do anything but replicate the effect of earlier sanctions and strengthen this ongoing dependency on the Asia region. (This is not to mention the vast accumulated funds that Burmese state capital has at its disposal to weather such a storm.[29]) Meanwhile, the burden of the broader economic fallout will continue to fall upon the working-class in the form of job losses and austerity.

Min Aung Hlaing has also consolidated his position within the officer corps by continuing to promote a younger generation of field commanders and generals who are loyal to him and purging moderate elements who worked closely with the ousted NLD government, limiting the prospects of a palace coup. He has also sought to "reform" Myanmar's first-past-the-post electoral system, which benefited the NLD. The result of the reforms will not only help the USDP and the generals rebuild themselves electorally but also enable a plethora of minority parties in ethnic states to challenge the NLD's electoral dominance. Meanwhile, the ongoing trial of Suu Kyi and other high-ranking NLD officials serve as a useful bargaining chip in the long term should the situation turn against the Tatmadaw.

---

29. It is estimated that Myanmar Oil and Gas Enterprise has at least 7 years' worth of precautionary savings while the Myanmar Gems Enterprise has 172 years' worth. See Bauer et al 2018.

## The left and the democratic transition

If there was a rupture with "discipline flourishing democracy" it was the February and March uprising against the coup. The uprising was a clear refusal to collaborate with both the military leadership and the ruling class more broadly. Much of this was made possible by years of militant organising by workers, students and the rural poor against the civilian-military governments and strikes against the previous military dictatorship.[30] Despite the limitations of the liberalisation process, the widening of democratic freedoms under civilian-military rule created a space in which workers and other oppressed layers could organise more openly against the deeply entrenched inequalities that characterise the country and attempt to advance their own class interests.

The legalisation of trade unions, the institutionalisation of collective bargaining, and the establishment of an arbitration body stacked with former army personnel and representatives of capital was a concession. The hope was to prevent strikes like those that had broken out across the garment sector in 2009–10 at the end of Than Shwe's dictatorship. But almost as soon as the first piece of labour legislation passed in 2011, the Hlaing Tharyar, Shwepyithar and Hmawbi industrial districts on the outskirts of Yangon erupted in a further wave of strikes, leading to the creation of dozens of new factory-based unions.[31]

Another wave of strikes engulfed the garment sector in 2015–17, including a 2017 riot in which hundreds of workers descended on the Hangzhou Hundred-Tex Garment factory on the outskirts of Yangon, damaging factory vehicles, breaking windows, wrecking machinery, attacking management and taking several managers hostage. (The riot followed a 15-month strike over unpaid overtime that resulted in

---

30. In an email exchange with Stephen Campbell he has pointed out that majority of strikes against Than Shwe's military dictatorship have been undocumented and there are no readily available accounts except for oral accounts by participants given to him. However, a 2009–10 strike wave of garment workers did receive some attention from both the media, activists and researchers. And while the 2007 uprising against the previous military junta did not achieve any immediate changes, it is reasonable to suggest that the fear of similar uprisings was a factor behind the transition to civilian-military rule in 2010. For more on the 2007 uprising see Callahan 2009b.

31. Campbell 2013.

the factory's union leader being fired.) Then, in 2019, garment workers led another wave of wildcat strikes before COVID-19 was used to crack down on militancy.

The expansion of the right to strike and form a trade union helped give space for activists to create hundreds of new unions during the transition. And unlike countries in which trade unions are well established, with entrenched bureaucracies and passive leaderships, many of these unions were established through wildcat strikes and even riots.

Similarly, the establishment of a land disputes body stacked with former state officials by Thein Sein's USDP government sparked a number of struggles waged by small farmers over land that had been confiscated under Than Shwe's dictatorship. These struggles were most acute in areas across the Irrawaddy Delta, the Monywa and Sagaing regions, and in a number of ethnic-minority areas. Aung San Suu Kyi and the NLD were just as repressive against these small farmers as their counterparts in the USDP, and strengthened the laws that give big business access to large swathes of occupied land.

Student activists fought to re-establish student unions, which had been banned under the previous dictatorship. These activists faced stiff resistance from university administrations and supporters of the old regime. The combative climate generated by this activism also led to the creation of a range of political associations where students could discuss and debate political topics openly for the first time in over five decades. A number of more explicitly radical forums also flourished, including Marxist discussion circles in Yangon.

Radical students in major cities also built networks with workers and supported strikes and riots whenever they broke out. In more regional areas, student activists built similar networks with small farmers around questions of land dispossession and environmental issues. And student opposition to state-sanctioned crimes against ethnic minorities (such as the atrocities committed in Rakhine state against the Rohingya and other groups in the periphery) was an important aspect of student activism during the transition, particularly in Yangon.[32] Again, many of the same repressive laws being used to

---

32.  Narai 2021a.

persecute NLD officials under the new dictatorship were used against left-wing activists during this period.

It was radical students and garment workers who launched the 6 February demonstrations that helped catalyse the initial actions by healthcare workers (many of whom were former student activists) and acted as the social detonator for the revolutionary movement that followed.[33] A garment worker from Yangon later explained that the joint solidarity between students and workers over the years is what enabled them to join forces on 6 February and throughout the coming weeks:

> We are used to strikes at the factories but striking against the military with guns is different. We have not engaged in political strikes before. But the students have plenty of this experience. And around these parts, many workers know that the students always support the workers when they strike.[34]

The targeting of these activists and the practical outlawing of most trade unions in Myanmar since the coup has been a calculated move to uproot these networks and deny them the capacity to act. One of the effects of the repression has been the severing of these links, albeit not entirely. Underground organising of workers at the point of production continues under the new military regime, despite the extreme difficulties and danger involved.[35] But the overall trend among the left has been to abandon the promotion of working-class self-activity and join the proliferation of armed groups that have emerged after the defeat of the March general strike.

## A "people's revolutionary war"?

The wing of the ruling class that was overthrown in the February coup has regrouped as the National Unity Government (NUG). While led by the NLD, the NUG contains a number of politicians from ethnic minorities, and has sought to move beyond the conflict between the centre

---

33. Maung 2021.
34. Wai 2021.
35. This includes the establishment of a new working-class newspaper known as *Workers' Journal*, which is linked to the underground organising that continues.

and the periphery through a political programme for a new Burmese state: a new constitution and a federalist political system that grants autonomy to ethnic minority regions as well as citizenship for the Rohingya. A component of the NUG's strategy for power is the "people's revolutionary war", which seeks to hegemonise the various militias ("people's defence forces" or PDFs) that have emerged in opposition to the coup, alongside drawing in the ethnic armed organisations (EAOs) who have either been at war or maintained ceasefires with the Burmese regime prior to the coup.[36]

There are two types of PDFs currently fighting Min Aung Hlaing's regime: autonomous local defence forces and those directly linked to the NUG's ministry of defence. The local groups developed out of grassroots struggles against security forces, and largely operate independently from the NUG. Meanwhile, the other armed groups maintain stronger connections to the NUG: some have been directly created by the NUG, while others have sought to associate themselves more closely with the parallel government.

At the time of writing, there are as many as 500 PDFs operating across the country with most acting as township-level militias. The size of each unit ranges from large groups comprising several hundred personnel to small cells of two or three dozen. Estimates of their numbers range from 25,000 armed fighters to as many as 100,000, including those in training or seeking to enlist. These numbers can be added to the 30,000 guerrilla fighters who make up the ethnic militias currently engaged in combat against the regime.

These numbers pale in comparison to the Tatmadaw's estimated 400,000 troops, Border Guard Forces, and pro-government militias. Yet they have placed Min Aung Hlaing's regime under pressure, stretching it thin in a number of outlying regions, inflicting an estimated 4,000 casualties and producing a steady flow of defections. Many of these defectors help train and lead the armed insurgents and play a prominent role in carrying out extensive propaganda opera-tions aimed at promoting defections and mutinies within the ranks of the Tatmadaw.

---

36. The following is based on the analysis put forward by Hein and Meyers 2021 and conversations with participants in various PDFs.

The resistance forces currently predominate along five main "fronts": the western corridor of Sagaing and Chin states; Kachin state where the Kachin Independence Army operates; the eastern front of Kayah and Kayin states where PDFs fight alongside factions of the Karen National Union (KNU) and the Karenni National Progressive Party; northern Shan state where the Myanmar National Democratic Alliance Army and its Northern Alliance have been engaged in fighting; and across the Irrawaddy Delta and central plains where a mosaic of urban and rural guerrillas are engaged in a diffuse and urbanised insurgency involving bombings and assassinations of military personnel.

Meanwhile, the NUG is based in Kayin state under the protection of the KNU, with the forces in the other areas largely outside its operational control or command. Importantly, the Arakan Army in Rakhine state and the United Wa State Army and its partners in Shan state have maintained their ceasefires and adopted a position of armed neutrality in relation to Min Aung Hlaing's regime.

In their report for the Wilson Centre, "Seizing the State: The Emergence of a District Security Actor in Myanmar", Ye Myo Hein and Lucas Meyers argue that there are two main factors currently hindering the NUG's "revolutionary war". The first is their lack of heavy armaments, which makes it difficult for the PDFs to capture and hold territory and counter the Tatmadaw's superior ground and airpower. The other is their lack of a centralised command and control structure able to overcome that of the Tatmadaw. Given these advantages, the Tatmadaw can concentrate their forces against isolated and uncoordinated insurgents, reducing and defeating them over the course of months, if not years. Meanwhile, many of the EAOs are rightly distrustful of the NLD-led NUG given previous treatment of the ethnic minorities and have not yet engaged beyond the borders of their ethnic areas to save besieged PDFs.

Historically, the Tatmadaw adopted a similar strategy against the Communist Party of Burma (CPB) by containing them to the borderlands while wiping out isolated pockets in the central regions; a similar approach was adopted against the All Burma Students' Democratic Front in the aftermath of the 1988 uprising.

Indeed, armed struggle is nothing new on the Burmese left and has played a fundamentally destructive role. The CPB's turn to armed struggle during the Second World War and the early independence period was disastrous, helping to subordinate the working class to bourgeois-nationalist forces, creating a highly militarised political terrain that excluded the working class from independent action, and giving the Tatmadaw a reason to construct a centralised repressive apparatus that could be used against workers and the poor.[37] This reflected a broader shift in Stalinised Communist parties internationally, where the goal of working-class self-emancipation was replaced with class collaboration and the substitution of other class forces (such as armed groups inspired by Maoism). In this respect, those on the Burmese left who are joining the armed popular militias have not yet broken with this disastrous legacy.

Hein and Meyers argue that in order to overcome current limitations, the militias will need to find a way to gain access to heavy artillery, most likely through regional powers such as China, bring the local and national groups under centralised command structures and find ways to address the NLD's poor record with the ethnic minorities. In other words, the "people's revolutionary war" is a form of capitalist restoration from above: a *stagist* strategy that seeks to limit the struggle against Min Aung Hlaing to the restoration of bourgeois democracy. Such an approach necessarily subordinates the class interests of workers and the poor, delaying their demands and grievances until the distant future when a stable democracy has been achieved.

The militarised approach represents a fundamental rupture with the revolutionary movement seen in the early weeks of February and March 2021. Where strikes and mass demonstrations gave other workers confidence and drew them and broader layers into the struggle, bombings, targeted assassinations and gunfights achieve the opposite. Tragically, the increasing militarisation of the resistance is helping consolidate a political terrain that excludes the democratic and popular participation of the working class and "the people".

It is unlikely that the military struggle can topple the Tatmadaw.

---

37.  Lintner 1990.

However even if the "people's revolutionary war" is successful, the NLD's record in power has clearly indicated that the NUG will not confront the many problems facing workers and the poor. There have been no indications made by the NUG that it would provide a solution to the concentration of wealth among the capitalist class; nor have they made any indication that they will repeal the laws that persecute small farmers and push them off their land; and the NLD's deplorable track record with the ethnic minorities means that a democratic solution to the national questions, complete self-determination over land and labour is unlikely, since the borderlands are a key site of capital accumulation for the domestic and regional capitalists they seek to represent. This is because challenging any of these conditions means taking on the economic and political power of the Burmese ruling class, which we know the forces coalesced around the NUG have no interest in doing. Instead, the NUG would seek to privatise larger sections of state capital in order to weaken the officer corps, as indicated in the NLD's economic reform agenda prior to the coup.[38] Yet any switch to a more fully marketised economy would simply open up the country to more parasitic domestic and foreign investment by big capital. These measures would only further exacerbate the tendencies toward land dispossession in rural areas that has underpinned the growth of low-wage employment in urban centres.

All of this points to the problems with such a stagist view of revolution that seeks to limit the struggle against Min Aung Hlaing's regime to the narrow conquest of capitalist state power by a broad alliance between workers, the poor and disaffected parts of the urban elite. This is not to deny that some armed component will be necessary to overthrow Min Aung Hlaing; but the goal for those committed to seeing the tasks of Myanmar's unfinished revolution succeed (political and economic democracy, land to small farmers and self-determination for the ethnic minorities) should not be aiding the construction of a new "bureaucratic-military machine" that is unable to solve any of these problems.

---

38. Liu 2020. It should be noted that privatisation of state assets has been a persistent policy concern of NLD governments that have been repeatedly resisted by the USDP and military-appointed representatives in parliament.

## From combined and uneven development
## to permanent revolution

Leon Trotsky's theory of permanent revolution[39] offers an alternative to stagist views of revolution. It does this by combining democratic and socialist challenges to the existing order of things. In Myanmar these include: the acquisition of the land by small farmers against the big landed interests bound up with former military personnel, state officials and their cronies; the resolution of the national question; and, of course, the reintroduction of parliamentary democracy through the overthrow of Min Aung Hlaing's regime. None of these demands are, in themselves, incompatible with capitalist social relations; but achieving them in the context of Myanmar's combined and uneven development necessarily raises the possibility of social revolution in order to break the nexus of class forces through which Min Aung Hlaing's junta is held together.

Trotsky's theory argues that only the working class can offer a solution to these tasks by challenging the entire basis of capitalist social relations. Although the working class may be young and small in number, their concentration in large, modern enterprises, in sectors of the economy crucial to the state and regional networks of capitalists, gives them the necessary social weight to take up the political leadership of the "democratic revolution" against the military dictatorship. Instead of voluntarily handing political power back to the bourgeoisie, which is incapable of leading the struggle against the Tatmadaw, the working class can turn the democratic revolution into a socialist revolution, bypassing the need for a phase of bourgeois democracy. The isolation of such a revolution in Myanmar would need to be ended by the internationalisation of the revolutionary process through similar struggles across the broader Asia region.

Trotsky's theory is also closely connected to the Marxist attitude to the capitalist state and revolutionary crisis. All revolutions that have involved a significant working-class component have produced situations of "dual power": a stand-off between organs of workers'

---

39. See Trotsky 1931.

power against a severely weakened capitalist state. These institutions of workers' power emerge organically from revolutionary struggle itself, such as the need to coordinate strikes, formulate political demands, defend the masses against capitalist state violence and continue to provide essential services under the control of workers themselves. But the existence of dual power and institutions of workers' power alone are insufficient to defeat the capitalist state; a revolutionary organisation with the goal of a working-class seizure of power is necessary to ensure that the capitalist state is unable to regroup.

With this in mind: why was Myanmar's working class unable to topple Min Aung Hlaing's regime during the great wave of strikes throughout February and March? Two factors stand out:

**1. The inability to create a second governmental power of the toiling masses.** The general strikes of 8, 15 and 22 February had united workers with the urban and rural poor, making them the driving force of the revolutionary struggle. The extended general strike that began on 8 March took the next step, and began to pose the question of who should govern Myanmar in a more direct way. Through each of these general strikes it was possible to capture glimpses of a revolutionary government of the toiling masses.

For example, the CDM support networks that stretched from trade unions to community groups and helped sustain striking workers illustrates the power of ordinary people to draw on their own collective resources and provide the necessities often carried out by the state: food, water, welfare, medical aid, alongside shelter for those avoiding arrest. Similarly, the neighbourhood self-defence organisations and streetfighters acted as militia that carried out protection and surveillance against the repressive arms of the state.

But the core of the general strikes were the committees organised directly by striking workers themselves. In some places these committees took direct control over production: electricity workers in Yangon occupied their workplaces to prevent security forces from conducting night-time raids in early February; seafarers, truckdrivers and shipyard workers at Yangon terminal began organising the transport of food, medicine and other essential goods in late February and early March.[40]

In their most developed form, strike committees fused with neighbourhood self-defence organisations, such as that which took place in a housing compound near Ma Hlwa Gone station in Yangon's Mingalay Taung Nyunt township.[41] The strike committee became the main political authority in the area, involving railway workers, nurses, doctors, teachers, civil servants, students and other locals in joint struggle against the coup, organising pickets and occupations of workplaces (such as the regular confrontations with security forces at a number of train stations and railyards throughout Yangon), attempted to fraternise and negotiate with soldiers, performed night-time security patrols of the area, alongside providing necessities to locals. While similar bodies remained isolated geographically in pockets of Yangon, locals in Mandalay and Bago also reported the existence of neighbourhood strike committees.[42]

Unfortunately, these revolutionary initiatives never congealed into a coherent system of collective self-management. In order to rise to the level of a revolutionary government of the toiling masses these experiences would need to be generalised at both a local and national level. They would also need to penetrate into the centres of capital accumulation that remained largely unscathed by the strikes, in particular the gas fields of the Andaman Sea and the jade mines of Kachin state. In doing so, they could have begun to provide a basis for a network of workers' councils that could eventually challenge for power.

It is reasonable to suggest that the General Strike Committees formed in mid-February could have played such a role had they been able to develop. Through the strike committees, it might have been

---

40.  Lwin 2021.
41.  This following is based on the account given to me in Zaw 2021.
42.  Ko Ko Zaw pointed out that a number of state sector employees in Mandalay had created similar bodies; Zaw 2021. Thar Yar Than, a local militia fighter in Bago, used the term "revolutionary government" to refer to the political authority that had been established in the eastern parts of the city that was routed by security forces in the massacre of 9 April; Than 2021. For an account of the Bago massacre see Narai 2021b.

possible to form both township strike committees and a national body that could place the working class in a better position to answer the questions raised by the 8 March extended general strike. If fuel and energy supplies ran out, workers could restart production under their own control to power working-class and popular districts while continuing to paralyse Min Aung Hlaing's regime and the capitalist class. The farms, food-processing plants and markets could have been run along similar lines. In general, a self-consciously pro-revolutionary leadership of the workers' movement would find ways to extend and deepen the movement while continuing to meet the needs of its popular base and the wavering middle layers. If workers started occupying and seizing their workplaces to carry out these tasks, other questions would have been raised; in particular the "sacred" right of private property and management's right to manage could be challenged. In contrast to the CRPH, this kind of political authority would have been an organic expression of the people involved in the day-to-day struggles against the dictatorship: one capable of posing a direct challenge to the political and economic power of Min Aung Hlaing's regime.

Meanwhile, the inability of forms of workers' power to take hold in the capital city of Naypyitaw, the seat of government, meant that the military could ride out the most difficult days. By constructing an artificial capital city, far away from the urban hub of Rangoon (Yangon), the military successfully prevented the masses from applying the type of pressure that forced a section of the officer corps to break with the BSPP regime in 1988.[43] Any strategy that does not seek to confront and ultimately destroy the heart of Min Aung Hlaing's regime in Naypyitaw cannot succeed, as it leaves the core of the officer corps intact and enables them to continue functioning.

Similarly, the movement has been doomed by its inability to promote mass mutinies inside the Tatmadaw. To deprive the state of its repressive apparatus, or at least to weaken it fundamentally, has been crucial to the success of most modern revolutions.

Many have tried to argue that the Tatmadaw is a military like

---

43. Mon and Weston 2021.

no other, impervious to such appeals. Bertil Lintner, writing in the *Asia Times*, argued that a combination of factors ensured that no cracks opened in the regime. He lists its "dual-function" ideology, which justifies the military's prominent role in economic and social development as well as national defence (the "Three Main Causes"); its powerful economic interests through military-controlled companies; and a fear of retribution for their many crimes, whether previous atrocities in ethnic regions, or the recent ones carried out while crushing the uprising.[44] But the cracks that have emerged through defections to the anti-coup movement reveal the same class divisions that structure any modern military.

"There is a huge gap in the wealth between the upper and lower ranks of the Tatmadaw", explains former military Captain Nyi Thuta, one of several hundred defectors and a founder of the group People's Soldiers, which has been at the forefront of aiding defections.[45] The upper ranks of the Tatmadaw are drawn overwhelmingly from the ruling class and retain economic, family and social ties with that class, while the middle and lower ranks are drawn from the urban and rural poor. "Only the top-level officials are associated with the business sector of the military", he says. "These officials get the profits from these businesses, while the rank-and-file personnel do not get any share. Although they [the generals] always speak about 'state-building', it appears to many of us that they are simply 'building' for themselves."

Furthermore, Captain Thuta says that out of 400,000 soldiers, only 20 percent have been deployed to commit violence against civilians. Throughout February and March, the bulk of the violence was committed by the military-controlled riot police, while most soldiers remained in the barracks. This suggests the rank and file are unreliable, or at least perceived to be so by their officers.

Further proof of this is demonstrated by the means through which loyalty has been maintained. Soldiers and their families live a tightly controlled existence, residing in military compounds that require permission to leave, resulting in what Captain Thuta describes as a

---

44. Lintner 2021.
45. The following is based on correspondence in Thuta 2021.

"hostage" situation. "Many soldiers wish to defect", he explains, referencing the 75 percent of soldiers who reportedly reject the coup.

> But they fear for the safety and lives of their families who remain on the military bases. For those that have a family to worry about, they are not prepared to live on the run as defectors presently do. Under this system, the rank-and-file members of the military and their families are suffering as much as the people.

Identification with the "Three Main Causes" ideology is contingent upon the Tatmadaw's ability to present itself as the only legitimate and sovereign state power. It follows that a rival body with similar claims to popular legitimacy has the ability to break large sections of rank-and-file soldiers away from their commanding officers. This helps explains the number of defections that have taken place to the various resistance forces, an estimated 2,000 soldiers and 6,000 police. These numbers are not enough to topple the regime, but neither are they insignificant. For defectors such as Captain Thuta, their ideological commitment to the idea that Min Aung Hlaing's regime could be overthrown – combined with personal circumstances such as the absence of family living on a military base – underpins their ability to tolerate the material hardships defectors face. For others who wish to defect, the absence of a clear alternative means they see no other option but to stay within the grip of the Tatmadaw.

If such an alternative had existed in February and March – a revolutionary "government of the toiling masses" – the picture could have been much different. The isolated instances of fraternisation between workers and soldiers – such as the workers outside the Central Bank of Yangon who posed with soldiers for group photos while urging them to join CDM – could have become coordinated and more widespread.[46] Through these bodies it might have been possible to formulate appeals targeting the grievances rank-and-file soldiers feel toward their superiors: concerns over wages and conditions; the extension of democracy into their own ranks; the nationalisation of the military-owned

---

46. Paddock 2021.

conglomerates under workers' control and channelling its resources into essential services for workers and the poor; and amnesty for rank-and-file soldiers for atrocities committed while following orders. Combined with mass land seizures in the countryside and the backing of the ethnic minorities, the lack of "peace" and "stability" in the borderlands, which provides justification for the Tatmadaw's ongoing operations in these areas, could be turned on its head: only the revolution could solve the perpetual conflict and bring about a just peace. Rank-and-file soldiers could have been presented a clear choice: do they commit to a corrupt, unequal and brutal state run by Min Aung Hlaing and his cronies? Or do they commit to a democratic, liberating and popular alternative organised by "the toiling masses"?

## 2. The absence of a revolutionary organisation.

Only a revolutionary organisation with deep roots in the working class and poor could have acted towards this end. Revolutionary organisation is not only a prerequisite for the goal of workers' power – its existence is also necessary to try to maximise the gains of partial struggles prior to that goal. During February and March there existed real potential for even small revolutionary organisations to make serious gains and play a leading role in the unfolding struggles. There were many signs that significant numbers of workers were open to revolutionary ideas; and train drivers, nurses, truck drivers, seafarers, teachers and other advanced workers were acting as a vanguard leading others in the struggle. The fact that many of these advanced workers took a lead from – or worked alongside – radical students also illustrates that a revolutionary organisation with roots among students could play an important role in such struggles. The tragedy is that all of these advanced layers were doing so spontaneously and were not united by a common political project and organisation.

A revolutionary organisation rooted in these advanced elements could have drawn on the spontaneous wave of militancy that was unleashed in February and tried to generalise from it; it could have communicated the experiences of the most advanced workers who had developed strike committees with the aim of raising every struggle to the level of the most developed; it could have linked these up through the strike committees on a local, regional and national basis; and it could have transformed the engine of revolutionary struggle into a government of the toiling masses capable of posing a direct challenge to the entire ruling class.

If these factors had existed in February and March, it is very likely that some form of compromise deal would have been struck between a section of the officer corps and the CRPH (most likely the outcome of a counter-coup carried out by middle-ranking officers under the weight of mutinies from below) in order to regain control over the situation. It is hard to predict what would follow such a move, but it is unlikely that the resulting situation would be stable. The social forces unleashed through such a process would have produced a situation of dual power: on one side, a provisional government made up of the CRPH and the officer corps claiming to represent "the people"; and on the other, a revolutionary movement with incipient organisations of self-management.

Hence, there are two senses in which the revolution would need to "grow over" from a democratic to a socialist revolution to fulfill the aspirations of the Burmese people.

Firstly, any newly installed "bureaucratic-military machine" would not be able to provide a solution to the concentration of wealth among the officer corps, state officials and their cronies. Nor would such a government be able to solve the agrarian question (land to the small farmers); nor provide a just solution to the national question. This is because challenging any of these conditions means taking on the economic and political power of the ruling class as a whole, which the officer class – even it's most radical sections – will never do.

Secondly, any assault on the Burmese ruling class is also an assault on the ruling class of neighbouring China, Thailand and Singapore, and a security concern to the Indian and Bangladeshi states. Faced with a revolutionary situation in Burma, these regimes would become a regional base of counter-revolution with the backing of other imperial powers. Yet such a scenario opens up the revolutionary potential of struggles for democracy within these neighbouring regimes; only the toiling masses of the region would be able to the rescue the Burmese people by launching similar assaults on their own ruling classes.

None of these tendencies were allowed to develop since the CRPH – as representative of the liberal sections of Myanmar's ruling class and the ethnic minority leaders that aspire to join them – were able to assume political leadership over the strikes. In doing so they limited the weight of the revolutionary process through three crucial interventions. Firstly, they contained the demands of the struggle to cosmetic political reforms that failed to address the underlying social concerns motivating workers and the poor. Secondly, the sabotage of the strike committees by members of the NLD who argued these bodies could develop into a rival base of power to the CRPH. Finally, by promoting the "right to self-defence" in mid-March (after a month and a half of calling for "peaceful protest" in the face of massacres by the Tatmadaw) they helped channel widespread sentiment that Min Aung Hlaing would need to be overthrown by armed force into abandoning the struggle at the point of production for the "people's revolutionary war".[47] In this way the NLD and CRPH played an important role in the defeat of the extended general strike.

The strategy pursued by the Confederation of Trade Unions Myanmar (CTUM) and the Myanmar Labour Alliance (the 16-member trade union body that launched the 8 March extended general strike) also bears responsibility for the defeat. They showed no desire to channel the creative energy from below into incipient forms of workers' power. The unions instead asked imperial powers to place trade sanctions on the regime, which history shows savage the living conditions of the poor while leaving the rich untouched. They systematically limited their demands to what was acceptable to the CRPH, thus transforming the extended general strike into an auxiliary of the CRPH. This can be seen in the countless working-class demonstrations throughout February that were led to the offices of the United Nations, the US consulate and the International Labour Organization.[48] Despite the youth and militancy of many unions in Myanmar, which are not as bureaucratised as their Western counterparts, and despite the

---

47.  James 2021.
48.  These are well documented on the CTUM's Facebook page throughout February and March 2021.

central role that countless working-class activists played in leading and catalysing the strike wave, the heroic movement was squandered. The dominant politics pushed by the CTUM bureaucracy blocked the path to more radical conclusions that were being drawn by sections of workers, and ensured the Tatmadaw could regain control of the situation.

The counter-revolutionary terror used to crush the extended general strike bears witness to the words of the French revolutionary Saint Just – those who make only half a revolution do no more than dig their own graves.

## "Until the end of the world"

The instincts of the movement opposed to the junta are sound: the battle cry of all those who continue to resist Min Aung Hlaing's regime – "until the end of the world" – contains within it the promise of a never-ending struggle against military rule. But the question remains: what force in society is capable of ending military rule and creating an outcome that can begin to address the vast inequalities that characterise Burmese society? This article has argued that the working class must become the leading class in the revolutionary process. This is because of the class power that arises from their position within the mass of the Burmese people: a power that arises from capitalism's dependence upon workers to produce the goods and provide the services that keep society functioning, and a material interest in overcoming the forms of oppression that characterise the treatment of the rural poor and ethnic minorities.

The ongoing instability that characterises Min Aung Hlaing's junta can open up the possibility for future crises and assaults upon his regime. In particular, the ongoing flash demonstrations against the regime must find a way to connect working class demands over wages, conditions, trade union rights, health, education and welfare and those related to the rural poor and ethnic minorities with the broader political goal of overthrowing the dictatorship. Similarly, those committed to advancing the position of the working class under the military dictatorship will need to break with the politics of sanctions being pursued by the CTUM bureaucracy, since it is acting as a substitute for the immensely difficult task of continuing to organise workers at the point of production.

The key task for revolutionaries in Myanmar today has to be laying the foundations for a socialist organisation that can cohere the most advanced workers into a fighting force capable of leading the mass of workers and drawing behind them the broader oppressed layers in a revolution that smashes the entire Burmese ruling class. Such an organisation will not be built overnight; nor will it be able to influence or lead mass struggles against the dictatorship in the near future. But such an organisation must be built in advance of the type of revolutionary crisis that erupted in February 2021. This type of organisation will necessarily start with small numbers of dedicated individuals convinced of the need to overthrow Burmese capitalism through a revolution led by the working class. These revolutionaries will need a high level of political clarity, in particular in relation to the disastrous effect of Stalinism and Maoism on the Burmese left, and a clear understanding of which forms of working-class organisation can give them the best chance of transforming a political revolt against military rule into a social revolution.[49]

This is because the working class are not just the gravediggers of Min Aung Hlaing's regime; they are the gravediggers of the entire social order upon which the power of the ruling class rests. In this land built with martyrs, only they can deliver on the promise: "We will not be satisfied until the end of the world".

---

49. The discussion circle that has been built around the blog *Revolutionary Marxism* and their recently launched publication *The Struggle* have made important moves in this direction. Due to the history of Stalinism and Maoism, they are allegedly the first Trotskyist group to emerge organically out of the Burmese left and, alongside attempting to develop a genuine Marxist understanding of Burmese capitalism, have made translations of a number of Trotsky's writings available in Burmese for the first time.

# References

Bauer, Andrew, Arkar Hein, Khin Saw Htay, Matthew Hamilton and Paul Shortell 2018, "State-Owned Economic Enterprise Reform in Myanmar: The Case of Natural Resource Enterprises", *Natural Resource Governance Institute and Renaissance Institute Report*. https://resourcegovernance.org/ sites/default/files/documents/state-owned-economic-enterprise-reform-in-myanmar_0.pdf

Blazevic, Igor 2021, "Tatmadaw casualties in clashes with EAOs and PDF/LDF", Facebook post, 20 November. https://www.facebook.com/ photo/?fbid=10159795338031473&set=a.10151665185261473

Cady, John F 1958, *A History of Modern Burma*, Cornell University Press.

Callahan, Mary P 2004, *Making Enemies: War and State Building in Burma*, Singapore University Press.

Callahan, Mary P 2009a, "Making Myanmars: Language, Territory, and Belonging in Post-Socialist Burma" in Joel S Migdal (ed.), *Boundaries and Belonging: States and Societies in the Struggle to Shape Identities and Local Practices*, Cambridge University Press.

Callahan, Mary P 2009b, "Myanmar's Perpetual Junta: Solving the Riddle of the Tatmadaw's Long Reign", *New Left Review*, 60, November–December.

Campbell, Stephen 2013, "On Labour Organisations in Myanmar", *Global Labour Column*, 22 July. http://column.global-labour-university.org/2013/07/ on-labour-organisations-in-myanmar.html

Campbell, Stephen 2021, Email correspondence with Robert Narai.

Galache, Carlos Sardiña 2020, *The Burmese Labyrinth: A History of the Rohingya Tragedy*, Verso.

Galache, Carlos Sardiña 2021, "The all-out war of the Burmese military against its own people", *Position Politics*, 30 March. https://positionspolitics.org/ carlos-sardina-galache-the-all-out-war-of-the-burmese-military-against-its-own-people/

Harkins, Benjamin, Daniel Lindgren, Boonsita Ravisopitying, Shawn Kelley, Thet Hin Aye and Tin Hlaing Min, 2021, "From the rice paddy to the industrial park: Working conditions and forced labour in Myanmar's rapidly shifting labour market", UNOPS Livelihoods and Food Security Fund report, 6 August. https://reliefweb.int/sites/reliefweb.int/files/resources/ myanmar_forcelabourstudy_lift_2021.pdf

Hein, Ye Myo and Lucas Meyers 2021, "Seizing the State: The Emergence of a Distinct Security Actor in Myanmar", *Wilson Centre Asia Program*, November. https://www.wilsoncenter.org/publication/seizing-state-emergence-distinct-security-actor-myanmar

International Labour Organization 2021, "Employment in Myanmar since the military takeover: A rapid impact assessment", *ILO Brief*, July. https://www.ilo.org/global/about-the-ilo/newsroom/news/WCMS_814686/lang--en/index.htm

The Irrawaddy 2021, "Myanmar Junta Loses 1,300 Soldiers Killed Over Last Month: NUG", *The Irrawaddy*, 11 November. https://www.irrawaddy.com/news/burma/myanmar-junta-loses-1300-soldiers-killed-over-last-month-nug.html

James 2021, Correspondence with Robert Narai.

Jones, Lee 2014, "The Political Economy of Myanmar's Transition", *Journal of Contemporary Asia*, 44:1.

Lintner, Bertil 1990, *The Rise and Fall of the Communist Party of Burma (CPB)*, Cornell Southeast Asia Program.

Lintner, Bertil 2021, "Why the Tatmadaw won't crack in Myanmar", *Asia Times*, 20 April. https://asiatimes.com/2021/04/why-the-tatmadaw-wont-crack-in-myanmar/

Liu, John 2020, "Myanmar reform plans fail to reach worst COVID-hit sectors", *Myanmar Times*, 10 December. https://www.mmtimes.com/news/myanmar-reform-plans-fail-reach-worst-covid-hit-sectors.html

Lwin, Phyo Moe 2021, Correspondence with Robert Narai.

Maung, Ko 2021, "Myanmar's Spring Revolution: a history from below", *Open Democracy*, 15 December. https://www.opendemocracy.net/en/beyond-trafficking-and-slavery/myanmars-spring-revolution-a-history-from-below/

Mon, Thurein and Fred Weston 2021, "Myanmar: a balance sheet of the 1988 uprising", *In Defence of Marxism*, 3 December. https://www.marxist.com/myanmar-a-balance-sheet-of-the-1988-uprising.htm

Myint, Me Mint 2021, Correspondence with Robert Narai.

Myint-U, Thant 2019, *The Hidden History of Burma: Race, Capitalism and the Crisis of Democracy in the 21st Century*, Atlantic Books.

Narai, Robert 2021a, "Myanmar's anti-coup movement", *Red Flag*, 31 March. https://redflag.org.au/article/myanmars-anti-coup-movement

Narai, Robert 2021b, "Revolution and counter-revolution in Myanmar", *Red Flag*, 20 April. https://redflag.org.au/article/revolution-and-counter-revolution-myanmar

Narai, Robert 2021c, "The coup and Myanmar's COVID-19 crisis", *Red Flag*, 31 July. https://redflag.org.au/article/coup-and-myanmars-covid-19-crisis

Paddock, Robert C 2021, "'We Can Bring Down the Regime': Myanmar's Protesting Workers Are Unbowed", *New York Times*, 15 February. https://www.nytimes.com/2021/02/15/world/asia/myanmar-workers-coup.html

Revolutionary Marxism 2021, Correspondence with Robert Narai.

Than, Thar Yar 2021, Interview with Robert Narai, 11 April.

Thuta, Captain Nyi 2021, Correspondence with Robert Narai.

Trotsky, Leon 1931, *The Permanent Revolution*. https://www.marxists.org/archive/trotsky/1931/tpr/pr-index.htm

UNDP 2021, "Impact of the twin crises on human welfare in Myanmar", *People's Pulse Survey*, November. https://www.undp.org/publications/impact-twin-crises-human-welfare-myanmar

Wai, Ma Su Su 2021, Interview with Robert Narai, 23 March.

World Health Organisation 2021, Myanmar, WHO Emergency Dashboard. https://covid19.who.int/region/searo/country/mm

Woods, Kevin 2017, *The War to Rule: Ceasefire Capitalism and State-Making in Burma's Borderlands*, PhD Thesis, University of California.

Z 2021, Correspondence with Robert Narai.

Zaw, Htet Naing 2020, "Younger Myanmar Military Officers Promoted to Key Roles in Reshuffle", *The Irrawaddy*, 11 May. https://www.irrawaddy.com/news/burma/younger-myanmar-military-officers-promoted-key-roles-reshuffle.html

Zaw, Ko Ko 2021, Interview with Robert Narai, 24 March.

SERGIO GARCÍA AND MARIANO ROSA

# Argentina: Opportunities for the left grow amid debates within the FIT-Unidad

**Sergio García and Mariano Rosa** are members of the national leadership of the MST and of the national coordination of the FIT-Unidad of Argentina.

A RGENTINA HELD ITS GENERAL LEGISLATIVE ELECTION on 14 November 2021. The government was defeated but it managed to avoid the collapse that it had faced in the primary elections – PASO[1] – on 12 September. The Left Front[2], of which the MST[3] is a member alongside three other organisations, came out as the third most voted for force nationally, winning new national, provincial and municipal legislative representation. These results foreshadow the prospect of a country with a growing social and economic crisis and with new processes, struggles and possible ruptures in the base with Peronism.

The political year closed with an important event: the FIT-Unidad called a national action in Plaza de Mayo and all the squares of the country to reject the agreement with the IMF which is the main issue on the bourgeois political agenda nationally. With about 50,000 people and 100 organisations responding to the call, the action contrasted with a rally held the day before, called in reaction by the

---

1. Mandatory primary elections that are held two months before the general elections. Only the forces that exceed 1.5 percent of the votes in the PASO can go to the general elections. In other words, they are a proscriptive electoral measure.
2. Frente de Izquierda y de Trabajadores Unidad, often referred to as FIT-Unidad or FIT-U.
3. Movimiento Socialista de los Trabajadores (Workers' Socialist Movement).

national government in support of the general orientation of the ruling coalition, which was significantly smaller. All this poses a huge challenge for the FIT-Unidad, which has positive aspects and is well positioned politically with its anti-capitalist and socialist program. But it also has contradictions, problems and debates on the type of project. We share our vision about all this and the political debates that we have been having in the MST, so that the anti-capitalist and socialist left can take a leap towards building a great alternative of power in our country.

## 1. Introduction: a brief overview of the political history of contemporary Argentina

To better understand the current situation and perspectives of the country it is useful to have as a starting point a series of historical references about modern Argentina. We develop a brief synthesis below.

### a. The formation of capitalist Argentina as a nation-state and the bourgeois democratic regime

The year 1880 marked a turning point in the configuration of the national capitalist state. The process of expropriation of land from the first peoples of the central-southern Patagonia was completed and the structure of the latifundio – enormous, privately owned farming estates – and the position of Argentina in the international division of labour as a supplier of raw materials to the industrially developed capitalist centres, especially to Great Britain, was consolidated. This period, dominated by the landowning oligarchy of the original capitalist accumulation, had, on the political side, a type of institutional regime based on a single party with different fractions of the oligarchy in both tension and agreement.

It was not until 1916 that the secret, universal and mandatory vote for male adults was sanctioned by law. In parallel, a combative working class had developed since the end of the nineteenth century. It was politically dominated by the tendencies of anarchism, the Socialist Party and after the Russian Revolution, the Communist Party, the latter became the founder of the first and most powerful workers' trade union federation in the country: the CGT (Confederación General del Trabajo). In the bourgeois camp, the UCR (Unión Cívica Radical) emerged as a national party of the urban petty bourgeoisie and the small farmers, which managed to defeat the conservative party of the landed oligarchy and ran the government from 1916 to 1930. In that year the first classic military coup of the twentieth century in the country took place. The decade of the 1930s saw the agrarian and world crisis, mass southern European immigration (mainly from Italy and Spain) and migration from the countryside to the big cities, which combined to feed a capitalist orientation that is the process known as industrial development by import substitution. The accumulation of reserves from international trade as a result of Argentina's neutrality in the two World Wars allowed it to fund an incipient industrial development out of which the modern working class emerged from the countryside and European migration from the impoverished south.

In this context of the late 1930s and mid-40s Peronism arose as a bourgeois-nationalist party which sought to organise the working class into large, industrial unions – no longer by trades, as was the case with anarchism and the left previously. It won political and union leadership over the workers' movement, based on handing down important economic concessions and democratic rights, fundamentally displacing the Communist and Socialist parties which were aligned with US imperialism. Peronism expressed a current that opposed the penetration of US imperialism in a country that, until that moment, was essentially located in the orbit of British imperialism. It ruled until 1955, when it was displaced by a pro-US military coup. During this period it consolidated itself as the leadership of the labour and mass movement in the country. Thereafter, it was banned for 18 years.

### b. The dynamics of the political regime until 1982 and 2001: the pendulum between bipartisanship and military coups

With the emergence of Peronism, Argentine capitalism ruled based on a combination of two alternating regimes until 1982:

• Short periods of bipartisan bourgeois democracy (led by Peronism and the UCR).

• Military coups, which interrupted those periods of bourgeois democracy, in order to contain polarisation or pre-revolutionary situations.

The coups which apparently displaced the UCR or Peronism from the government, had, however, the purpose of saving those parties from falling due to a revolutionary ascent, that is, of being brought down by the independent action of the mass movement. Thus, during the periods of military rule the army gave the two bourgeois parties time to recompose themselves, doing the "dirty" work of repression and reversal of workers' gains, to then return to some form of bourgeois reopening and again, to the radical-Peronist alternation.

This pendular dynamic lasted until 1982. Then, the last dictatorship, whose capitalist, pro-imperialist, neoliberal and genocidal character – with 30,000 disappeared – and, in addition, with a military defeat in the Malvinas on its back, precipitated a process of mass mobilisation, with a general strike and confrontation in the streets. This process threw the dictatorship from power and forced an improvised bourgeois-democratic exit, which lasted until 2001 with, once again, alternation between Peronism and the UCR.

What was new about this period was that, as the military dictatorship had been swept away by a profound process of mass irruption, the army was politically disabled from being brought to power in favour of the bourgeoisie in the event of a crisis. In fact, the movement for *memory, truth and justice*, which to this day continues to mobilise against those responsible for the genocide is a very powerful factor of mobilisation in the country. It has won the imposition of life imprisonment on some of those responsible, and remains an obstacle to the bourgeoisie's ability to repress the workers and mass movement.

The bourgeoisie and imperialism have thus been forced for almost 20 years to administer capitalism in crisis with the battered radical-Peronist alternation, which has exposed before the mass movement the reality that in the end both applied the same plans of austerity at the service of the IMF and big capital. This experience ended with the crisis of 2001 and a triumphant semi-insurrection that brought down five presidents in a week and forever buried traditional bipartisanship.

## c. From 2001 to the present: from the Argentinazo to the regime of weak bourgeois coalitions

In the heady days of December 2001, the streets were filled with songs that said "Out with them all, not one should remain" and "without *radicales* or *Peronistas*, we are going to live better". With a bipartisan regime discredited by the mass movement, and lacking confidence in the success of a military coup, the bourgeoisie improvised a new scheme: bourgeois coalitions based on the old parties, but now prettified by their alliances with components from the more recent period. Thus, from 2003 to 2015, Kirchnerism ruled presenting itself not as "Peronist" but as the "Front for Victory". It capitalised on the tailwind of the international economy with very high commodity prices and the lowering of labour costs due to a brutal 400 percent devaluation of the peso and the use of an idle industrial capacity of around 50 percent. At the same time, it deployed a modernised image of itself in tune with the Latin American progressive wave, discursively taking up banners of the left such as the struggle for human rights, anti-imperialism, the denunciation of corporations, Latin Americanism as an identity, etc.

Thus, for a period, Kirchnerism managed to pause the profound shift to the left that started in 2001. But, as it did not provoke any structural changes in the dependent capitalist matrix, the changing winds in the world economy after the 2008 crisis led to its electoral defeat in 2015, at the hands of a moderate right-wing coalition with a pro-business, anti-populist profile referenced in what would later become the "Lima Group". The right-wing was immediately confronted in government by a mass movement in the streets. It barely managed to complete its term, saved by the complicit role of Kirchnerism in parliament and, above all, in the workers' federations. In 2019 a new coalition with Kirchnerism as a central component snatched the presidency, capitalising on a strong desire to "punish" the disastrous Macri government.

This is how we got to the current government, with a mass movement yet to be defeated, with an accumulated experience against the right, with relative expectations in the new government that denounced the "fraudulent debt of Macri with the IMF" and promised to "recover all the rights lost in four years". None of this happened, but rather the opposite is true. That is why the current context is defined by the beginning of a *thaw* of the elements or tendencies of a left turn that, incipiently, have been expressed in the FIT-U vote (with the logical distortion of being in the bourgeois democratic electoral terrain), but also in the streets with actions such as that of 11 December against the IMF called by our Front.

The current moment, the post-electoral scenario and the challenges and debates within the left, are the subject of the rest of this article. A final comment before moving forward: we consciously ignored developing the history of the revolutionary left in the country, which in any case can be the subject of another work.

## 2. The defeat of Peronism and the prospect of more crisis and social convulsions

Argentina has now lived through two years of Peronism, via its governmental coalition: the Frente de Todos (Front of All).[4] All sectors of the old Justicialista (Peronist) party came together, along with progressive organisations, centre-left sectors and a sector called the Frente Patria Grande (Great Fatherland Front) that calls itself the "independent left", but lost all its independence by joining a bourgeois front. Also Maoism and the Communist Party of Argentina are part of this capitalist coalition. It has the open support of all the trade union bureaucracy of both the CGT and the CTA (Central de Trabajadores de la Argentina).

That great unity formed in the Frente de Todos was consummated to take advantage of the sentiment of millions of working families, popular sectors and even middle-class sectors and part of the industrial bourgeoisie against Macri and his right-wing political project. From 2015 to 2019, four years of the Macri government caused the economy to collapse, increased levels of poverty and unemployment and brought the IMF back to the country, indebting it to the tune of US$44 billion. This money was extracted from the country by a model that favoured the financial system, the big exporting agrarian bourgeoisie and the extractive corporations.

---

4. Frente de Todos is the governing coalition led by the historic Partido Justicialista with all the wings of Peronism inside, plus a series of organisations that come from the left such as the PCR (Revolutionary Communist Party), PC (Communist Party) and the Patria Grande (Great Fatherland) front, among other sectors.

The Frente de Todos had won the presidential election of October 2019, promising profound changes and to leave behind the Macrista model. When, almost two years later on the night of 12 September 2021, the results of the legislative primary elections came out showing a strong defeat for the government, the message from the polls was clear: these changes and improvements had not taken place. The results expressed a punishment vote and the strong disappointment of the masses, opening a new situation. The Frente de Todos suffered a significant loss of votes, falling from 48 percent in 2019 to roughly 30 percent at the national level, even though all the wings of Peronism were united, making it one of its worst elections in many years.

However, this decline in votes did not feed the right-wing opposition. A large part of them went to the left and to an expression of the extreme right (third and fourth force respectively), to the blank or null vote and to electoral abstention. Juntos por el Cambio (Together for Change), the right-wing opposition coalition, won the primaries in 17 provinces but without growing its voter base. It maintained its electoral space, unified its voters and social base, but without qualitative changes. The recent experience with Macrismo and the right in the government was enough to dissuade an important sector of the population from seeing it as an alternative, despite their anger with the current government. Another phenomenon appeared to the right, the so-called libertarians, who combine neoliberal "Austrian School" economic policies with an anti-political discourse. This includes Javier Milei[5] in the city of Buenos Aires, another neoliberal economist, José Luis Espert in the province of Buenos Aires and minor expressions in the rest of the country.

The general elections of 14 November dealt a new blow to the ruling Peronism that lost in all the main districts of the country. But it managed to recover in the largest one, the province of Buenos Aires, regaining some of its losses in the primaries. Therefore, despite having lost, it avoided a collapse and thus has a little more room to manoeuvre

---

5.   Milei represents a new liberal approach, using anti-political caste discourse, encouraged by the media, to attract the attention of the population dissatisfied with the traditional parties and prevent that dissatisfaction from only going to the left.

going forward. Since its defeat in September, the Peronist government had gone from crisis to crisis, with a number of very public faction fights. In that dispute, a new cabinet emerged, with increased representation for the more right-wing and traditional figures from what remains of the Partido Justicialista apparatus, the provincial governors of the country, all with the support of Cristina Kirchner, the vice-president. This confirms that the decisive sectors of the coalition realise they must remain united to manage a government that can resist social pressure in the coming period.

In the midst of this internal crisis, the social and economic reality dealt a new blow: an inflationary jump, a devaluation with the dollar reaching 200 pesos, and the country-risk rate skyrocketing. The daily life of millions of working families is marked by extremely low wages, unemployment and the inability to make ends meet on meagre incomes. In this context, the internal disputes of the government were seen by a large part of the population as bureaucratic politicking unrelated to their urgent problems. Thousands of workers and young people who supported the Frente de Todos two years ago, have begun to walk away in disappointment.

Faced with this situation, the government prepared a series of announcements trying to convince the population that the worst of the crisis had already passed, and spent millions in the last month before the general elections. With this it tried to temper the unfavourable social mood. Now it is sailing in "troubled waters", the political regime as a whole is in crisis and new economic tensions are looming.

The context of this situation is marked by the latest agreement with the IMF, whose negotiations overshadowed the electoral campaign. The government has advanced towards signing an agreement that legalises a $50 billion scam, and an ongoing submission to the IMF's designs, and its illegal and illegitimate debt. The right-wing opposition obviously supports this path, although it hides behind theatrical parliamentary "debate". Indeed, within the framework of this new agreement, the right also wants to stage an offensive over working conditions. It is not by chance that, together with influential capitalist sectors, they are arguing the need for a labour reform to remove more rights and make employment conditions more precarious.

With an agreement with the IMF on the horizon, the country is now moving towards a major crisis. Argentina is part of the global and regional capitalist crisis that started years ago and that the irruption of the pandemic has exacerbated. It is no coincidence that in the last two years, Latin America has experienced rebellions, revolutions, social polarisation, and electoral and political experiences that reflect a search towards the left in various countries.

Our opinion is that this whole process will deepen, creating the conditions for new actions of class struggle, more opportunities to challenge for the leadership in the organisations of the labour and student movements, and a greater opening of the political space for the left. This does not mean that we are going into an easy situation, nor do we encourage unilateral or over-optimistic perspectives. There will always be strong disputes, clashes with other leaderships connected to the government, and political struggles against all the possibilist and reformist sectors that will argue that the right can return to the presidency in 2023 to try to contain their bases. But in the midst of this dispute we will clearly have better conditions to move forward because of discontent and ruptures in the Peronist working-class base, a process which will be amplified as the government moves towards more austerity and an agreement with the IMF.

The government will walk on the ledge. On the one hand, it will want to rebuild its strength. But, we cannot rule out the hypothesis that the country could move towards a major crisis with abrupt changes or even early elections, because the presidential figure is very weakened by the profound erosion of the last months. We must not lose sight of the fact that we are talking about a country that twenty years ago had the Argentinazo, a semi-insurrection that liquidated the bipartisan model as it had existed before and brought down five presidents in one week. A similar process, now under a Peronist government, would have much greater consequences and new phenomena would emerge. Of course it is not certain that this will happen, but it is a possibility worth taking into account.

Our party is preparing for this new situation of crisis and volatility. That is why throughout the electoral campaign we waged a political struggle and called to vote and strengthen the FIT Unidad and to organise with the MST. Our argument is that the left needs to be prepared for this coming crisis. As always in Argentina, the situation will be very dynamic, it will open up new phenomena that will change the situation and generate repercussions throughout the region.

## 3. The left in the September primaries and in the November general elections

One of the main facts that emerged from the 2021 electoral process is that the left consolidated its position as the third national force. The FIT-Unidad obtained over 5 percent of the vote nationally – more than one million votes – in the September primaries. This was a very important political achievement of which we are proudly part, having contributed our campaign in the primaries and our own votes for that result.

Among the important numbers obtained by the left there were some very prominent votes, such as those achieved jointly by the two lists that competed in the FIT-U primaries: Jujuy 23 percent, Province of Buenos Aires 5.2 percent, CABA 6.2 percent, Chubut 9.4 percent, Neuquén 7.8 percent, San Juan 6.9 percent, Santa Cruz 7.8 percent, Salta 5 percent, La Rioja 5 percent and Mendoza 4.9 percent, among others. They are signals that in the face of the austerity applied by the previous and current governments, and in face of the debates between both sides of that false divide, an important section of the population opted for the left that is united in our Front.

### Progress of the MST within the FIT-U

The important number of votes obtained in the primaries by the FIT-U are a product of both the votes of List 1A (PTS of Bregman and Del Caño, PO, IS[6] and other sectors) and the novelty of the 10(R) "Revolutionise the Left" list that we promoted with Alejandro Bodart, Cele Fierro and other MST referents throughout the country, that obtained more than 280,000 votes, almost 30 percent of the total votes of the Front. Thus the MST has clearly become one of the main forces of the FIT-U, as the

---

6.    PTS: Partido de los Trabajadores Socialistas; PO: Partido Obrero;
      IS: Izquierda Socialista.

other list ("1A"), formed by three parties and several other organisations, got the rest. This amount is not divided equally, there are clear differences in strength between the three groups.

Among the results obtained by the MST lists within the FIT-Unidad, the most important victories were achieved in Salta, San Juan, La Rioja and Entre Ríos, together with the important growth in provinces like Mendoza (above 30 percent) and in Jujuy. We also achieved very important results in Río Negro, Chubut, Neuquén, Santa Fe, Córdoba, Catamarca and La Pampa, among others, a good electoral result in the City of Buenos Aires and the important result in the province of Buenos Aires.

These results, as a whole, reflect progress by those of us who propose that the FIT-Unidad advances on the basis of its anti-capitalist and socialist program, opens up, changes and surpasses its current existence. That is why we believe that now, in light of the results, neither the specific weight that the MST represents nor the ideas and proposals that we defend, and with which we achieved a more than respectable amount of electoral support among workers and the youth throughout the country, can be ignored.

This support we received for our politics, and which gained a lot of visibility throughout the campaign, contrasts with a more blurred campaign of the PO comrades, who lost positions and visibility, in addition to a strong defeat in Salta. And it contrasts even more with the position of Izquierda Socialista, which almost everywhere remains submerged behind the politics and the candidacies of the PTS and the PO without any political influence. The IS uses conservatism and an anachronistic discourse that denies the different perspectives and tries to cover them under an artificial single mindset. In short, a regrettable politics that is not at all related to what we must do on the left if we want to move towards becoming a great alternative. One more important point, very relevant for us: the political and electoral contribution of the MST added an amount of votes so that in the final result the FIT-U was the third and not the fourth national force.

The results also show the weakness of the forces that are outside of FIT-U, who paid the price for their divisive stance. The MST also came out of these elections with greater support than the Nuevo MAS,[7] which obtained about 130,000 votes, less than half of what the MST obtained in the primaries and slightly more than 10 percent of what the FIT-U obtained. Another sector that came out defeated in the elections is the one headed by Jorge Altamira (a split from PO), with 0.2 percent of the vote.

### The Left Front in the general elections

We arrived at the general elections on 14 November with common lists of the FIT-U and achieved a very important result. We were again the third national force, increasing the overall vote by around 20 percent, reaching 1,300,000 votes, or about 6 percent of the national vote. For the first time we won four seats in the national Congress: two for Buenos Aires, one for the City of Buenos Aires and one for Jujuy. The FIT-U also won two seats in the state legislature of the province of Buenos Aires and two in the city of Buenos Aires. In a historical event, for the first time the left entered the legislative Councils of various municipalities in Greater Buenos Aires, a clear sign that the relationship between Peronism and parts of its social base is beginning to crack, with parts of the latter beginning to look towards the left.[8]

In addition, very important results were obtained in different provinces, reaching 25 percent in Jujuy, in Chubut 8.5 percent, in Neuquén 8.1 percent, in Santa Cruz 7 percent, in Buenos Aires 6.8 percent, in the City of Buenos Aires 7.7 percent, among others.

The important result obtained by the FIT-U is a great political accomplishment which was achieved through the unity of the anti-capitalist and socialist left and is at the service of the working class and the youth. Our party is a prominent part of these results, not only because we had an important role in the campaign and the dispute against the capitalist parties, but also because we will be part of the

---

7.  Nuevo MAS (Nuevo Movimiento al Socialismo) is a small and very sectarian party on the left, whose main public figure is Manuela Castañeira, that refuses unity and persistently attacks the FIT-U.
8.  The municipalities of Greater Buenos Aires, where around 15 million people live, have always been a terrain dominated by Peronism and the left has never managed to place council members there. This election is the first time that this barrier has been broken in five major municipalities.

rotation of the national, provincial and municipal legislative seats, with some exceptions. The result of the FIT-U confirms that there is progress and a search by important sections of the population outside of the traditional parties and that this process can advance much more in the coming times if we are able to attract new sections towards the left. Hence the importance of the debates that we are having inside the Front, that in light of the results will gain much more relevance and importance.

We need to have the greatest audacity to intervene in the FIT-U without fearing the debate of ideas and proposals within the left. We believe that it is positive that more voices were heard in the primaries of the FIT-U, a result of the understanding that if there is no agreement on the formation of the electoral lists, or even on the criteria to do so, the correct political path was for our party to present its own list in the primary. This also allowed the sum of both lists to make the Front the third force in the country and also in key places such as the province of Buenos Aires. If we truly believe that we can be an alternative of power, a reference and organisational channel for thousands in all areas of struggle, far beyond the elections, we must continue building our Front in unity, but without hiding debates, without impositions and understanding that there can be differences and nuances on the base of a common program and agreements.

## 4. Positive elements, potential and limits of the Left Front

As we have said, the general elections of 14 November marked a turning point, and a conjuncture of greater social and political upheaval will come, in tune with the winds of rebellion, shifts to the left and social polarisation that blow in the world and the continent. The very good election result of the Left Front is an important step in preparing ourselves for that perspective.

At the same time, as the MST has been proposing in this campaign and since we joined the Front, we need a stronger, bigger, more convincing and open Left Front. In this sense, as we anticipated in the opening lines of this article, 2021 ended with an important event that had the FIT-U as the protagonist: the call for a national day of mobilisation on 11 December against the agreement with the IMF, with its epicentre in

Plaza de Mayo and reproduced throughout the country, that mobilised more than 50,000 people and 100 organisations in Buenos Aires alone. This came the day after the national government had called a rally, hastily improvised, in support of the ruling party's orientation, supporting the agreement with the IMF. It was a petty demonstration composed of the clientelist apparatus without the least enthusiasm and smaller than the one we did with the Front. The image of the two squares, showing a polarisation between the government and the FIT-U around the axis that organises all national politics (the agreement with the IMF), and to the advantage of the left, could not be silenced by the large bourgeois media and had an impact on national discussion.

We place this event as a point of reference and political turning point, because it showed all the political potential of the FIT-U as a motor for street action and a pole of attraction for organisations that oscillate between governing progressivism and the revolutionary left. In a general sense, it was the confirmation of all our insistent strategic proposal as orientation for the Front: to overcome the limited – although important – electoral front stage, to transform ourselves into a political pole in the process of class struggle that appears as an alternative, seen by millions as an option in the face of the decline of the ruling progressivism.

Obviously this was just one action, but it reflects our political approach. We believe we need to strongly push for these kinds of actions and spaces of coordination against the IMF and all the austerity plans, with the perspective that it is only the starting point for a broader orientation of the FIT-U beyond the electoral process.

If we were to outline the debates around the project within our coalition, we would say the following:

a. The MST is committed to making the Front a great political movement based on its correct anti-capitalist and socialist program. We are convinced that, facing the evident fact that no organisation within the left has its own hegemony or mass influence, it is crucial to act in united fashion beyond the bourgeois elections in all fields of the class struggle. We propose that the FIT-U evolve towards a political movement or party with freedom for tendencies, that fights for the leadership of organisations and key sectors of the labour movement, the youth and social movements, that debates in its meetings a common intervention in all of these spaces for struggle. At the same time, we should design forms of organic participation for thousands of independent activists who sympathise with the FIT-U and today are not part of any of its parties, but who could be part of the Front if there were institutions such as assemblies, plenaries or other forms to channel the enormous energy and potential militant contribution militant contribution which exists in reality.

Unfortunately, in spite of our insistence on this proposal, until now the comrades of PTS, PO and IS have refused to move forward with such a plan. For example, the PTS knows that the FIT-U is still only an electoral front but doesn't have any proposal to overcome this. Every once in a while they speak of forming a single party with democratic centralism, which is not viable in the current reality. PO only speaks of a united front in the struggles and a FIT-U Congress. IS, the smallest force, sees its position threatened by any bold shift in orientation by the FIT-U, and so does not have any proposal on this matter.

The debates about how to build an important left alternative are logical and at the same time they are not new. It is worth mentioning that the integration of the MST into the Front and therefore the constitution of the FIT-Unidad, was only due to the combination between a relative electoral setback of the FIT in 2019 and an advance of our party in the elections at that time. Faced with that fact, the forces then involved in the Front accepted, for the first time, a political agreement and our integration into it. But this did not eliminate the debates over revolutionary strategy, over how to become a real alternative of power in the workers' and mass movement.

b. We want a Front with democratic mechanisms to make every decision, plurality of voices and a real representation of every organisation. It is worth noting that the MST values the unity achieved with the FIT-U, even if it is at the electoral level for now. It has served to challenge all the forces of the capitalist regime, be they of the right, centre or progressive-possibilists and, therefore, it has played an undoubtedly progressive role in that sense. All of this is based on a correct and profound program that points towards breaking with the system. That is why it appears as the only truly alternative force. It is why in this campaign the government was worried about it at times, because our Front could snatch an even greater section of its working-class and popular social base. The FIT-U could appear in key debates, such as on the issues of the IMF and foreign debt among others, as the only alternative with a program opposed to all the rest, clearly at the service of the working class and popular majorities.

However, having said all this, there is an important political debate for the orientation of the Front that expresses important agreements and also differences of conception and strategy, elements which have points of contact with international debates. If we want to become an alternative for millions we must start by taking advantage of the best elements of each organisation, their influence and insertion in every aspect of reality, and not from unnecessary disputes and unilateral electoral points of view. We have debates over this issue with the PTS comrades as they start from trying to impose a certain hegemony through their well-known electoral figures, when at the same time they are neither hegemonic in the labour movement (where they are very weak), nor in the student movement, nor in the social front, nor in the organic capacity of militant mobilisation. Their relative advantage in the electoral arena leads them to push so that everything that is done as a Front has electoral results as a point of reference. This conception borders on a very marked parliamentary adaptation that does not help the FIT-U. The PO and IS agree with this basic orientation of the PTS, expressing a conservative stance that seeks to defend their electoral positions in the Front. In spite of having differences on several issues, the three forces have a mistaken strategic point of agreement. This leads them in practice to try to impose a monolithic vision on the coalition, to reject the debates and ideas that the MST proposes as "factional or divisive". They also refuse the idea of making the Front a movement or party of tendencies with democratic mechanisms to decide everything.

In the pre-electoral debate, as a result of our decision to have our own list for the primaries since we defended the right to express our positions to improve the front, the other three parties agreed on a electoral regulation with a restrictive minimum of votes that in practice acted as a "punishment" for the "political sin" of publicly arguing for our positions in favour of an orientation for the FIT-U that we are convinced would help it grow, always on the basis of defending its program and existence.[9] These practices, which we hope will change and be corrected in the future, are an expression of a debate that exists throughout the left, not only in Argentina. And now more than ever, standing on the important position achieved by the FIT-U, we must argue for a Front without a forced consensus or hegemony. We need a FIT-U that builds forms of democratic political deliberation to decide and resolve. At the same time, we propose to open the Front by making it a movement, without dissolving the current parties or losing political and organisational independence, generating democratic mechanisms of deliberation and resolution that integrate sectors that sympathise with the FIT-U on the basis of its anti-capitalist and socialist program that we defend.

c. In short, we combine the analysis of where the country, the region and the world are going – *more crisis, discontent and ruptures from below* – with the necessary policy of intervening in this process, not ignoring it, and widely calling to strengthen a pole of the left. And that cannot be done if one only aspires to convince people to vote for the FIT-U, but doesn't give them any role in making our Front bigger, stronger, more capable of action. We have learned, following Trotsky, that when there are crises of other forces and competitors, our duty is to intervene in those crises, to generate more contradictions, to develop a clear line so that when there are more ruptures and detachments, we can attract sections towards the anti-capitalist and socialist left. Only in this way can progress be made with broad swaths of workers, women and popular sectors. The electoral result and the successful call against the IMF are two irrefutable proofs of the potential of this orientation that we propose.

---

9. The electoral regulations of the FIT-U were prepared by the PTS, PO and IS, and it prevents a list that does not exceed 20 percent of the votes in the PASO from being part of the first rotation of a position that comes out in the general elections, entering into the rotation only if a second seat is won. Thus, this undemocratic regulation attacks the rights of other lists in the primaries and tries to "punish" those who dare to present an alternative list. The MST presented an alternative regulation without any type of restrictive floor, as it should be on a left front. And we will demand that it be modified towards the next elections.

This debate is decisive for the future. With the current political orientation, even with our good recent electoral results, we will be limited to winning a few seats in congress and achieving a certain social influence. But there will be no qualitative change. On the other hand, if we revolutionise the politics of the Front and go all-out, united on the basis of a shared anti-capitalist and socialist program, to change the model of the electoral front towards that of a great political movement that openly and collectively discusses the way forward in all the areas of the class struggle, we could take great steps towards being a true alternative of power in the country, and really have an impact on future events of crisis and mass irruption in Argentina.

## A revolutionary or a conservative orientation

This debate is profound and takes on a particular aspect due to the composition and structure of the left in Argentina. With a strong tradition and influence of Peronism for decades, Trotskyism has also carved its own independent way, and we have gained a very important political and social influence, with real roots. This reality, together with the right turn of forces that came from other left traditions and were assimilated into Peronism, means that today the actually visible left is the Left Front, there is no other influential alternative.

Therefore, we are not in a country where a small group of revolutionaries have to decide whether to tactically enter for a period of time into a broader or programmatically diffuse project, something that might be correct to do in light of certain difficulties. In Argentina it is the other way around. We are the ones who can and must convene and incorporate and lead other sectors, convince their bases that we are a better leadership, that we have a better program and a better project. It is a key debate, because we can either have a bold and revolutionary orientation on this issue, or maintain a line with sectarian, conservative aspects that means nothing changes, that in the end shows a certain scepticism, of not believing in our forces or that the working class and the youth can advance by evolving politically.

Ultimately, we are discussing political strategy because there are two different projects and political orientations within the FIT-Unidad. The MST represents and fights politically for a revolutionary project, which sees what has been achieved up to now as a very valuable starting point, but seeks now to make a qualitative leap in the dispute between sections of the masses, and towards political power. We are and we will continue to be a left wing within the FIT-U that wants to transform everything that today limits the Front and wants to have an offensive policy. Among other reasons, there is a danger that the sectarian stance can lead to phenomena arising outside of the Front, that can become an obstacle to the advancement of the left. This reaffirms once again that sectarian politics always ends in opportunism and in strengthening competitors who are neither anti-capitalist or socialist.

The perspective for the Left Front may be one of greater advances and important leaps, and we will continue to put in all our militant strength and ideas towards this goal, working in unity on the basis of the important agreements we have with others in the FIT-U, despite our differences. But a qualitative leap forward towards the objective of conquering a workers' government not only depends on objective conditions and a search to the left by sections of the population. We must also try to overcome our subjective limits and contradictions, with the objective of truly transforming ourselves into an alternative of power for the working class and the people. That is our goal, and why we continue to argue our position, even as we jointly build the FIT-U with other comrades.

## 5. Strengthening the party and the International Socialist League, a key strategy

All this debate on the different projects within the left is not a matter of propaganda, nor is it a philosophical discussion. It is a very deep political struggle, which requires our greatest strength in its prosecution.

For this reason, although we place the task of advancing in the construction and growth of our party at the end of this text, we actually consider it to be a top priority. There is no way to advance in our orientation and project if the MST does not over the next period become much stronger and bigger than it already is in the country.

Scenarios of major struggles and very strong social convulsions will come. This will generate new opportunities and challenges for the revolutionary left, and at the same time will deepen the debates that already exist. We need to prepare for these moments, in order to have a greater chance that our ideas can advance within the FIT-U, and the broader movement. This is essential for a left-wing alternative like the FIT-U to play the role that it can play and overcome its present limited and electoral stage.

At the same time, building the party is not reduced to strengthening ourselves only within the Left Front. Rather, our task is to make a much more solid party, rooted in the processes of the labour movement, advancing in the leadership of unions, internal commissions and delegate bodies. Advancing in leading sectors of the student movement and intervening in the processes of struggle of the precarious youth. Advancing in our positions in the popular neighbourhoods and in the environmental and gender fronts that are very dynamic and generate a lot of left-wing activism.

This advance also has a priority task, that of politicising and forming a new and large layer of cadres in the strategy of a revolutionary party and in its internationalist character, politically nourishing ourselves with the analysis and contributions of the ISL, taking on the tasks and campaigns that are proposed and carrying out and helping in what we can to its development.

After the November elections, we entered a new situation with opportunities, risks and exciting challenges. Our task is to prepare and strengthen ourselves thoroughly to intervene in the entire period that is opening, with a stronger MST and contributing to the FIT-Unidad with our ideas for a revolutionary course in the politics and the orientation that the Front needs to assume.

JORDAN HUMPHREYS

# Red and black: How Australian communists fought for Indigenous liberation[1]

**Jordan Humphreys** is a socialist activist in Sydney and a regular contributor to the *Marxist Left Review*.

O N 1 MAY 1946 ABORIGINAL STOCK WORKERS walked off stations across the Pilbara region in Western Australia. This was the beginning of one of the first great Aboriginal strikes that rocked post-war Australian society. In taking this action, the workers were not merely fighting for improved wages and conditions, but were challenging more than one hundred and fifty years of oppression and exploitation.

Support for the strike flowed in from workers' organisations across the country. Don McLeod, the white Communist who helped organise the strike, had told the Aboriginal workers that they would have "power behind us". He was quickly proven right. Nineteen unions in Western Australia, seven national unions, four trades and labour councils and innumerable local trade union branches supported the strike and sent money. In 1949 the Communist-led Seamen's Union would bring the struggle to a climax with a boycott of wool shipping that broke the last resistance of the station owners.

This was no spontaneous expression of solidarity. The groundwork had been laid by almost two decades of work by Communist Party militants in trade unions and working-class communities across the

---

1.   Thanks to Bob Boughton for his comments on an earlier draft of this article.

country. This article is about how those foundations were laid, and the Indigenous and non-Indigenous activists who made it possible for the union movement to take such bold and widespread action in support of an Indigenous strike.

Most of the non-Indigenous activists involved in this work were working-class militants and members of the Communist Party of Australia (CPA). Throughout the twentieth century, the CPA made an important contribution to the struggle for Indigenous rights. For decades, Communists stood against the grain of racism in Australian society, criticised the mainstream of the labour movement for its failure to take Indigenous rights seriously and condemned the Australian Labor Party for its role in enforcing oppression and racism at both a state and federal level. These weren't just words; Communists sought to build solidarity with Indigenous struggles and promoted anti-racist ideas among the party's predominantly working-class membership and audience. No other predominantly non-Indigenous organisation contributed as much to the Indigenous struggle in Australia as the CPA.

The CPA was ahead of the curve, even compared to other Communist parties in countries with minority Indigenous popula-tions. Communists in New Zealand didn't start to organise around Maori rights until 1935.[2] The Canadian CP didn't adopt a program for Indigenous rights until 1937 (six years after the CPA, and its program was much more limited than the CPA's 1931 *Draft Programme*) and didn't begin to take up the question in a practical sense until after the Second World War. The contribution of the CPA to Indigenous struggles also significantly dwarfed that made by CP in America, where there are no examples of Communist-organised working-class support for Indigenous rights on the scale seen in Australia.[3]

The CPA's contribution has often been obscured or downplayed by those for whom the natural white allies of Indigenous communities are middle-class humanitarians, university-trained intellectuals and liberal members of the clergy.[4] Recently, some historians have sought

---

2.   McNeill 2015.
3.   Drachewych 2017.
4.   See Henry Reynolds' discussion of the Caledon Bay campaign during the early 1930s,

to correct this false narrative and draw attention to the contributions of the CPA and its working-class supporters.[5]

Yet much remains to be written. This article focuses on what might be called the pre-history of the more thoroughly documented examples of solidarity in the post-war period.[6] For it was in the turmoil of the Great Depression that Communist militants first began to integrate the struggle for Indigenous rights with working-class politics. At first, the contribution was mainly through propagandistic articles drawing attention to the terrible exploitation of Indigenous people and making arguments for why their struggle should be seen as a part of the movement for working-class self-emancipation. But as the Communist Party grew in influence throughout the 1930s they were in a position to turn the idea of solidarity into action, first in the unemployed movement, then the trade unions, and finally in broader political campaigns.

In the process, the CPA trained hundreds, if not thousands, of working-class activists to be sensitive to the oppression of Indigenous people and to be ready to show solidarity when Indigenous people fought back. Through the first half of the 1930s, the CPA conceived of the fight for Indigenous liberation as a potentially revolutionary and anti-capitalist struggle, situating it in the context of the rise of anti-colonial and anti-racist movements across the globe. They argued that the working class were natural allies of Indigenous people, much more so than the naive, vacillating and paternalistic middle classes and do-gooders. During the late 1920s and early 1930s, the CPA believed that while Communists should strive to combat racism and promote Indigenous rights in day-to-day struggles, the ultimate liberation of Indigenous people would only be possible with the overthrow of Australian capitalism and the establishment of a workers' state. This forthright position would be modified as the politics of the

---

in which he doesn't even mention the fact that Communist Party trade unionists played a leading role in the campaign both in Darwin and across the country. Instead he prefers to narrowly discuss the role of religious and middle-class figures. Reynolds 1998.

5.   In particular Boughton 2001, Townsend 2009, Bloodworth 2006, Wilson 2013 and Jordan 2011.

6.   For the post-war history of solidarity see Wilson 2013 and Scrimgeour 2020.

popular front took hold in the mid-1930s, a process that is also a part of the story presented here.

## Indigenous oppression, the labour movement and the socialist left before 1920

> Hitherto, the conditions of the aborigines have not been considered by workers in the revolutionary movement, and the rank and file organisation set up by the aborigines was allowed to be broken up by the A.P.B., the missionaries, and the police, but henceforth no struggle of the white workers must be permitted without demands for the aborigines being championed; no political campaigns without political programs applicable to our fellow exploited – the aborigines – being formulated.
>
> – Communist Party of Australia's 1931 *Draft Programme of Struggle Against Slavery*.[7]

The formation of the Communist Party of Australia is often presented as a radical break with the previous development of the socialist left and the labour movement in Australia. This is particularly the case in regard to the attitude of the left and the labour movement towards racism in general and Indigenous oppression in particular.

As Bob Boughton has argued:

> Communists who took up the cause of Indigenous rights in the 1920s were clearly reflecting concerns more widely held in non-Aboriginal society, concerns stimulated by Indigenous peoples' own struggles, but this does not explain why they adopted such "advanced" positions, nor why, alone among working class political organisations, the CPA consciously set out to become a major force in the movement for Indigenous rights. Australian communists were led to this position largely by the international movement of which they were members.[8]

---

7.  *Workers' Weekly*, 25 September 1931, p.2.
8.  Boughton 2001.

There is an important element of truth in this argument. The CPA developed a more advanced program and a more effective relationship with Indigenous struggles than the left-wing organisations that came before them. A major factor pushing them to do so was undoubtedly the politics of the international Communist movement. However, a one-sided emphasis on this point can obscure previous tendencies towards solidarity, however underdeveloped.

So this section begins with a discussion of the relationship between the socialist left, the labour movement and Indigenous people prior to the formation of the CPA in 1920, before moving on to the early history of the Communist Party itself.

While forming a small minority of the overall workforce, Indigenous involvement in the labour movement goes back to the 1800s, with Aboriginal miners present at protest meetings in the lead-up to the Red Ribbon and Eureka rebellions on the Victorian goldfields.[9] It was in the shearing industry though that it seems the first substantial numbers of Aboriginal workers became involved in union campaigning, and where the issue of Aboriginal involvement in the union movement was first seriously discussed. Aboriginal shearers were involved in the shearers' union movement from its very origins, and hundreds took part in the intense class battles of the 1890s. While exact numbers are hard to come by, a delegate at the 1891 Australasian Shearers Union (ASU) conference claimed that 60–70 Aboriginal shearers were members of the union in South Australia, while the Adelaide branch of the Australian Workers Union (AWU, into which the ASU had amalgamated) in 1913 had 5,000 members, of whom 400 were Aboriginal.[10]

While the shearers' unions were not immune from paternalistic or racist ideas, many unionists did express sympathy for the plight of Aboriginal people and at least some understanding that their dispossession was morally wrong and placed them in a disadvantaged position that should be changed.

The socialist groups that emerged in the early twentieth century drew on this history, occasionally addressing the conditions of Indigenous people in strident terms. Many of these articles railed

9. Howitt 2011, p.406 and Clark 2005.
10. Humphreys 2021.

against "slavery" in Western Australia and the exploitation, abuse and murder of Aboriginal workers by station masters, the police and government officials.[11] Others were concerned with the hypocrisy of religious missions which were interested only in profits.[12] Most articles were similar to those that had been published in the shearers' union newspapers. However, some did start to draw together the exploitation of Aboriginal workers, the nature of capitalism and the need for socialism. As an article in *The People*, the newspaper of the Australian Socialist League, put it:

> [T]he real working-class movement knows neither race nor color and detests and opposes oppression and injustice everywhere. The cause of this poor maltreated halt-caste girl is the cause of every worker, and their cause is hers. Only when the Social Revolution shall have accomplished itself, and christian capitalist "civilisation" shall have been relegated to the rubbish destructor, will the rule of justice and equity, untrammelled by class interests and free from the sordid debasement of character germinated in the capitalist muck-heap, be possible.[13]

Some articles described pre-invasion Aboriginal society as a form of primitive communism.[14]

Though the issue was not a focus of their work, the syndicalist Industrial Workers of the World (IWW) took an anti-racist and internationalist stance and published a few short articles supporting Aboriginal rights.[15] At times individual IWW activists did fight against the discrimination against Aboriginal workers. In Darwin a Filipino IWW activist who was married to an Aboriginal woman fought against racist discrimination on the docks in 1912.[16] It is unclear how many Indigenous members the IWW was able to recruit, or if there are other examples of them participating in action against

---

11.   *The People*, 10 August 1901, p.4.
12.   *The International Socialist*, 25 March 1911, p.3 and *The People*, 20 August 1910, p.2.
13.   *The People*, 28 August 1909, p.3.
14.   *The People*, 3 January 1918, p.3.
15.   *Direct Action*, 25 December 1915, p.3, 7 April 1917, p.2.
16.   Townsend 2009, p.9.

Indigenous discrimination, although at least one Aboriginal worker, Ted O'Reilly, was a prominent IWW orator, and Lucy Eatock joined while participating in the anti-conscription struggles during the First World War.[17]

Despite these not insignificant contributions, working-class consciousness about Indigenous oppression remained limited, and often intertwined with paternalistic or racist views. As the Indigenous population was quite small and marginalised in a profoundly racist society, their oppression did not present itself as a pressing strategic question for the workers' movement, nothing like the issues of immigration, or African Americans in the US. Another factor is that many of the most important union conflicts of the early twentieth century were either urban-based or in tightly knit mining communities such as Broken Hill, whereas at that time the vast majority of Indigenous people lived in rural areas.

This began to shift after Federation, when Indigenous communities came under increased attack from governments. State parliaments passed a series of new laws giving sweeping powers to Aborigines Protection Boards, who then demanded even more powers to control Indigenous communities. Rural communities and state officials intensified pressure to break up Indigenous landholdings or reserves that had been established on valuable land, and segregation and exploitation were further entrenched. Indigenous communities resisted these attacks in various ways, laying the basis for the emergence of the Aboriginal activist organisations of the 1920s and 30s.

At the same time as these attacks were increasing, significant sections of the leadership of the labour movement were becoming more incorporated into the running of capitalism. The AWU, which had united Indigenous and non-Indigenous workers earlier in the century, became the backbone of many state Labor governments. While some Labor MPs from rural backgrounds, many specifically from the AWU, criticised aspects of the treatment of Aboriginal communities, the vast bulk of Labor politicians happily participated in the brutal oppression of Indigenous people. When the NSW Labor government debated giving

---

17. Townsend 2009, p.15.

the Aborigines Protection Board greater powers to control Aboriginal communities in 1915 only three politicians, all Labor, opposed the amendment, while a fourth agreed to withdraw his opposition as a show of cabinet solidarity.[18]

Thus the situation in the lead-up to the founding of the CPA in 1920 was an intensification of racist oppression, and strong proof that Labor governments were no solution. While some traditions of solidarity had been built in certain sections of the working class, and anti-racist politics were accepted on the left, these processes were in a preliminary phase. There was little practical solidarity between white and Indigenous workers, and even less theorisation of the role of Indigenous people in Australian capitalism.

## The Communist Party of Australia, the Comintern, and Indigenous rights

The Communist Party took some time to go beyond the politics and practice of the left that preceded it. This is not particularly surprising given it spent much of the 1920s as a small and beleaguered organisation, numbering only in the hundreds, regularly wracked with internal crises, splits and a high turnover of both rank-and-file members and its political leadership. Despite these challenges, from 1923 the CPA's paper *Workers' Weekly* began publishing articles about Indigenous oppression. One article about the exploitation of Torres Strait Islanders on Badu Island ended by stating: "facts show that wherever the capitalist system plants itself the native population is subjected and ruthlessly exploited. Let us speed the day when the workers – black, white or brindle – will be free from the blighting influence of brutal Capitalism".[19] An article in 1924 criticised the mainstream labour newspapers the *Worker* and the *Labour Daily* for whipping up a hysterical campaign "denouncing the blacks as treacherous murderers" in the Northern Territory. The author, C Arfeldt, while accepting the idea that Indigenous people were a "dying race", also pointed to the benefits that capitalism had gained out of exploiting the Aboriginal population in the Northern Territory.[20]

---

18. Horner 1974, p.10.
19. *Workers' Weekly*, 23 November 1923, p.1.
20. *Workers' Weekly*, 7 November 1924, p.3.

From 1925 *Workers' Weekly* regularly reported about the condi-tions of Aboriginal workers. Articles from 1925–27 criticised Labor state governments for not stopping the exploitation of Aboriginal domestic servants[21] and attacked the AWU for refusing to organise Aboriginal workers in Western Australia and the NT.[22] In January 1928 they published an interesting account of a conversation between a Communist Party member and some Aboriginal workers in Western Australia. According to the account, the Aboriginal workers said that they were "treated very harshly by some white people". When the Communist replied that this would change when workers "woke up and ruled Australia", the Aboriginal workers reportedly said "we wish they would hurry up and do it". The Aboriginal workers also said they wanted control over their own land, to which the Communist replied that when the "white worker would control Australia...then they would have land and freedom too".[23] Whether this account is accurate or embellished for propaganda purposes, it reflects that the party was starting to think about the issues. Unfortunately during this period their theoretical journal, *The Communist*, published a series of anthropological articles that approached the Indigenous question from a racist standpoint common in the academy at the time.[24]

From 1928 the CPA was thrown into disarray by a factional struggle, out of which a new leadership, backed by the Stalinised Communist International, came to power.[25] The victory of this new leadership spelt the end of the CPA as a revolutionary socialist organisation, and saw it transformed into a Stalinist organisation in line with Communist parties across the globe. This would have important consequences for how the party came to understand the question of Indigenous oppression.

The approach of the CPA to Indigenous oppression in the 1920s has often been criticised as being economistic, meaning that they had a narrow focus on the economic aspects of Indigenous exploitation

---

21. *Workers' Weekly*, 20 February 1925, p.2.
22. *Workers' Weekly*, 20 July 1926, p.3.
23. *Workers' Weekly*, 27 January 1928, p.2.
24. See articles in *The Communist*, September–October 1925, November–December 1925, January–February 1926 and March 1926.
25. The general analysis of the CPA in this article comes from O'Lincoln 1985.

rather than any consideration of broader political issues.[26] It is then argued that this shifted from 1928 onwards due to the influence of the Comintern, which pressured the Communist Party to take the issue of Indigenous oppression more seriously and to develop a political analysis of that oppression and strategies to combat it.

While there is some truth to this argument, most writers on the subject end up avoiding examining the broader context in which debates around colonialism, racism and anti-imperialism took place within the Comintern, in particular the impact that the rise of Stalinism had on the formulation of its policies towards colonially oppressed and Indigenous peoples.

Unlike the old Socialist International, which maintained ambiguous positions on colonialism, the Comintern was established on a clearly hostile basis. This was important because in the aftermath of the First World War a series of national independence movements had erupted across the globe. The Bolshevik Party in Russia and the leadership of the Comintern saw an alliance between the revolutionary workers' movements of the advanced capitalist countries and the anti-colonial movements of the oppressed nationalities as a key strategic question.

At first the Comintern essentially split the world between the large imperialist powers like Britain, Germany, and the colonies that they oppressed and controlled. The colonial world was seen as relatively homogeneous, with only limited attempts to differentiate between different categories of oppressed nations.[27]

At the Fourth Comintern Congress in 1922 the Indian Communist MN Roy argued for a more sophisticated analysis of different colonial nations. Roy distinguished between three different "tiers" of colonial societies. First there were the "countries in which capitalism has reached a rather high level of development", such as Australia and Canada. In these countries "industry has developed due to the inflow of capital from the great centres of capitalism", and a "native capitalism has gained strength". Second were those countries where capitalist development has occurred but "it is still at an elementary level" and "feudalism" was supposedly still economically dominant. Lastly there

26. Townsend 2009, p.7.
27. The following is largely drawn from Drachewych 2019.

were countries where capitalist development had barely started at all, "primitive conditions still prevail, and the social order is dominated by patriarchal feudalism".[28]

In this schema Australia's position was still ambiguous. While it was seen as having a high level of capitalist development and a native capitalist class, it was still a colony of Britain and therefore the fight for Australian independence was presumably progressive. This was at any rate how leading members of both the CPA and Comintern officials in charge of Australian affairs chose to interpret Roy's schema. For the CPA this fit conveniently with the strong current of Australian nationalism dominant in the socialist left and the wider labour movement.

It wasn't until 1928 that the nature of Australian capitalism, and the place of Indigenous people within it, was further clarified. The Sixth Comintern Congress argued that it was

> necessary to distinguish between those colonies of the capitalist countries which have served them as colonising regions for their surplus population, and which in this way have become a continuation of their capitalist system (Australia, Canada, etc.) and those colonies which are exploited by the imperialists primarily as markets for their commodities... The colonies of the first type, on the basis of their general development, became "Dominions", that is, members of the given imperialist system with equal or nearly equal rights. In them, capitalist development reproduces among the immigrant white population the class structure of the metropolis, at the same time that the native population was, for the most part, exterminated.[29]

Australia was now understood not as a colony, but an independent capitalist power with "equal or nearly equal rights" with Britain, and a social structure that reproduced the main features of class society in the advanced capitalist world, albeit with the added feature of the Indigenous inhabitants. While this was an important development in the analysis of countries like Australia, the political strategies put

---

28. Riddell (ed.) 2012, p.687.
29. Quoted in Drachewych 2019.

forward for combating racism and imperialism were negatively influenced by the growing Stalinisation of the Comintern.

From 1925 the Comintern became dominated by the "right-centre" bloc of Stalin and Bukharin, with Bukharin in charge from 1926. He pursued a policy of alliances with national liberation movements on whatever basis possible. When criticised for this opportunism, he argued that Communists across the globe should subordinate themselves to anyone willing to ally with the USSR, whatever impact this might have on the development of class struggle within the country itself. This policy was pursued in the interests of the new Soviet bureaucracy, who were concerned about increasing pressure on the USSR from the Western powers. Even after Bukharin was driven out of the leadership, the Soviet bureaucracy largely maintained the policies on race and colonialism entrenched during Bukharin's time.

What does this have to do with the CPA and the question of Indigenous oppression? At a meeting of the Comintern Information Department in 1926, CPA member Hector Ross was grilled over his attitude towards the Indigenous populations in Australia and New Zealand. The questions reflected little concern for combating racism, but were instead about clarifying whether the Indigenous populations in the two countries could generate national movements that the USSR could support in order to undermine British imperialism. Ross appears to have been confused by this line of questioning and vaguely replied that while the Maori were antagonistic to the British, "the Australian natives are not to be reckoned with at all".[30]

The shift to seeing Indigenous Australians as a colonised national minority striving for national independence, and therefore a potential ally for the Communist movement, took place sometime between 1928 and 1931. This change was shaped by the broader shift in Comintern thinking in regard to various oppressed peoples across the globe. The origins of this shift appear to be in the intervention of the Comintern officials Nikolai Nasanov and Max Petrovsky, although it has been argued that it was directly influenced by Stalin himself and his writings

---

30. Quoted in Drachewych 2017, pp.226–7.

on the national question.[31] In several countries with a history of colonialism or racism, Petrovsky and Nasanov proposed that the Communist parties adopt new demands to relate to these questions. For South Africa, Petrovsky and Nasanov developed the Native Republic thesis and for the US the Black Belt thesis. While both theses would shape the CPA's response to Indigenous oppression, it is the Black Belt thesis that was drawn on most directly. This was a perspective which argued that African Americans concentrated in the South constituted an oppressed nation with tangible borders within the US, and that they should fight for their national right to self-determination, up to and including the right to secede from America.

For revolutionary anti-Stalinist critics, there were several points of concern with the Black Belt idea.[32] The first was that they believed the motivation behind it had little to do with developing serious concrete strategies for combating racism and strengthening Communist working-class forces. Instead what lay behind the thesis was a desire to propose demands that would allow Communist forces to relate to middle-class layers within oppressed groups. This criticism related to the broader shift in Comintern policy towards anti-colonial movements raised by Trotsky and others in the 1920s.

Secondly, the demand for a Black Belt was criticised as yet another example of the Comintern coming up with reasons to endlessly defer the socialist revolution. This approach was outlined at the Sixth Comintern Congress, where the world was divided between countries where proletarian revolution was on the agenda and countries where the immediate goal should be a so-called "democratic dictatorship of the workers and the peasantry" distinct from a revolutionary workers' state. This was the beginning of the Stalinist revival of the Menshevik two-stage theory of socialist revolution. The US Trotskyist Max Shachtman in his book *Communism and the Negro* drew out how the Black Belt demand accepted the idea that there "is still room in the United States for a national-democratic revolution

---

31.  See Zumoff 2014, pp.342–52 for a detailed discussion about the origins of the Black Belt thesis.
32.  For a more modern critique of the Black Belt see Sustar 2012. For anti-Stalinist critiques from the time see Shachtman 2003, Trotsky 1994 and James 2018.

distinct from the proletarian revolution". However for anti-Stalinists like Shachtman,

> no other revolution, intervening between the present rule of finance capital and the final proletarian upheaval, is conceivable in the United States. A theory which does conceive of one is utopian and reactionary. Yet it is precisely such an "intermediate" revolution which is visualised by the new theory.[33]

While the Native Republic thesis did at least have the effect of pushing the South African Communist Party to orient more seriously towards the black working class, something previously resisted, it similarly envisaged the creation of a Native Republic rather than a socialist revolution. This republic was conceived of as "a stage towards a workers' and peasants' republic with full rights for all races", and saw the party develop a mostly uncritical alliance with the middle-class leadership of the African National Congress.[34]

The third problem with the Black Belt thesis is that it conceptualised African Americans as an oppressed nation engaged in a movement for national liberation. As the leading Black Communist Harry Haywood put it:

> The Negros in the United States reveal amongst themselves all the characteristics of a nation... Therefore, the struggle of the Negro masses for liberation...must take the form of a movement for national liberation.[35]

For anti-Stalinists like Max Shachtman and CLR James, this argument did not stack up. While they did not rule out the possibility of African Americans developing a nationalist consciousness, they saw this as still explicable within the framework of understanding African

---

33. Shachtman 2003, p.86.
34. South African Communist Party 1928. Also see Zumoff 2014, pp.345–6 for a discussion about the relationship between the Black Belt thesis and the Native Republic slogan in South Africa.
35. As quoted in Shachtman 2003, pp.68–9.

Americans as an oppressed racial minority rather than a nationally oppressed group striving for national independence. The idea that African Americans constituted a "nation" was undermined by numerous factors, including their mass migration from the South to North, the diverse social and economic conditions in which they lived, and the lack of any precedent for a campaign to create a Black nation. But aside from its lack of sociological grounding, the theory had big political problems. It pushed against the idea of trying to unite Black and white workers together in militant struggle, something which would in fact take place throughout the 1930s and again later with the civil rights movement. It also went against the grain of early Comintern thinking on African Americans, which Shachtman acknowledges to be sometimes unclear and imprecise, definitively did not raise the demand for national self-determination nor consider them to be a nation. Thus for Shachtman and other Trotskyist critics, the theory was further proof of the Stalinist desire to seek alliances with middle-class layers in the Black community, and to move away from a class-based analysis of Black oppression towards a race- or nationalist-based one.

There isn't direct evidence of the Comintern developing a comparable strategy for the CPA. Instead it seems that they developed their policy on Indigenous issues through internal discussion, although their approach was obviously shaped by the Native Republic and Black Belt theses. You can see this in the first major writing by the CPA on the Indigenous question, *Communist Party's Fight for Aborigines: Draft Programme of Struggle Against Slavery*, published by CPA leader Bert Moxon in September 1931.[36] The *Draft Programme contains* a systematic overview and denunciation of the exploitation and oppression of Aboriginal people. It then presents a long list of demands for "full economic, social and political rights", the abolition of the Aborigines Protection Boards, the release of all Aboriginal people from prison and their trial by Aboriginal juries and other quite advanced and radical slogans.

The *Draft Programme* was strongly shaped by local conditions.

36. *Workers' Weekly*, 25 September 1931, p.2.

A number of its demands were very similar to those put forward by the Australian Aboriginal Progressive Association (AAPA) founded by Aboriginal activist Fred Maynard in 1924, and the *Programme* itself positively references the existence of the AAPA.

Moxon would also have been influenced by his own direct experience and those of other CPA leaders. In 1931 he went on a semi-clandestine tour of Indigenous communities in central and northern Australia. The tour was not announced publicly in the Communist press, presumably because of their fear of alerting authorities to his project. However, it came to the attention of the public anyway when South Australian CPA secretary and future Trotskyist Giles Roper was arrested at a public meeting in the Botanical Gardens at which Roper reported on the findings of Moxon's tour, in particular the abuses of station owners and police. Roper was found guilty of offensive behaviour for criticising police attacks on Aboriginal communities and fined.[37] After the tour, Moxon wrote an article about his experiences for the Communist press.[38] Norman Jeffery, a leading Communist who showed a particular interest in Indigenous issues, was reportedly influenced by his time working alongside unionised Aboriginal workers in rural NSW.[39] Similarly, Tom Wright had some experience with Aboriginal working-class activists in the Unemployed Workers Movement in Glebe – in particular the irrepressible Eatock family. EA Knight, Sydney district secretary of the CPA-led Militant Minority Movement during the 1930s, similarly noted that his views on Aboriginal oppression were shaped by "personal experiences in my youth".[40]

However, the *Draft Programme* also raised a demand directly influenced by broader Comintern thinking:

> The handing over to the aborigines of large tracts of watered and fertile country, with towns, seaports, railways, roads, etc., to become one or more independent aboriginal states or republics.

---

37. *The Advertiser*, 18 December 1931, p.26, *Workers' Weekly*, 27 November 1931, p.3, and *Workers' Weekly*, 25 December 1931, p.3.
38. *Workers' Weekly*, 11 September 1931, p.1. This was also republished in two parts in *Red Leader*, 11 September 1931, p.4 and 25 September 1931, p.2.
39. Macintyre 1998, p.266.
40. *Workers' Weekly*, 7 April 1939, p.2.

> The handing back to the aborigines of all Central, Northern, and North West Australia to enable the aborigines to develop their native pursuits. These aboriginal republics to be independent of Australian or other foreign powers. To have the right to make treaties with foreign powers, including Australia, establish their own army, governments, industries, and in every way be independent of imperialism.[41]

The Aboriginal republics section of the *Draft Programme* has often been dismissed as a kooky idea that, while misconceived, had no negative impact upon the CPA's practical approach to Indigenous issues. Some have even celebrated it as evidence that they were starting to take the question seriously.[42] Other writers see the demand as confused but expressing a commitment to a demand for Indigenous self-determination that foreshadowed the struggles of the 1960s and 70s.

But to what extent are the criticisms of the Black Belt thesis applicable to the CPA's 1931 *Draft Programme*? The problem of relating to a middle-class Indigenous leadership was not a concern, as during this period it was basically non-existent. Nor does the CPA's demand for Aboriginal republics seem to have been conceptualised as part of a two-stage theory of revolution. The CPA insisted that the establishment of Aboriginal republics would only come after the socialist revolution and the creation of a workers' state.[43]

The main problem with the *Draft Programme*'s Aboriginal republics demand was that it was not based on a serious analysis of Australian conditions, but represented a mechanical adoption of a cynical slogan created by the Comintern bureaucracy. The adoption of the demand created a series of confusions and ambiguities regarding the Indigenous question which would make it difficult for them to understand the changing dynamics of Indigenous struggle.

Like the Black Belt thesis, it conceptualised Indigenous people as a national minority, striving for national independence. But this threw up some difficult questions for the CPA. After all, most of the

---

41. *Workers' Weekly*, 25 September 1931, p.2.
42. Townsend 2009, p.13.
43. See for instance *Workers' Weekly*, 6 May 1932, p.3 and *Proletariat*, August 1934, p.14.

Aboriginal population did not live in the Northern Territory or Western Australia. Some had become integrated, to varying degrees and not without significant racist discrimination, into Australian society. The 1931 *Draft Programme* dodged this dilemma by arguing that the "fifty thousand aborigines in the Federal territories, the few hundred in each State, and the tens of thousands of half-caste workers in each State and the territory must be mobilised" around all the demands in the *Draft Programme* – for civil rights and Aboriginal republics.

Compare this for instance to the actual development of the Australian Aboriginal Progressive Association (AAPA). The AAPA was influenced by the black nationalist ideas of Marcus Garvey, which had filtered through to Aboriginal people via African American sailors landing in Sydney. Unlike Indigenous activist organisations in the 1930s, the AAPA did not narrowly advocate the ending of discriminatory laws in order for Aboriginal people to assimilate into white society. Though it did campaign against racist discrimination and called for the abolition of the Aborigines Protection Boards, the AAPA also argued for the protection of Aboriginal cultural independence, the right to plots of land for Aboriginal families due to their prior ownership before invasion and strongly rejected the idea that Aboriginal culture was inferior. As Maynard wrote in his 1927 letter to NSW premier Jack Lang:

> I wish to make it perfectly clear, on behalf of our people, that we accept no condition of inferiority as compared with the European people. Two distinct civilisations are represented by respective races. On one hand we have the civilisation of necessity and on the other the civilisation co-incident with courteous supply of all the requirements of the human race. That the European people by the arts of war destroyed our more ancient civilisation is freely admitted, and that by their vices and diseases our people have been decimated is also patent, but neither of these facts are evidence of superiority. Quite the contrary is the case. The members of [the AAPA] have also noted the strenuous efforts of the Trade Union leaders to attain the conditions which existed in our country at the time of invasion by Europeans – the men only

worked when necessary – we called no man "Master" and we had
no king.[44]

Maynard's letter goes on to explain that while Aboriginal people have
"accepted the modern system of government which has taken the
place of our prehistoric methods" this did not mean the AAPA had
any intention of abandoning either Aboriginal culture or a distinct
Aboriginal identity.

This assertion of Aboriginal identity was not connected to a demand
for national separation. In fact, when white sympathisers proposed to
campaign for a "Model Aboriginal State" in the Northern Territory the
AAPA explicitly rejected the idea, twice. As the Indigenous historian
John Maynard explains, the "AAPA's fight was not for a separate and
segregated Aboriginal state but for the provision of enough land for
each and every Aboriginal family in Australia".[45] Of particular concern
to members of the AAPA was the fear that if such a state was created the
entire Indigenous population would be forcibly resettled there, setting
up a segregationist state. So while the AAPA saw itself as connected to
the worldwide struggle against racism and colonialism, it was able to
do so without mechanically applying demands from other countries
and different contexts.

This raises a number of problems with the CPA's *Draft Programme*
and other writings. The leadership of the AAPA, and many of its
hundreds of members, had some European heritage. Many engaged in
work alongside white workers. They wanted both an end to discrimination and a positive affirmation of their identity and culture. On the
other side of the equation, in the pastoral industry in north-western
Australia and the cattle industry in the Northern Territory, hundreds of
Indigenous workers were employed by capitalist landowners. Though
the conditions Indigenous workers faced were uniquely terrible, they
were nevertheless participating in a capitalist labour process. At the
same time, they were able to keep alive more of their cultural traditions, including their connection to country, than Indigenous people
in the eastern states. The example of the AAPA also didn't fit with the

44. Maynard 2007, pp.104–5.
45. Maynard 2007, p.83.

1931 *Draft Programme*'s conception of Aboriginal people as a national minority striving for the establishment of Aboriginal republics.

Throughout this period, the CPA attitude towards Indigenous struggle went through important changes, with substantial shifts of substance and emphasis. However, despite the various changes, for most of the 1930s the CPA strongly associated the struggle for Indigenous rights with a revolutionary working-class struggle against capitalism. The *Draft Programme* was an extremely radical and intransigent document. It connected the struggle for Indigenous rights to a revolutionary fight against capitalism and imperialism, while also raising several politically advanced demands that had not been raised widely, or in some cases at all, in Australia beforehand. It was reprinted in the Comintern publication *The Negro Worker* in 1932 as part of an overview of revolutionary movements against imperialism and colonialism across the globe.[46] The CPA would bring this militant spirit into the class battles of the Great Depression.

## The Unemployed Workers' Movement

It was in northern Australia that the CPA first systematically organised around Indigenous rights. In doing so, they were forced to challenge the approach of the established labour movement in Darwin. The union movement in the NT, centralised under the leadership of the Northern Australian Workers' Union (NAWU) often had an antagonistic attitude towards the multiracial working class that it was supposed to represent.[47] Chinese labourers were an early and persistent target of the NAWU, which successfully lobbied to restrict their employment from 1911 onwards. During the 1920s, the NAWU leadership was also often dismissive of Indigenous workers. Even when the NAWU argued that they should be covered by union agreements, this was usually in the hope that this would lead them to be replaced by white workers.

Seizing the latent possibilities for multiracial working class solidarity would thus take a sharp break in the development of the Darwin labour movement. Two things made this possible: the existence of an

---

46.  *The Negro Worker*, April 1932, Vol. II, No. 4, pp.10–12.
47.  The two best accounts of Indigenous workers and the Darwin labour movement are Martínez 1999 and Brian 2001.

increasingly frustrated left-wing opposition within the NAWU, and the establishment of a small CPA branch, the two of which quickly merged.

A key role in bringing the two together was played by Lawrence James Mahoney and his friend and comrade John Waldie. Mahoney and Waldie had been a part of a growing left-wing opposition within the NAWU, trying to unseat the conservative NAWU leadership of Robert Toupein. The issue of Indigenous workers came to the fore during a union boycott campaign of local pubs over the employment of Aboriginal workers. While some NAWU members argued for the boycott on the basis that the workers were being underpaid, the majority of the union supported the boycott, more or less explicitly, with the goal of driving the Aboriginal workers out of the industry and replacing them with white workers. As the boycott went on the tensions over this started to come to the fore.

Mahoney had played a prominent role during the boycott, demanding heavy penalties for workers who drank at the pubs against the moderation of the NAWU leadership. This support for the boycott though sat uneasily with Mahoney who was friends with Aboriginal workers through his position as a referee at the local football club.[48] As the boycott came to an end he started to raise the issue of Indigenous exclusion. This came to a head in the aftermath of the boycott's victory, when the NAWU leadership proposed that it be extended to Chinese merchants who employed Aboriginal workers. Mahoney and his friend Waldie raised a stink, pointing out that it was hypocritical of the union to do this when Aboriginal workers were excluded from NAWU membership and when NAWU members personally employed Aboriginal workers. Mahoney and Waldie pushed for a vote on allowing Aboriginal workers and some other "coloured" workers to join the union, although it was unsuccessful.[49] Mahoney also organised union support for a strike of Malay pearlers and protested against racist discrimination in the football league.

---

48. See *Northern Standard*, 20 December 1928, p.1. Mahoney was also arrested in Jan 1928 for drunkenness and obscene behaviour while driving with Aboriginal footballers Fred Saunders and Robert Shepard after a game: *Northern Standard*, 24 January 1928, p.4.
49. *Northern Standard*, 28 August 1928, p.5 and 1 March 1929, p.5.

Mahoney and Waldie's arguments dovetailed with those being made by the CPA. *Workers' Weekly* had criticised the boycott campaign from the beginning, and the broader hostility of the NAWU towards Aboriginal workers which underpinned it.[50] In theses passed at a CPA Central Committee meeting in June 1930, it was proclaimed that in "such places as Darwin, where there are masses of coloured workers, our Party must become the leader of these masses and bring them into political struggle against their capitalist exploiters". The theses noted the strikes by Indigenous workers in the pearling industry and went so far as to argue that:

> The majority of our Party members in such districts should be coloured. Let the contemptible scoundrels of social fascism scornfully sneer at us as a "coloured party" in such districts. We will accept it as a tribute to our revolutionary determination to unite the working class for the destruction of capitalism.[51]

The CPA would never achieve this goal in Darwin, but it would fight admirably for an anti-racist working-class culture in the city. It is unclear exactly when Mahoney and Waldie joined the CPA. By November 1929 they had resigned from the Darwin ALP,[52] though they had already been active in various Communist-led organisations and campaigns. As Mahoney and Waldie started attacking the NAWU leadership more stridently around a range of issues, including its racism, the NAWU moved to punish them by pushing them out of delegate and organiser positions.

Having been essentially isolated from the centre of the union movement in Darwin, Mahoney, Waldie and their supporters instead

---

50. *Workers' Weekly*, 13 April 1928, p.4. It is worth comparing the arguments in *Workers' Weekly* in 1928 to those made by NAWU leader Robert Toupein in *The Pan-Pacific Worker* in 1929. While Toupein acknowledged that Aboriginal people were "one of the most oppressed and intensely exploited people on the face of the earth", he puts forward no actual demands for them other than stating that governments need to end the "competitive menace to white workers". *The Pan-Pacific Worker*, 1 September 1929.
51. Communist Party of Australia 1930, p.39.
52. *Northern Standard*, 6 November 1929, p.1. This is unclear because the CPA still had some members in the ALP in the late 1920s.

focused their attention on unemployed struggles, where they would find an easier audience both for their militant tactics and their arguments about racism. They established an Unemployed Workers' Movement branch and engaged in a number of high profile and militant actions. The most famous saw Mahoney climb onto the roof of a local government building occupied by the unemployed and fly the red flag.

Mahoney and the Darwin Communists also brought the CPA's support for Indigenous rights into the unemployed struggle. In July 1929, the local Communists promoted a mass meeting at Police Paddock, an area where much of the local Aboriginal and non-white community lived. The meeting demanded that the government give ownership of the area over to the local community, end racist discrimination and grant them full citizenship rights.[53] When Police Paddock was raided by the police the Communists organised an open-air meeting denouncing the repression.

Many Aboriginal workers were involved and arrested at the militant unemployed protests. Photos show several Aboriginal and Asian workers participating in the infamous unemployed occupation of government offices in January 1931. One of these Aboriginal workers was Joe McGinness, the future national president of the Federal Council for Aboriginal and Torres Strait Islander Advancement.[54] At a meeting of the Darwin UWM in 1931, a motion was adopted supporting the "complete emancipation" of Aboriginal people from economic and political oppression.[55] Mahoney would regularly write letters to the *Northern Standard* about Aboriginal oppression.[56]

While Mahoney and Waldie had some success building anti-racist sentiment among the unemployed, the mainstream labour movement remained mostly hostile. They had some success getting the NAWU to protest at the banning of "half-caste" workers from drinking at Darwin pubs.[57] However, at the NAWU annual conference in 1930, their motion

---

53.  *Northern Standard*, 16 July 1929, p.3.
54.  Brian 2001, p.125.
55.  *Workers' Weekly*, 6 Nov 1931, p.4.
56.  See *Northern Standard*, 1 July 1932, p.4.
57.  *Northern Standard*, 1 September 1931, p.2.

to end all racial discrimination in union membership was ruled out of order.

Over time opposition from the NAWU leadership and police repression began to take their toll on Mahoney and Waldie. The NAWU whipped up a slanderous campaign accusing them of plotting to replace the white workforce with their "coloured" allies.[58] They both spent considerable time in jail over various offences related to the unemployment protests. The NAWU leaders effectively abandoned them and manoeuvred to limit their support within the Darwin workers' movement, with some success. The repression reached its farcical climax when Mahoney was arrested while waving goodbye to a friend on an outgoing ship. His crime? Standing on the wrong side of the wharf.[59]

In January 1933 Mahoney left Darwin, and Waldie followed suit shortly afterwards. They would both remain active in Communist politics in Sydney,[60] but clearly felt defeated in Darwin and that their efforts to build an anti-racist working class movement had been in vain. But within a few years a new generation of Darwin Communists inspired by Mahoney and Waldie would continue their fight for militant unionism and anti-racism.[61]

It wasn't just in Darwin that Communists took up the issue of Indigenous oppression within the unemployed struggle. At the beginning of the Depression, the CPA membership was primarily concentrated in the capital cities, particularly Sydney, plus a handful of mining communities. But as the Depression forced hundreds of thousands of people out of work, the unemployed struggle opened up opportunities for the Communists to spread into new areas.

One of these was country NSW. Most readers are probably inclined to think about rural NSW – then and now – as an undifferentiated reactionary mass. After all, it was in the country towns that the fascistic Old Guard drilled its militias in preparation for the overthrow of

---

58. *Workers' Weekly* 30 May 1930, p.2 has a reply to these accusations.
59. *Northern Standard*, 13 September 1932, p.4.
60. *Sydney Morning Herald*, 13 March 1934, p.5.
61. *Northern Standard*, 13 May 1941, p.4 notes that "names such as Waldie and Mahoney are still spoken with respect by workers here".

the Lang Labor government. Rural newspapers were filled with dire warnings about the Communist hordes gathering in the industrial cities, and some advocated for rural regions to separate from NSW in protest. When the rural elite heard that Communists were attempting to build a base in country towns they hit back with a wave of attacks on Communist activists, culminating in an estimated 3,000-strong protest in Dubbo that surrounded the home of local Communists and demanded their immediate expulsion from the town limits.[62]

Throughout the 1920s and 30s, there was also a wave of racist agitation against Aboriginal communities, with a number of country towns pushing for greater levels of segregation in schools, cinemas and public spaces, as well as the further removal of Aboriginal missions. As the Depression set in, the NSW government issued instructions that unemployed Aboriginal workers should receive rations instead of the dole.

Aboriginal people didn't accept these attacks without a fight. In 1931 Aboriginal unemployed workers protested in Wellington, NSW, demanding the dole instead of rations.[63] The *Yass Tribune-Courier* reported that the change was "much resented by the colored people", and that strikes were being advocated by Aboriginal communities and petitions organised to be sent to Jack Lang.[64] According to historian Heather Goodall, these actions culminated in a wave of "stop-works, protest and strikes at Wallaga Lake, Menindee, Burnt Bridge, Brewarrina and Purfleet from 1936 to 1938".[65]

In the face of these attacks, Indigenous and non-Indigenous working-class activists started to draw together in some places, with a key role often being played by Communists. In June 1931 a meeting was organised in Dubbo by a small group of Communist activists to launch a local Unemployed Workers' Movement branch. It was immediately controversial with the conservative Dubbo establishment, who condemned it as a Communist front.[66] Criticism also came from

---

62. *Wellington Times*, 23 November 1931, p.3.
63. *Newcastle Morning Herald and Miners' Advocate*, 23 September 1931, p.6 and *The Northern Miner*, 3 October 1931, p.2.
64. *Yass Tribune-Courier*, 15 June 1931, p.2.
65. Goodall 2008, p.218.
66. *The Dubbo Liberal and Macquarie Advocate*, 21 November 1931, p.6 and *Dubbo*

the local ALP leadership who attempted to stop Communist activists from dominating the movement, and when that failed, set up a rival unemployed organisation. The mayor repeatedly refused to give the UWM permission to hold public rallies.

As the unemployed struggle in Dubbo took off it intersected with the local Aboriginal community. Aboriginal activists Tom Peckham and Ted Taylor both got involved in the unemployed protests. They then spoke to the white unemployed about the discrimination of the Aborigines Protection Board and asked them to take up Aboriginal issues.[67] The Peckham family would be involved in trade union and socialist politics for many decades.

Their appeal had an impact. At a mass meeting in 1932, the unemployed movement carried a motion demanding full rations for Aboriginal workers and urged the labour movement to take up the issue more generally.[68] During the 1932 municipal elections, the Dubbo CPA branch platform included the demand for the "enfranchisement of aboriginals and foreign workers of all races", and the "right of all aboriginals to own property and participate in municipal affairs".[69] There was also a small Communist group in the nearby town of Wellington (the CP got only nine votes in the town during the 1934 election), which supported unemployed Aboriginal workers through the local UWM branch.

At a meeting of western NSW unemployed organisations and unions in Orange in 1936, the Wellington and Dubbo UWM branches initiated a discussion about the treatment of Aboriginal people which led to the conference deciding that "a definite campaign be launched throughout all areas to demand equal treatment for all classes and colors".[70]

This activity wasn't confined to western NSW. The Waratah-Mayfield UWM branch in Newcastle repeatedly discussed the issue of Aboriginal rights. In February 1932 it sent a letter to the local branch of the Australasian Society of Patriots drawing their attention to the

---

*Dispatch and Wellington Independent*, 20 November 1931, p.1.

67. Goodall 2008, p.218–19.
68. *Workers' Weekly*, 1 July 1932, p.4.
69. *Dubbo Dispatch and Wellington Independent*, 8 January 1932, p.2.
70. *Wellington Times*, 27 February 1936, p.3.

abuses of Aboriginal people in the Northern Territory.[71] In March of the same year, it sent a protest to the Queensland government over reports of attacks on Aboriginal communities, and in July it protested against the different dole rates for unemployed Aboriginal workers. At a meeting of the Kempsey Unemployed League in 1932 a Mr Stevens, who was at the very least a close supporter if not a member of the CPA, argued in favour of equal rights for the Aboriginal unemployed workers – and won the debate.[72] In 1932 Communists tried to organise a joint protest of Aboriginal fisherman and wharf labourers at Port Kembla after they were all kicked off the dole.[73]

This support for unemployed Aboriginal workers spread further still, with the Innisfail, Queensland branches of the UWM, the Australian Railways Union, the Waterside Workers Federation and the Mourilyan Mill Workers demanding at a meeting in May 1933 that "aboriginals and other colored workers be placed on the same footing as other unemployed as regards rations and relief work". The meeting also protested "against the police intimidatory methods which are used with these workers".[74] The motion was moved by CPA member Pat Clancy. By 1938 even the Tasmanian unemployed movement was passing motions about Aboriginal rights.[75]

What Darwin, Dubbo, the working-class suburbs of Newcastle, and Innisfail had in common is that the CPA had built up a base of support among working-class activists through the unemployed struggle and in some cases trade union activity that then opened up the space for them to pursue anti-racist arguments and activity.

## Evolving Communist theory on Indigenous oppression

The Communist contribution to the struggle for Indigenous rights in the first half of the 1930s wasn't confined to practical activity. There was also a wide-ranging discussion in the Communist press about the origins and nature of Indigenous oppression. As has already been

71.  *Newcastle Morning Herald and Miners' Advocate*, 23 February 1932, p.4.
72.  *The Macleay Chronicle*, 14 September 1932, p.6.
73.  *Workers' Weekly*, 3 February 1932, p.3.
74.  *Cairns Post*, 26 May 1933, p.12.
75.  *The Mercury*, 13 August 1938, p.13.

noted, in the 1920s this discussion had been mainly of an anthropological nature, often with strong paternalistic or racist undertones due to the influence of the academic framework around these issues. However, during the 1930s Communist writers pushed past this to a more serious examination of the relationship between Indigenous oppression and Australian capitalism.

Communists were well placed to reject the founding myths of Australian capitalism. While the shearer unionists, socialists and some liberals had in the past acknowledged that the establishment of the colonial government had rested on a morally unjustifiable invasion that resulted in death and misery for Indigenous people, Communists took this further.

The 1931 *Draft Programme* had laid out the general arguments, but these were now expanded upon in numerous articles. One of the most advanced statements on Indigenous issues came from a 1934 article in *Proletariat*,[76] a publication of the Melbourne University Labor Club run by CPA members. The article begins by noting that "there has been a great awakening of interest in Australian Aborigines over the last two or three years". However while noting the growing interest in the conditions of Aboriginal people shown by humanitarian, religious and scientific organisations – and more cynically by the "smug bourgeois" – the article argues for a specifically Communist approach to the question of Indigenous oppression.

The *Proletariat* article argues forthrightly that Indigenous oppression is embedded in the capitalist system. Due to the integration of Indigenous workers into certain sectors of the economy such as the pastoral industry, Indigenous exploitation was "now part of the economic life of the country". The exploitation of Indigenous peoples, much like those in Australia-controlled New Guinea, was the ground from which "the colonial super-profits of the Australian bourgeoisie" arose. The article also argued that Indigenous oppression is not just economic but political in nature, explaining that "the aborigines, like the million masses of Asia and Africa, suffering from European and Japanese imperialism, are robbed of all political rights", as they had no

---

76. *Proletariat*, August 1934, p.12–14. All quotes in this section are from this article.

political representation, constitutional recognition or legal control over their own land.

At the time this oppression was often justified with the idea that the British invasion was beneficial for the Indigenous population, and that at any rate, they were a "dying race". The *Proletariat* article took issue with both of these arguments, further revealing the distance between Communists and middle-class humanitarians. On the question of the supposed benefits that British imperialism gave to Indigenous people, the article is very clear. According to the article, British capitalism came to Australia already, in the words of Marx, "dripping from head to foot...in blood and dirt".[77] The Indigenous experience of British colonisation was one of massacres and exploitation in which "the aborigines have been brought very close to total annihilation at the hands of the imperialists". However this annihilation was not total and the article argues that it wouldn't be if working-class forces threw themselves into the anti-racist struggle. "We must decisively reject the bourgeois theory that aborigines are doomed to extinction. Even without Socialism, they may be saved from extinction" by concerted political action.

The involvement of the working class, and the CPA, in particular, was seen as vital for the advancement of Indigenous rights. The capitalists were "not concerned with the emancipation of the aborigines". Bourgeois academics, while feigning concern about Indigenous people, were content "to see they depart in peace". The work of religious missionaries had been a total failure in regard to protecting the Indigenous population, and while sympathetic anthropologists might help to gather scientific evidence of the exploitation of Indigenous people, the reality was that "we already possess sufficient information... What is wanted... [is] political action to prevent further oppression".

Despite this quite brilliant polemic, when it came to solutions *Proletariat* was still trapped in the framework provided by the *Draft Programme*. It envisioned the establishment of an "autonomous aboriginal republic under the leadership of the working class" as the only fundamental means of achieving emancipation. This "aboriginal republic" however was not seen as an achievable goal under capitalism,

---

77.  Marx 1887, Chapter 31.

but rather its success was "contingent on the formation of a Soviet Australia". As evidence for the viability of this strategy, the article pointed to the experience of the national minorities during the 1917 Russian Revolution which showed that "where the working class succeeds in emancipating itself from capitalism it simultaneously emancipates all oppressed peoples within its territories".

## Solidarity and struggle

As the CPA drew young militants towards it through its work in the unemployed workers' movement, it also began to rebuild a left-wing current within the unions. A key role in this was played by the Militant Minority Movement, modelled on overseas examples of rank-and-file initiatives. As they rebuilt a class struggle wing within the labour movement the CPA also sought to integrate their support for Indigenous rights into trade union battles.

*Red Leader*, the publication of the Minority Movement, published extensively on Indigenous oppression.[78] While other Communist publications focused more on developing a platform for Indigenous rights, *Red Leader* articles were more agitational, highlighting particular examples of exploitation and oppression. These articles were important in popularising support for Indigenous rights among a layer of left-wing militants, alongside the more local publications of the CPA. As Communist influence increased within the union movement, they were then able to take practical steps in solidarity with Indigenous struggles on a number of fronts.

In 1932 the Communist Party's "Agit-Prop" committee proposed pro-Aboriginal slogans for that year's May Day.[79] The CPA also organised for Anna Morgan, an Aboriginal activist, to speak at a meeting of the International Women's Day Committee and at the Women's Anti-War Conference in 1935, and published one of her articles in the CPA's publication *Working Women*.[80] When Aboriginal shearers were refused award wages by an employer in Mukinbudin, Western Australia, the

---

78. For example *Red Leader*, 11 September 1931, p.4, 25 September 1931, p.2, 9 October 1931, p.2.
79. *Workers' Weekly*, 1 April 1932, p.2.
80. *Workers' Weekly*, 15 February 1935, p.6, 22 February 1935, p.2, 21 June 1935, p.3.

CPA took up the issue with the state government. Norman Jeffery, the Communist organiser of the Pastoral Workers' Industrial Union, used his time visiting rural workers committees to urge workers to support Indigenous rights and investigate conditions at local Aboriginal missions. Another member of the Pastoral Workers' Industrial Union wrote a report to *Red Leader* detailing multiple examples of the exploitation of Aboriginal workers in Queensland, and the *North Queensland Guardian* reported on the arrest of an Aboriginal man called "Rupert" who had been deported to Palm Island for agitating among Aboriginal workers.[81] Communists in Northern Queensland also built support for the 1936 strike by Torres Strait Islanders in the pearling industry, and after the Second World War a CPA organiser and writer Gerald Peel wrote the book *Isles of the Torres Straits: an Australian responsibility*, which exposed the conditions of the Islanders and advocated for a radical break with government policy.[82]

The CPA had the greatest impact through its intervention into two of the most significant and sustained union-backed Indigenous campaigns of the time, the Caledon Bay campaign of 1932–34 and the Day of Mourning and Protest in 1938.

### The Caledon Bay campaign

In September 1932 five Japanese fishermen were killed near Caledon Bay in the Northern Territory. Suspicion fell on the local Yolngu Indigenous community. One of the police officers dispatched to investigate also turned up dead. In Darwin establishment opinion demanded that a significant police expedition be sent to arrest those accused. The Melbourne *Herald* captured the mood:

> The Administrator...and the Superintendent of Police...consider that unless prompt action is taken to punish the natives, it will be unsafe for any white man or trepangers [fishermen] to call at any part of the north-eastern portion of Arnhem Land.[83]

---

81. *Red Leader*, 9 October 1931, p.2, North *Queensland Guardian*, 8 May 1937, pp.1–2.
82. See Boughton 2005 and Peel 1947.
83. Quoted in Gray 2007, p.115.

In August 1933 a committee was set up in Darwin to campaign against the police expedition to arrest the accused Aboriginal men due to fears it could lead to a massacre.[84] The CPA immediately campaigned across the country to build opposition to the police expedition. In September a large meeting of waterside workers in Sydney voted to condemn the expedition.[85] While the committee's action managed to stop a police attack, Dhakiyarr Wirrpanda and three other Aboriginal men were brought back to Darwin by a group of missionaries, and a trial began.

The campaign continued right through the trial and into 1934. In June 2,000 attended a rally at the Sydney Domain organised by the International Labor Defense (ILD) to demand a retrial after Dhakiyarr Wirrpanda was sentenced to death and the three other Aboriginal men to 20 years' hard labour.[86] Throughout the year the campaign received support from unemployed organisations in Brisbane, Punchbowl, Redfern and Bankstown, from branches of the Australian Railways Union and other unions, and a further two rallies of thousands were organised in Sydney during August.[87] The Aboriginal men were eventually released due to the pressure of the campaign. But Dhakiyarr Wirrpanda disappeared soon after he was released from Fannie Bay jail, possibly murdered by the police.

The work that the CPA did around this campaign brought it into greater contact with Indigenous people. A report on the work of the party in Western Australia in June 1934 noted that due to the campaign "aborigines are in contact with the D.C. [District Committee] – they write to the party and party members go down to where they are preparing facts to present to the Royal Commission when it meets".[88] The widespread opposition to the police in Darwin over the incident was a turning point. For a long time after 1932 governments would no longer feel confident of having the public support or indifference necessary to launch large-scale police expeditions into Indigenous communities.

---

84. *Workers' Weekly*, 19 August 1933, p.3.
85. *Workers' Weekly*, 15 September 1933, p.2.
86. *Workers' Weekly*, 8 June 1934, p.6.
87. *Workers' Weekly*, 10 August 1934, p.1, 7 September 1934, p.5.
88. Docker 1934, p.17.

## The anti–Sesquicentenary and the 1938 Day of Mourning and Protest

The Sesquicentenary of the arrival of the First Fleet was intended by the bourgeoisie to be a celebration of Australian nationalism, conservatism and loyalty to the British empire. It immediately came under criticism from the workers' movement, the socialist left and sections of the progressive middle class. After all, what version of Australian history was going to be celebrated in 1938? The struggles of the Eureka Stockade, the 1890s strikes and the anti-conscription campaign? Or the ties to British empire, the values of colonialism and the Australian ruling class?

The CPA initially supported the day's festivities, arguing that the history of working-class and democratic struggle should be the focus. In this vein they argued that Aboriginal people should be included in the official celebration as an acknowledgement of their continued existence.[89] This shameful outlook was shaped by the CPA's turn to what became known as the Popular Front, a shift that pushed the CPA to abandon its former hostility to all forms of Australian and British nationalism, and instead to frame the Communist movement as a continuation of a progressive Australian national tradition.

The CPA was forced to change its perspective on the day as it became clear that Indigenous activists were organising to demonstrate against the celebrations. On 30 November 1937 *Workers' Weekly* reported that Aboriginal activists were planning to hold a day of protest and argued: "The Australian people should make it a day for heaping coals of fire on their own heads and at the same time a day of determining that white chauvinist beastliness be relegated to the past".[90]

One of the Aboriginal activists who played a key role in organising the Day of Mourning and Protest was William Ferguson. In 1937 Ferguson founded the Aborigines' Progressive Association (APA) at a meeting in Dubbo. Ferguson had a long history in union and Labor Party activism. He had been a delegate for the AWU, a member of the

---

89. *Workers' Weekly*, 10 December 1937, p.3.
90. *Workers' Weekly*, 30 November 1937, p.3.

ALP during the anti-conscription campaign and involved in union committees across rural NSW.[91]

The CPA had welcomed the creation of the APA and promoted its activities in *Workers' Weekly*.[92] In October 1937 Ferguson spoke at a public meeting in Sydney organised by the CPA.[93] Afterwards Ferguson was invited by Tom Wright, the Communist leader of the Sheet-Metal Workers' Union, to a meeting of the Sydney Labour Council to talk about Indigenous oppression. The Labour Council then voted to endorse a list of progressive demands around Indigenous issues proposed by Wright. Alongside Wright, a number of Communist union leaders played an important role in getting the Labour Council to endorse this position, including Lloyd Ross, state secretary of the NSW Australian Railways Union and Bill Orr, the CPA leader of the Miners Federation.[94]

In the lead up to the Sesquicentenary, a meeting of the Labour Council passed a resolution moved by Ross that condemned the celebration and urged the labour movement to organise its own pro-working class, anti-Sesquicentenary events. The resolution noted the slap in the face to Indigenous people embedded within the official celebrations:

> We seize the opportunity to draw the attention of the Government and the people to the tragic position of the aboriginals, and declare that immediate attention must be given to their needs. We demand that the perversion of history in the celebrations should cease and a correct view be given of the treatment of the aboriginals, the place of the convict, and the role of the masses. We appeal to the Trade Unions to feature working-class history and analysis in their journals and meetings.[95]

Coverage of the Day of Mourning and Protest itself was front page news for *Workers' Weekly*, and the various meetings and events held over

91.  Horner 1974, pp.1–26.
92.  *Workers' Weekly*, 23 July 1937, p.3.
93.  *Workers' Weekly*, 8 October 1937, p.4 and 15 October 1937, p.4.
94.  Holt 1988, p.299.
95.  Holt 1988, p.301.

the week by Indigenous activists were reported on as historic events. However several articles pointed to tensions which had arisen between the CPA and the APA.

On 25 Jan *Workers' Weekly* published a reply to media reports that Ferguson was accusing the CPA of refusing to hand over money raised at one of the meetings he spoke at. The CPA argued that this had arisen over a misunderstanding; however it was a foreshadowing of future debates.[96] The Day of Mourning was organised by the APA with the support of the Australian Aborigines' League, based in Victoria. Its organising meetings were open to Aboriginal people only, and while white supporters were encouraged to attend a meeting afterwards, the Day of Mourning and Protest itself was also to be an Aboriginal-only event.

The CPA was very critical of this approach. While they positively covered the Day of Mourning and Protest in detail, they also published articles criticising the "separatist" politics of the organisers. One article laid out the general argument:

> It is most admirable that a movement should take place among the aborigines on their own behalf, but that movement must not be limited or confined in any way. All progressive and democratic people must be rallied to their cause. Their struggle is ours as well as theirs. While praising the aborigines for taking up the fight, we, the whites, must help them, fight for them, use all means in our power to see that they get justice. Representatives of the trade unions, of all progressive bodies, should be present on their platforms, present in the Australia Hall with them on their Day of Mourning. Whoever tries to limit their movement is foe, not friend, of this fine and terribly maltreated people.[97]

These debates have been seen by some as a precursor to arguments over autonomous organising and black nationalism in the second half of the twentieth century. While concern about white influence over the

---

96. *Workers' Weekly*, 25 January 1938, p.4.
97. *Workers' Weekly*, 25 January 1938, p.1. Also discussed in *Workers' Weekly*, 1 February 1938, p.2.

movement by Indigenous activists probably played some role, there were other factors at work as well.

In the lead-up to the Day of Mourning considerable conservative pressure was building on Indigenous activists. David Unaipon, a prominent Aboriginal figure, pulled out of the protest a few days before it was to start on the basis that the Lyons government had contacted him to assure him that changes were to be made to Aboriginal policy. The Lyons government also accepted a proposal to meet with a delegation from the protest, provided that it only included Aboriginal people. This was motivated by a desire to exclude representatives from the socialist left and the unions. Some white people did attend the meeting, but they were handpicked by the government.[98]

There were other conservatising pressures on the Indigenous activists. While establishing the APA, Ferguson and another Aboriginal activist, Jack Patten, had come into contact with the publisher William Miles and the writer PR Stephensen. Stephensen had once been a CPA member but had drifted away. Both were now part of a tradition of nationalist politics that had some sympathy for Indigenous people, such as John J Moloney, editor of the nationalist newspaper *The Voice of the North*, who had supported the Australian Aboriginal Progressive Association.[99] Later Miles and Stephensen would found the proto-fascist Australia First Movement.

While Ferguson had initially been friendly to Miles and Stephensen, he became increasingly suspicious of their motives.[100] This was heightened when they arranged the funds to have a newspaper called *Abo Call* published with Jack Patten as the editor. Divisions started to open up within the APA between Ferguson, who was closer to the union movement and the socialist left, and Patten, who looked to nationalist allies. Patten used *Abo Call* to publish articles attacking Ferguson,[101] and sent a letter to *Workers' Weekly* explaining that the APA would no longer be accepting "unsolicited" donations. There was also pressure

---

98.  *Workers' Weekly*, 4 February 1938, p.2.
99.  Maynard 2007, pp.39–40.
100. See Horner 1974, pp.68–80 for an overview of the dispute between Ferguson and Patten.
101. For instance *The Australian Abo Call*, 1 June 1938, p.2 and 1 May 1938, p.1.

on Ferguson by ALP members like Albert Thompson to put limits on his relationship with the Communists.[102]

Despite arguments between the CPA and the APA, they continued to work with each other after the Day of Mourning. On May Day four months after the protest, the APA accepted an invitation from Communist union leaders to march in the parade, and Tom Wright spoke alongside Ferguson at a massive meeting on the Domain at the end of the march. The CPA also worked with the APA in establishing a new group, the Campaign for Aboriginal Citizen Rights, which included CPA member Jean Devanny, Ferguson from the APA, and Mark Davidson and Albert Thompson representing the ALP state executive.[103]

The political divisions within the APA would also shape, and unfortunately ultimately undermine, the important struggle at Cummerajunga in southern NSW. Cummerajunga had long been a site of Aboriginal resistance and unrest, with tensions coming to a head in February of 1939 when Jack Patten was arrested while agitating amongst the Aboriginal people at the station. Several hundred Aboriginal people living at Cummerajunga then staged a walk-off in protest and crossed over the Murray River to Victoria.

The walk-off was highly controversial in both Indigenous and non-Indigenous activist circles. The issues involved were muddled due to the tensions between Patten and other Indigenous leaders, and Patten's relationship with the far-right nationalists in Sydney. William Ferguson opposed the walk-off and made it known to those involved in Aboriginal campaigning that he believed Patten had stirred up trouble for his own purposes. The Campaign for Aboriginal Citizen Rights which had brought together Ferguson, the CPA and the ALP left in Sydney "claimed that Patten represented no known Aboriginal organisation and disassociated itself from his methods".[104]

In Victoria however the situation was somewhat different. PR Stephensen's Australia First organisation seems to have collapsed shortly before the walk-off began, and with the Sydney left quite hostile, the walk-off found support among the socialist left and the

---

102. Horner 1974, p.71.

103. *Workers' Weekly,* 22 April 1938, p.4.

104. Attwood 2021, p.187.

workers' movement in Melbourne. William Cooper and the Australian Aborigines' League in Melbourne were more supportive of the walk-off. In March the League brought the issue to the attention of the ACTU, which passed a motion calling on the NSW government to hold an inquiry into the conditions that led to the walk-off. The Victorian CPA branch started to run a series of articles about the walk-off and protest meetings were held at the Yarra Bank with socialist, CPA and Aboriginal speakers. A new organisation, the Aborigines' Assistance Committee, was formed with a number of Aboriginal representatives as well as socialists like JF Chapple, general secretary of the Australian Railways Union. Young Aboriginal members of the Committee such as Margaret Tucker "were keen to accept the support of socialists and communists".[105]

However after nine months the walk-off eventually ended in defeat. The NSW government rejected any demands for a public inquiry and successfully convinced the Victorian government to refuse to give aid to the protesters who had crossed the state border.

## The Popular Front and "New Deal for the Aborigines"

From 1934 onwards a significant shift in the politics of the international Communist movement and therefore the CPA was underway. This was the turn to what became known as the "Popular Front". For the first half of the 1930s, the Comintern had argued for a policy of "class versus class", emphasising the immediacy of proletarian revolution and denouncing the reformist left as "social fascists". This was a period of extreme sectarianism that in some cases led to important defeats for the workers' movement, such as the rise of Hitler in Germany, and placed limits on the growth of Communist parties elsewhere, including during the radicalisation in NSW under the Lang government. At the same time, it saw the CPA lead hundreds and then thousands of working-class fighters in battles on the streets and in the workplace.

The turn towards the Popular Front involved a shift away from this perspective, but it was a shift even further away from revolutionary Marxist politics. The emphasis was now on winning over sections of the

---

105. For left-wing support for the walk-off see Attwood 2021, pp.187–94.

progressive middle class and even the capitalists to a common struggle against fascism. Within the workers' movement, this involved a toning down of criticisms of the ALP and "left" trade union leaders, which led ultimately to the adoption of a reformist and left-nationalist ideology.

A growing orientation towards the middle class was already present in the latter half of the Caledon Bay campaign and the 1938 Day of Mourning protest. Compared to the Third Period's insistence on a sharp distinction between middle-class and working-class approaches, there was a greater emphasis on winning over anthropologists, scientists, religious leaders and middle-class humanitarians. This is not an inherently negative approach, but it did open up the CPA to be more influenced by the politics of the liberal middle classes. The CPA began to adapt to the assimilationist currents growing in these layers. This was particularly notable in Tom Wright's 1939 pamphlet *New Deal for the Aborigines*.

The 1939 pamphlet marked a shift in CPA policy towards a much stricter separation between Indigenous people still living on the fringes of Australian society and "half-castes" who had become more integrated. The CPA now adopted essentially two different strategies for Indigenous people:

> It would be an important step towards a better understanding of the aborigines question if it were clearly recognised that there are two separate problems.
>
> The most urgent problem is that of the Aborigines proper, the full-blooded natives, thousands of whom still live under tribal or semi-tribal conditions, and who could be saved from extinction if appropriate measures were adopted immediately by the Australian people. It is this problem, the real aborigines problem, that is the subject of this pamphlet.
>
> A second problem, often wrongly referred to as the aborigines problem, is that of the half-castes and others of mixed blood. Most half-castes and their descendants are denied social equality with other Australian citizens, and are subjected to social indignities that are a disgrace to our community. This second question

has only passing reference in this pamphlet. It is a separate problem, not the aborigine problem, and requires a different and separate treatment.[106]

Wright doubled down on this distinction in a 1947 report to the CPA Central Committee:

One of the demands of the party is that the terms "Aborigine", "Aboriginal" and "native", used in the various acts and ordinances, should not apply to persons of mixed blood. However, we find people of mixed blood, particularly in NSW and Victoria, who think it is necessary and correct to represent themselves as Aborigines in conducting a campaign for full civic rights. These persons of mixed blood confuse the right of the Aborigines with their own problems, which is not the Aborigine fight.[107]

Wright's distinction was an attempt to respond to the divergent experiences of Indigenous people in Australian capitalism at the time, however this rigid distinction between sections of the Indigenous population created new problems. It will be obvious to contemporary readers that it is mistaken to deny the Aboriginality of those with mixed ancestry or those who live in urban settings. This is not simply because doing so means uncritically accepting a reified, capitalist understanding of race and racial identity. Politically speaking, it also produces a schematic understanding of Indigenous oppression and excludes the possibility of urban and regional communities being inspired by each others' struggles and grievances.

It also dovetailed with assimilationist ideas being promoted by middle-class sympathisers with Indigenous suffering at the time. While assimilation wouldn't become official government policy until 1951, from the late 1930s onwards there was a growing assimilationist wing within academic and government circles, particularly the Australian National Research Council that funded most anthropological research into Indigenous communities.

106. Wright 1944 [1939].
107. Wright 1947.

In April 1937 a conference of Commonwealth and state Aboriginal authorities was organised which made a recommendation that so called "half-caste" Indigenous people should be assimilated into Australian society by abandoning any connection to their Indigenous heritage. The rest of the Indigenous community was divided between "detribalised", "semi-civilised" and "uncivilised." So called "detribalised" Indigenous people would also be assimilated into Australian society under this recommendation, while the "semi-civilised" and "uncivilised" would be segregated from the rest of society, with strict limits on contact with both whites and assimilated Indigenous people.[108]

These recommendations were endorsed by figures such as anthropology professor AP Elkin, who had spoken on platforms alongside Communists during the campaigns of the mid to late 1930s.[109] Wright was particularly influenced by the outlook of two dissident anthropologists: Donald Thomson and Olive Pink.[110] Thomson, who had become friends with Tom Wright during the 1930s, was more on the outer of the academic establishment than Elkin. However their proposals for government policy on the Indigenous question were both marked by paternalism. Thomson's main difference with mainstream assimilationist thought was that he placed a much greater emphasis on the need to rigorously segregate the still "tribalised" Indigenous communities from the rest of society, in order, in his view, to prevent the total destruction of the last remains of true Indigenous pre-invasion culture and society.[111]

This acceptance of middle-class prejudices towards Indigenous people was not the only problem with Wright's writings. The 1931 *Draft Programme*, despite some of its problems, had been a *radical* document emphasising the revolutionary nature of anti-racist solidarity, the role of the working class and the need for a socialist revolution to destroy the roots of Indigenous oppression in the capitalist imperialist system.

*New Deal for the Aborigines* and its various reprints however made not a *single* reference to class struggle or socialism, capitalism or

---

108. Commonwealth of Australia 1937.
109. *Workers' Weekly*, 10 August 1934, p.1.
110. Macintyre 1998, p.266.
111. For the views of Thomson, Pink and Elkin see Gray 2007, pp.115–71.

imperialism. It also makes not a single reference to the role that unions or the working class can play in the struggle for Indigenous rights. As Hannah Middleton has argued:

> CPA policy was weakened by the introduction of bourgeois, reformist ideas. The anti-imperialist essence of the struggle for Aboriginal rights, the recognition of Aborigines as members of the working class and the key importance of land rights were replaced by *New Deal for the Aborigines*... The pamphlet offered not radical changes but measures to alleviate the conditions of the Aborigines. It viewed their position as static rather than a process of change and development and did not consider the active role that the Aborigines themselves were playing and would have to play in their own struggle.[112]

For the so-called "half-caste" Indigenous population Wright proposed a civil rights campaign with no class content whatsoever. Wright's main criticism was that the government had failed to follow through on its promise to assimilating them into white society:

> The Conference of Commonwealth and State Aboriginal Authorities held in April 1937 resolved that, in regard to people of mixed aboriginal and white blood, they must aim at their "ultimate absorption by the people of the commonwealth". No explanation is given for delay in acting on the resolution, and conceding full social equality.[113]

At the same time, Wright also downplayed the working-class character of Indigenous people in the Northern Territory and Western Australia. In the 1947 report to the CPA Central Committee Wright positively notes the Aboriginal strikes in the Pilbara and Darwin but goes on to argue that they have no particular working-class content.[114]

While the idea of Aboriginal republics had its problems, Wright

---

112. Middleton 2008.
113. Wright 1944 [1939].
114. Wright 1947.

redefined the strategy for Indigenous people in the NT and Western Australia in a much more conservative direction that was deeply influenced by mainstream liberal academics. He took up the idea proposed by Thomson that Indigenous groups that had not yet been "detribalised" should be completely segregated on reserves not just from white people but also from the influence of "half-caste" Aboriginal people as the only way to preserve what remained of their traditional way of life.

Wright had reframed the struggle for Indigenous rights as an essentially liberal one and simply one piece of the general advance of the broad front of democratic progressive forces against fascism and the power of monopolies. While this could serve as a guide for CPA members in campaigning for equal rights for some Indigenous people in day-to-day struggles, it could not lead to developing a revolutionary Marxist perspective on Indigenous struggle.

You can see the impact of this more liberal orientation in how Communist activists organised around Indigenous issues in the lead-up to the 1946 Pilbara strike.

The ALP was in power in WA from 1933 until 1947, and outside the brief period of the Hitler-Stalin pact, the CPA believed that it was in a united front with the ALP from the late 1930s until 1947. This impacted how they understood the relationship between the ALP and Indigenous rights. For instance, in 1935 the CPA's Western Australian paper *The Red Star* had ruthlessly criticised the failures of the WA Labor government on Indigenous issues.[115] Yet by 1939 *Workers' Weekly* welcomed the inclusion of Bob Coverly and Emil Nulsen into the Labor cabinet as they were apparently strong supporters of Aboriginal rights.[116] In fact, Coverly was a consistent mouthpiece for the white station owners who exploited Aboriginal people in the Pilbara. At the Moseley Commission in 1934 Coverly had voiced his opposition to any government regulations on the exploitation of Indigenous workers, criticising what he called the "stupid system of protecting the aborigines to the detriment of the settlers as a whole".[117] He would be one of the most hostile politicians to the 1946 Pilbara strike, and contrary to the CPA's article, was

---

115. *The Red Star*, 8 March 1935, p.2.
116. *Workers' Weekly*, 11 April 1939, p.3.
117. Scrimgeour 2020, p.20.

only a critic of the Commissioner of Native Affairs in so far as Coverly believed he was organisationally and financially ineffective and not doing enough to protect the rights of the station owners.

The white Communist Don McLeod played a key role in preparing Aboriginal workers for the 1946 strike. However in 1945, despite Aboriginal workers being seemingly ready and willing to go on strike, McLeod convinced them to delay it by a year in order not to undermine the "progressive" war effort.[118] In the initial aftermath of the war McLeod found new reasons to oppose an immediate strike. He argued that the Aboriginal workers would be defeated without access to resources, and instead must focus on winning control over some areas of land from the government.

This attitude was shaped by the extremely optimistic perspective of post-war Australia promoted by the CPA, heavily informed by its Popular Front politics. They saw huge opportunities for social and economic advancement under a post-war federal Labor government and emphasised that this would be possible through an alliance of middle-class, working-class and even "progressive" capitalist forces. As Ken Mansell has argued, the CPA "entered the post-war period with a positive attitude towards reconstruction and its own version of the peoples' anti-monopoly democratic revolution based on a gradualist perspective".[119]

Influenced by this framework, McLeod believed that in the Pilbara the large station owners were detested by the majority of the population. He envisaged uniting together the small business owners and small farmers, the rural workers and urban business interests around a program for economic development in the Pilbara. Such a program would benefit all except the larger station owners, and would include provisions for greater autonomy for the local Indigenous population.[120] McLeod thus focused his efforts on winning over the North-West and Kimberley Advancement Association.[121]

Unsurprisingly, the organisation – which was the representative

---

118. Scrimgeour 2020, p.86.
119. Mansell 1980, p.23.
120. Scrimgeour 2020, pp.86–9.
121. The following account is based on Scrimgeour 2020, pp.87–9.

of small and large business interests in the region – was not receptive to McLeod's ideas. At the first convention of the Association, Harry Greene, the owner of Talga Talga Station and a strong opponent of McLeod, was elected chairman and the meeting endorsed the interests of the pastoralists. McLeod then tried to set up a more sympathetic branch of the Association in Marble Bar which had a broader social basis. However at the first meeting of this branch a motion was moved to effectively censor McLeod. The motion passed overwhelmingly. In the aftermath of the meeting, Department of Native Affairs Inspector Lawrence O'Neill wrote that McLeod had "no standing in the community but...a small following among poor class whites".[122] The North-West and Kimberley Advancement Association would go on to vigorously oppose the 1946 strike and advocate for the segregation of Indigenous children in schools. The WA CPA branch endorsed McLeod's orientation towards the North-West and Kimberley Advancement Association and published his program in the *Workers' Star* newspaper.[123]

McLeod's Popular Front-inspired program crashed up against the realities of capitalism in the region. While small business owners and farmers might not particularly like the large station owners, they were utterly dependent upon them. Nor did they have any particular interest in campaigning against the racist controls on Indigenous people. After being rejected by Pilbara polite society, McLeod soon refocused his efforts back on planning for the 1946 Pilbara strike. This was helped by the revival of class struggle with the end of the Second World War and the growing rift this produced between the CPA and the ALP federal government.

Wright's pamphlet quickly replaced the half forgotten 1931 *Draft Programme* as the guide to the Aboriginal question for Communists. Many of the positions in *New Deal for the Aborigines* would be challenged by important developments in Indigenous struggle during the post-war era, leading to further changes in CPA policy. In particular Wright's insistence on a strict separation between different Indigenous peoples would be progressively abandoned by the CPA through the 1950s and early '60s.

---

122. Scrimgeour 2020, p.89.
123. *Workers' Star*, 1 June 1945, p.5, 8 February 1946, p.6 and 5 April 1946, p.4.

## Conclusion

Throughout the 1930s Communist militants across the country rebuilt a fighting labour movement that had been all but destroyed by the initial impact of the Great Depression. As they did so they infused militants with a deeper appreciation of the nature of Indigenous oppression.

No one can discount the positive contribution that the CPA made to popularising support for Indigenous justice among a significant layer of working-class activists across the country. But the CPA's Stalinist politics undermined its attempts to develop a Marxist perspective on Indigenous struggle that both accurately understood the nature of Indigenous oppression and clearly linked this struggle to the broader fight for socialism. This reinforces the argument that anti-Stalinist revolutionaries have always made. Stalinism not only tied Communist parties across the world to an authoritarian dictatorship masquerading as socialism, it also deformed socialist attitudes on a range of important political questions. For revolutionaries in Australia today then, the history of the CPA's involvement in Indigenous struggle leaves us with a dual legacy to be grappled with.

## References

Attwood, Bain 2021, *William Cooper: An Aboriginal Life*, The Miegunyah Press, Melbourne University.

Bloodworth, Sandra 2006, "Aboriginal rights & trade unions in the 1950s and 1960s", *Marxist Interventions*. https://sa.org.au/interventions/kooris_unions.htm

Boughton, Bob 2001, "The Communist Party of Australia's involvement in the struggle for Aboriginal and Torres Strait Islander Peoples' Rights 1920–1970", *Labour and Community: Historical Essays,* University of Wollongong Press. https://ro.uow.edu.au/cgi/viewcontent.cgi?referer=https://www.google.com.au/&httpsredir=1&article=1012&context=labour1999

Boughton, Bob 2005, "Assimilationism and anti-communism. A Reflection on Gerald Peel's 'Isles of the Torres Strait'", *Contesting Assimilation: Histories of Colonial and Indigenous Initiatives,* Perth: API-Network. https://www.academia.edu/15758192/Assimilationism_and_anti_communism_A_Reflection_on_Gerald_Peels_Isles_of_the_Torres_Strait

Brian, Bernie 2001, *The Northern Territory's One Big Union. The Rise and Fall of the North Australian Workers' Union, 1911–1972*, PhD thesis, Northern Territory University. https://ris.cdu.edu.au/ws/portalfiles/portal/22706059/ Thesis_CDU_6353_Brian_B.pdf

Clark, Ian 2005, *Another Side of Eureka – the Aboriginal presence on the Ballarat goldfields in 1854 – Were Aboriginal people involved in the Eureka rebellion?*, Working Paper, University of Ballarat Business School, https://citeseerx.ist.psu.edu/viewdoc/ download?doi=10.1.1.693.6129&rep=rep1&type=pdf

Commonwealth of Australia, 1937, *Aboriginal Welfare: Initial conference of Commonwealth and State Aboriginal Authorities*. https://nla.gov.au/nla. obj-52771316/view?partId=nla.obj-88456768#page/n0/mode/1up

Communist Party of Australia 1930, *Australia's Part in the World Revolution: Theses of the Central Committee Plenum, Communist Party of Australia, June 28th and 29th*. https://www.reasoninrevolt.net.au/objects/pdf/d0885.pdf

Docker, Comrade 1934, "Work in Districts 5 & 6", *Communist Review*, Vol. 1, No. 3, June. https://www.reasoninrevolt.net.au/objects/pdf/d0170.pdf

Drachewych, Oleksa 2017, *The Comintern and the Communist Parties of South Africa, Canada, and Australia on the questions of Imperialism, Nationality and Race, 1919–1943*, PhD thesis, McMasters University. https://macsphere. mcmaster.ca/bitstream/11375/22007/2/drachewych_oleksa_m_2017september_ PhD.pdf

Drachewych, Oleksa 2019, "Settler Colonialism and the Communist International", *The Palgrave Encyclopaedia of Imperialism and Anti-Imperialism*, second edition, Palgrave MacMillan.

Goodall, Heather 2008, *Invasion to embassy: land in Aboriginal politics in New South Wales, 1770–1972*, Sydney University Press.

Gray, Geoffrey 2007, *A Cautious Silence: The Politics of Australian Anthropology*, Aboriginal Studies Press.

Holt, Stephen 1988, *A Veritable Dynamo: Lloyd Ross, the Australian Railways Union and left-wing politics in inter-war Australia*, PhD thesis, Australian National University.

Horner, Jack 1974, *Vote for Ferguson for Aboriginal freedom: a biography*, Australia and New Zealand Book Co.

Howitt, William 2011 [1855], *Land, Labour and Gold: Two Years in Victoria: with Visits to Sydney and Van Diemen's Land*, Cambridge University Press.

Humphreys, Jordan 2021, "Aboriginal unionists in the 1890s shearers' strikes: a forgotten history", *Marxist Left Review*, 22, Winter. https://marxistleftreview.org/articles/aboriginal-unionists-in-the-1890s-shearers-strikes-a-forgotten-history/

James, CLR 2018, *C.L.R. James and Revolutionary Marxism: Selected Writings of C.L.R. James 1939–1949*, Haymarket Books.

Jordan, Douglas 2011, *Conflict in the Unions: The Communist Party of Australia, Politics and the Trade Union Movement, 1945–1960*, PhD thesis, Victoria University. https://vuir.vu.edu.au/16065/1/Douglas_Jordan_PhD.pdf

Macintyre, Stuart 1998, *The Reds: The Communist Party of Australia from origins to illegality*, Allen & Unwin.

Mansell, Ken 1980, *The Marxism and Strategic Concepts of the Communist Party of Australia 1963–1972*, honours thesis, La Trobe University. https://labourhistorymelbourne.org/wp-content/uploads/2019/03/cpa-thesis-ken-mansell.pdf

Martínez, Julia 1999, *Plural Australia: Aboriginal and Asian labour in tropical white Australia, Darwin, 1911–1940*, PhD thesis, University of Wollongong.

Marx, Karl 1887, *Capital*, Vol. 1. https://www.marxists.org/archive/marx/works/1867-c1/ch31.htm

Maynard, John 2007, *Fight for liberty and freedom: the origins of Australian Aboriginal activism*, Aboriginal Studies Press.

McNeill, Dougal 2015, "Maori and Communism in the 1930s", *ISO Aotearoa*. https://iso.org.nz/2015/07/09/maori-and-communism-in-the-1930s/

Middleton, Hannah 2008, "Reflections on the Aboriginal Movement", *Australian Marxist Review*, 47, January. https://archive.cpa.org.au/amr/47/amr47–04-reflections-on-the-aboriginal-movement-middleton.html

O'Lincoln, Tom 1985, *Into the Mainstream: The Decline of Australian Communism*, Stained Wattle Press. https://www.marxists.org/subject/stalinism/into-mainstream/index.htm

Peel, Gerald 1947, *Isles of the Torres Straits: an Australian responsibility*, Current Book Distributors.

Reynolds, Henry 1998, *This whispering in our hearts*, Allen & Unwin.

Scrimgeour, Anne 2020, *On Red Earth Walking: The Pilbara Aboriginal Strike, Western Australia 1946–49*, Monash University Publishing.

Shachtman, Max 2003, *Race and Revolution*, Verso Books.

South African Communist Party 1928, *The South African Question*, resolution adopted by the Executive Committee of the Communist International following the Sixth Comintern congress. https://www.marxists.org/history/international/comintern/sections/sacp/1928/comintern.htm

Sustar, Lee 2012, "Self-Determination and the 'Black Belt'", *Socialist Worker* (US). https://socialistworker.org/2012/06/15/self-determination-and-the-black-belt

Townsend, Terry 2009, *The Aboriginal Struggle & the Left*, Resistance Books.

Trotsky, Leon 1994, *Leon Trotsky on Black Nationalism and Self-Determination*, Pathfinder Press.

Wilson, Deborah 2013, *Different White People: Communists, Unionists and Aboriginal Rights 1936–1972*, PhD thesis, University of Tasmania.

Wright, Tom 1944 [1939], *New Deal for the Aborigines*, Current Book Distributors, Sydney. https://www.marxists.org/history/international/comintern/sections/australia/1944/19440531.htm

Wright, Tom 1947, "Fight for Aborigines", *Communist Review*, April. https://www.marxists.org/history/international/comintern/sections/australia/1947/19470214.htm

Zumoff, Jacob 2014, *The Communist International and US Communism, 1919–1929*, Haymarket Books.

MICK ARMSTRONG

# Property is sacred: How Proudhon moulded anarchism

**Mick Armstrong** has been actively involved in socialist politics since the late 1960s. He is the author of numerous pamphlets and articles on revolutionary organisation and the Australian labour movement, including *The Industrial Workers of the World in Australia*, and *The Labor Party: A Marxist analysis*.

THE *ANARCHIST FAQ* WEBSITE, which is reasonably reflective of broad anarchist opinion, lists Max Stirner, Pierre-Joseph Proudhon, Michael Bakunin and Peter Kropotkin as the major anarchist thinkers.[1] In this article I intend to focus on Stirner and Proudhon, as they played a decisive role in establishing the anarchist world view and moulding the outlook of subsequent anarchists including Bakunin and Kropotkin. Indeed we can't understand the outlook of the anarchist movement today without coming to grips with Stirner and Proudhon. So what did they stand for?

Let's start with the German writer Max Stirner, most famous for his 1844 book *The Ego and His Own*. There is no doubt that Stirner still exercises a major influence on anarchist writers. According to *An Anarchist FAQ* "his ideas remain a cornerstone of anarchism",[2] while the sympathetic historian of anarchism George Woodcock stated that Stirner had "a considerable influence in libertarian circles during the present [twentieth] century".[3] The anarchist writer April Carter describes Stirner as "the next major anarchist theorist" after

---

1.  "Who are the major anarchist thinkers?", *An Anarchist FAQ*.
2.  "Who are the major anarchist thinkers?", *An Anarchist FAQ*.
3.  Woodcock 1962, p.88.

William Godwin,[4] and states that Stirner's book "had an impact on Bakunin just when the latter was being radicalized for the first time in Young Hegelian circles".[5]

In the words again of *An Anarchist FAQ*, Stirner argued for "an extreme form of individualism",[6] which placed the individual above all else. Stirner believed that the concept of workers' solidarity was "quite incomprehensible".[7] Indeed for Stirner there was no common humanity or social morality other than the demands of the individual Ego. He proclaimed; "I, the egoist, have not at heart the welfare of this 'human society'. I sacrifice nothing for it. I only utilize it".[8] Stirner glorified crime and exalted murder, declaring:

> I do not demand any right; therefore I need not recognize any either. What I can get by force I get by force and what I do not get by force I have no right to.[9]

As Woodcock puts it, Stirner

> sets forth his ideal the egoist, the man who realizes himself in conflict with the collectivity and with other individuals, who does not shrink from the use of any means in the "war of each against all", who judges everything ruthlessly from the viewpoint of his own well-being.[10]

There is nothing in any sense left-wing or progressive about such an approach. Stirner was a reactionary self-centred individualist. It is unsurprising that the reactionary philosopher Friedrich Nietzsche had high regard for Stirner. As Woodcock writes:

> There is no need to point out the resemblance between Stirner's

---

4.   Carter 1971, p.1.
5.   Draper 1990, p.114.
6.   "Who are the major anarchist thinkers?", *An Anarchist FAQ*.
7.   Blackledge 2008, p.134.
8.   Stirner 1844.
9.   Stirner 1844.
10.   Woodcock 1962, pp.88–9.

egoist and the superman of Nietzsche; Nietzsche himself regarded Stirner as one of the unrecognized seminal minds of the nineteenth century.[11]

Stirner was not in any serious sense anti-capitalist. Indeed he supported a market economy. He rejected political or social revolution in favour of individual ego rebellion, declaring:

> [M]y object is not the overthrow of an established order but my elevation above it, my purpose and deed are not political and social, but egoistic. The revolution commands one to make arrangements; rebellion demands that one rise or exalt oneself.[12]

Reflecting this reactionary outlook Stirner abstained from any involvement in the revolutions that swept Germany and much of Europe in 1848 and 1849. However on the basis of his extreme individualism Stirner was anti-state, anti-authority and anti-hierarchy.

To be fair there are some anarchists, for example Lucien van der Walt and Michael Schmidt in their book *Black Flame*, who reject the view that figures such as Stirner and for that matter Proudhon are part of the anarchist tradition. They argue that "individualist anarchism" and "lifestyle anarchism" are not genuinely anarchist and that "class struggle anarchism" is the only true anarchism. It would undoubtedly be an important step forward if this was true as it would bring anarchism much closer to a Marxist approach. However as van der Walt and Schmidt concede, their standpoint is very much a minority view among anarchists. They acknowledge that the views of Stirner and other reactionary individualists like Nietzsche have had a significant impact on the anarchist movement.

This is clearly reflected in *An Anarchist FAQ*, which repeatedly quotes Stirner favourably and is obsessed with the individual and the need for "individual sovereignty". It emphasises the individual much more than it does the collective struggle of the working class. *An*

---

11. Woodcock 1962, p.88.
12. Stirner 1844.

*Anarchist FAQ* states that "anarchists recognise that individuals are the basic unit of society and that only individuals have interests and feelings". And it proclaims the need for individuals to free themselves.[13] This represents an abandonment of a class analysis of society. There is simply no way that individuals as individuals can in any meaningful way free themselves from capitalist rule. The only freedom possible is *collective* freedom. Freedom can only be obtained by mass collective working-class struggle that overthrows the rule of the capitalist class and smashes the capitalist state.

And it is totally wrong to believe that only individuals have interests. The working class very much has its own collective class interests – to improve its living standards, increase its democratic rights and to liberate itself as a class, *not* as a series of discrete individuals. Moreover a series of the interests and rights that workers have fought for – including the legalisation of trade unions, the right to assemble, the right to hold mass meetings, the right to vote, a public health system, free education, the ending of wars – are not individual rights but mass collective rights. The ruling class also has collective interests, to maintain their domination over workers and the poor, to expand their profits and market share, and so on.

*An Anarchist FAQ* argues: "For anarchists, the idea that individuals should sacrifice themselves for the 'group' or 'greater good' is nonsensical".[14] But in any mass struggle or revolution that is precisely what workers and the oppressed have done time and time again – giving their lives in the hope that their sacrifice would help liberate their *class*. Just look at the recent protests in Myanmar, Kazakhstan or Hong Kong. Some brave people marched in the front rows knowing that they could well be tear-gassed, arrested, tortured or shot.

In virtually every strike individual workers make financial sacrifices for the good of the collective – both their own immediate workmates and often in the hope that any gains that they make will flow on to other workers they have never even met. They refuse to scab on a strike because they would be a traitor to their class. Similarly in the current COVID crisis, health workers and many other groups of

---

13. "Are anarchists individualists or collectivists?", *An Anarchist FAQ*.
14. "Are anarchists individualists or collectivists?", *An Anarchist FAQ*.

essential workers risk their lives on a daily basis out of a broader collective responsibility. This collective approach is central to what makes us human – not individual egoism.

The strong emphasis by anarchists on individualism is not simply some foible of *An Anarchist FAQ*. Woodcock states: "Democracy advocates the sovereignty of the people. Anarchism advocated the sovereignty of the person".[15] The anarchist historian Alexandre Skirda champions Stirner's individualism.[16] As has already been noted, Bakunin was strongly influenced by Stirner. Woodcock points out that among anarchists in the 1890s and the early twentieth century there was a significant revival of interest in Stirner and his book *The Ego and His Own* was widely read.[17] Proudhon saw freedom in individual terms, not in working-class collective terms as a product of mass class struggle. The prominent British anarchist Nicolas Walter declared: "Nearly all individuals live in society, but society is nothing more than a collection of individuals".[18] Similarly Emma Goldman, one of the best known twentieth century anarchists, insisted:

> Anarchism alone stresses the importance of the individual, his possibilities and needs in a free society... Anarchism insists that the center of gravity in society is the individual.[19]

She declared:

> I, too, will accept anarchist organization on just one condition: that it be based on the absolute respect for all individual initiatives and not obstruct their development or evolution.
>
> The essential principle of anarchy is individual autonomy. The International will not be anarchist unless it wholly respects this principle.[20]

---

15.  Woodcock 1962, p.30.
16.  Skirda 2002, pp.5–6.
17.  Woodcock 1962, p.91.
18.  Walter 1969.
19.  Goldman 2017, p.1134.
20.  Goldman et al 1907.

And as van der Walt and Schmidt note, even many anarchists who distance themselves from the extreme individualism of Stirner and accept the need for some form of organisation do so hesitantly, and advocate a loose organisation. This reflects a common anarchist idea that it is somehow authoritarian for an organisation to prescribe specific views and actions as a basis for membership, and to insist on a political program based on clear positions.

The ongoing influence of individualism among anarchists is also reflected in the fact that today's anarcho-syndicalists and anarcho-communists who claim to stand for class struggle politics generally refuse to make a sharp break politically from lifestyle anarchists and other individualist anarchists. And consequently by default they go along with various individualist ideas hostile to class politics. In particular identity politics, being currently the most common form of middle-class liberal individualism today, are dominant in anarchist circles.[21]

## Proudhon: "The master of us all"

As *An Anarchist FAQ* puts it,

> individualism by definition includes no concrete programme for shaping social conditions. This was attempted by Proudhon...who had a profound effect on the growth of anarchism.[22]

Pierre-Joseph Proudhon, famous for coining the phrase "property is theft", is widely recognised as the founder of anarchism. As Proudhon's anarchist biographer Woodcock states: "All the fundamental anarchist ideas are there [in Proudhon's writings]; it was only in matters of tactics that his successors have ever really differed from him".[23] *An Anarchist FAQ* agrees, stating: "It would be no exaggeration to state that Proudhon's work defined the fundamental nature of anarchism".[24] Anarchist historian Alexandre Skirda credits Proudhon with providing "the inception of the notion of abstention from politics" which is a key

---

21. For a critique of identity politics see Garnham 2021.
22. "Who are the major anarchist thinkers?", *An Anarchist FAQ*.
23. Woodcock 1987, p.xix.
24. "Who are the major anarchist thinkers?", *An Anarchist FAQ*.

pillar of anarchism.[25] Even left-wing anarchists like van der Walt and Schmidt, despite being very critical of Proudhon, acknowledge he influenced anarchism profoundly.

Both Kropotkin and Bakunin admired Proudhon. Kropotkin described him as "the father of anarchy", while Bakunin famously proclaimed that in his "instinct" for freedom Proudhon was "the master of us all"[26] and that his own ideas were simply Proudhon's ideas "widely developed *and* pushed *right to these*, its final consequences".[27] EH Carr in his biography of Bakunin argues that "it was Proudhon more than any other man who was responsible for transforming Bakunin's instinctive revolt against authority into a regular anarchist creed".[28] Eugene Pyziur in his study of Bakunin writes:

> [I]t must be stressed that it was due to the influence of Proudhon's ideas that Bakunin's instinctive rebellionism was transformed into a formulated, doctrinaire anarchist creed. It was Proudhon who provided Bakunin with the theorems and concepts which were essential to him in his later creation of a species of anarchist doctrine, when this became necessary for Bakunin in his duel with Marx.[29]

There is no doubt that Proudhon was one of the most influential radical figures in France in the 1840s and 1850s. He edited probably the most widely read paper in Paris around the time of the 1848 revolution, with a daily circulation of 40,000 copies at its peak.[30] This was quite an amazing achievement for the time. And this was no tabloid scandal sheet but a serious publication with lengthy articles. Proudhon's mass support was reflected in his election to parliament, first at a by-election and then again with an increased majority at the May 1849 general elections. His influence continued well after his death in 1865. The Proudhonist current, which he inspired, was the major radical

---

25. Skirda 2002, p.7.
26. van der Walt and Schmidt 2009, p.84.
27. McKay 2009.
28. Carr 1961, p.137.
29. Pyziur 1955, p.32.
30. Hyams 1979, p.97.

current in France for some decades, playing a substantial (if often quite negative) role in the 1871 Paris Commune.

Proudhon promoted a range of reactionary ideas that anarchists today would find highly embarrassing. I do not have the space to provide a full charge sheet, but here is a representative sample.

Proudhon was hostile to trade unions and to strikes, and at times called for them to be suppressed by the authorities. He condemned strikes for provoking hostility to employers and being contrary to the right of free competition. He viewed trade unions as an assault on individual freedom and denounced as outrageous trade union attempts to interfere with workshop management. As van der Walt and Schmidt comment: "From his Mutualist perspective, strikes were at best irrelevant and at worst a positive threat; they were not really a viable means of struggle for his constituency of petty commodity producers".[31] In his election campaign he called on workers to "offer their erstwhile employers the hand of friendship".[32] In his last complete work, *The Political Capacity of the Working-Classes*, he called on workers to form an alliance with the bourgeoisie and criticised them for having "been too busy with their own wrongs to understand the sorrows of the middle classes".[33]

He opposed voting rights for workers, declaring that "universal suffrage is the counter-revolution".[34] He supported the right of the slave-owning states of the United States to secede at the time of the US Civil War.[35] He opposed the abolition of capital punishment. He was stridently anti-Semitic, declaring:

> Jews. Write an article against this race that poisons everything by sticking its nose into everything without ever mixing with any other people. Demand its expulsion from France with the exception of those individuals married to French women. Abolish synagogues and not admit them to any employment... Finally,

---

31. van der Walt and Schmidt 2009, p.84.
32. Hyams 1979, p.126.
33. Quoted in Brogan 1934, p.82.
34. Blackledge 2010, p.144.
35. Hyams 1979, p.286.

pursue the abolition of this religion... The Jew is the enemy of humankind. They must be sent back to Asia or be exterminated... The Jew must disappear by steel or by fusion or by expulsion... The hatred of the Jew like the hatred of the English should be our first article of political faith.[36]

Proudhon idealised the nuclear family as a core unit of society that had to be protected at all costs. For that reason he opposed divorce and sexual freedom, especially for women. As Carter comments: "Proudhon, unlike most anarchists, sees a positive value in a marriage ceremony".[37] He was an extreme sexist, notoriously declaring that a "woman knows enough if she knows enough to mend our shirts and cook us a steak". According to Proudhon men must be the master in the house. Women should be denied all rights in money and business. As he put it: "Men must always be superior to the women, as three is to two".[38] Despite being hostile to the church, he thought religion a good thing for women given that they were supposedly incapable "of taking a place in the life of society in their own right".[39]

When it came to political strategy Proudhon was a reformist, making it clear in a letter to Karl Marx in 1844 that he opposed "violent revolution".[40]

Yet despite all this, Proudhon was upheld for decades by anarchists as a champion of human freedom against the supposedly authoritarian Marx. Such arguments ignore Marx's polemics in favour of democratic working-class organisation and the vital role of strikes against Proudhon's reactionary views.[41] Right up until the present day the litany of Proudhon's backward positions has been covered up or apologised for or brushed aside by numerous anarchist writers.[42]

---

36. Proudhon 1847. Bakunin was arguably a more vile racist and anti-Semite than Proudhon. See Mendel 1981, pp.330–31, 354, 381–87.
37. Carter 1971, p.48.
38. Quoted in Hyams 1979, p.271.
39. Brogan 1934, p.75.
40. Hyams 1979, p.58.
41. Marx 1976, pp.206–12.
42. A classic case being George Woodcock's 1969 *Encounter* article celebrating Proudhon's *Notebooks*, quoted in Draper 1969.

There are a few honourable exceptions among anarchists, such as van der Walt and Schmidt, who denounce and disown Proudhon. Murray Bookchin is also highly critical of him. However they are very much in a minority, with book after book by anarchists championing Proudhon. Most anarchists simply ignore Proudhon's hostility to strikes and tend to brush aside his sexism and anti-Semitism as unfortunate side issues. But to just take one example, championing the nuclear family was not some side issue for Proudhon. It was a central element of his whole world view, a cornerstone of his "small is beautiful" federalist standpoint. The great bulk of anarchists refuse to acknowledge that Proudhon's hostility to strikes and his sexism and anti-Semitism are integral to his overall petty-bourgeois populist politics and social base. The anarchist unwillingness to sharply disown Proudhon is but a reflection of the fact that many of Proudhon's core ideas remain central to anarchism right down to the present day.

## Abstract and classless anti-authoritarianism

At the centre of Proudhon's world view is a hostility to all forms of authority as an infringement of individual freedom, which, like Stirner, Proudhon upheld as an absolute principle. Proudhon declared that he was for the "complete freedom of every man for himself and his family, and to the association of fellow workers into which he enters under the terms of a contract".[43] As he wrote in *The General Idea of the Revolution in the Nineteenth Century*:

> The idea of contract excludes that of government... What characterises the contract, the mutual convention, is that in virtue of this convention man's liberty and wellbeing increase, whilst by the institution of an authority, both necessarily diminish.[44]

Proudhon saw all forms of authority, whether it be God or, above all, the state, as the fundamental problem in society. He viewed the state as hostile to the natural order of society. All that was needed to achieve human freedom was for the state to simply disappear or be abolished.

---

43. Quoted in Hyams 1979, p.122.
44. Quoted in Brogan 1934, p.60.

But this was simply utopian nonsense. As the Marxist theorist Hal Draper notes:

> [T]he state performed a necessary function for society, and was not a mere excrescence or cancer, and that therefore it could not be "abolished" until society was able to perform this function with different institutions. This is the stumbling block over which anarchism breaks its neck theoretically.[45]

Proudhon opposed all forms of representative democracy as hierarchical and authoritarian. He believed that democracy would usher in a period of retrogression that would bring the nation and the state to ruin. He also opposed the mass of workers exercising direct democracy as he argued it would lead to just another form of authoritarian rule.[46] This reflected his contempt for the masses who he believed would always support authoritarian leaders.

> The people...by reason of their ignorance, the primitiveness of their instincts, the urgency of their needs and the impatience of their wishes, they incline to summary forms of authority... They seek a leader whose word they trust, whose intentions are known to them, and whom they believe devoted to their interests; to him they give unlimited authority and irresistible power...all they have faith in is the will of a man.[47]

As Carter comments: "Proudhon argued in *The Federative Principle* that historically the aristocracy and the bourgeoisie have tended to protect liberty and federalism, whilst the masses have supported a despotic and unitary state". Consequently democracy, universal suffrage and the referendum must be opposed, as "the people as a whole must be protected from their own folly by a federal structure which limits the effects of their mistakes".[48]

---

45. Draper 1990, p.120.
46. Hyams 1979, p.183.
47. Quoted in Hyams 1979, pp.252–53.
48. Carter 1971, p.72.

Proudhon's classless opposition to authority and the state also led him to oppose inheritance taxes on the rich; indeed he saw any form of taxation on the rich as oppressive.[49] Wealth taxes would just concentrate the control of wealth in the state; much better just to leave it decentralised in the arms of the bosses. Similarly he opposed nationalisation of the banks and of giant corporations, even if it occurred under workers' control.

Following the same abstract anti-statism, Proudhon opposed making any demands on the state for reforms that would benefit workers. He opposed all government welfare payments for workers and the poor, including age pensions and free healthcare. Most controversially in terms of practical politics at the time of the 1848 revolution in France, Proudhon opposed the most popular demand of the workers of Paris that the government create jobs for them.

Proudhon's second core principle was opposition to all forms of centralism, which he spuriously claimed was innately authoritarian. He was for a completely decentralised, small-scale society which he believed was inherently progressive. He declared that "all of my political views can be stripped down to a similar formula: *political federation* or *decentralization*".[50] This fetish for decentralisation led Proudhon, as mentioned previously, to back the southern US slave states breaking away from Abraham Lincoln's centralised republic – the epitome of his classless world view. He praised the Austrian monarchy as it was moving towards a decentralised empire. His "small is beautiful" approach also led him to favour small reactionary monarchies over unified republics. He claimed: "In a little state, there is nothing for the bourgeoisie to profit from".[51] Consequently he opposed Italian unification, defended the Papal States and lamented the defeat of the armies of the ultra-reactionary King Francis of Naples by Garibaldi's rebel forces.

Proudhon's solution to society's ills was that workers and small producers should set up their own companies to compete on the

---

49. Hyams 1979, p.6. For the classic demolition of Proudhon's economic theories see Marx 1976.
50. Quoted in Skirda 2002, p.7.
51. Quoted in Woodcock 1987, p.246.

capitalist market. They would then ruin the big capitalists by out-competing them on the market, and by denuding them of a labour force. At the centre of this fantasy was a People's Bank to which ordinary people would loan their money and which in turn would provide cheap credit to finance the producer-owned companies. This schema, known as Mutualism, would succeed according to Proudhon by simply ignoring the state. Definitely there should be no recourse to violence by the oppressed, or expropriation of those with existing wealth. At most all that would be needed was a campaign of civil disobedience and passive resistance.

> The producer-owned companies would be federated together by mutual agreement. The state would become redundant. Freedom of trade and the market would, however, continue to exist and money would still circulate. Indeed Proudhon stridently opposed communal equality and collective working class ownership of industry, and "defended the rights of private property as a necessary bulwark of personal liberty".[52]

Proudhon's schema was a typical petty-bourgeois utopia reflecting the social class from which he came and sought support. As the anarchist writer April Carter puts it: "The type of anarchism developed by Pierre-Joseph Proudhon...idealized the sturdy independence of the small peasant proprietor or skilled craftsman".[53] Similarly Woodcock notes: "The ideal of the free peasant life was to become a shaping element in Proudhon's social and political thought".[54] Proudhon had owned a small printing business that went broke. And this libertarian very much saw the paper he edited as his own individual property, subject to his dictatorial control.[55]

As Marx wrote:

> From head to foot M. Proudhon is the philosopher and economist

---

52. Carter 1971, p.73.
53. Carter 1971, p.2.
54. Woodcock 1962, p.102.
55. Hyams 1979, p.176.

of the petty-bourgeoisie...he is dazed by the magnificence of the big bourgeoisie and has sympathy for the sufferings of the people. He is at once both bourgeois and man of the people. Deep down in his heart he flatters himself that he is impartial and has found the right equilibrium... A petty-bourgeois of this type glorifies contradiction [in his theorising] because contradiction is the basis of his existence. He is himself nothing but social contradiction in action. He must justify in theory what he is in practice.[56]

Proudhon decreed that under his schema, "Retail trade should be left to the small shopkeeper".[57] Indeed he championed the right to be a shopkeeper, the rights of other small business owners and he opposed consumers' cooperatives that were being set up to compete with them. Similarly Proudhon proclaimed that peasants would own their own patch of land and compete in a market economy. Property would be bought and sold but large landowners would not be permitted. So ironically, despite being famous for the phrase "property is theft" Proudhon, as one of his biographers DW Brogan notes, "explained, for twenty years, that he was a defender, not an enemy of property".[58] According to Proudhon it was only large-scale industry, which he did not view favourably, that would be run as producer-owned companies. However he opposed workers forcibly seizing capitalist companies as a violation of property rights, and also opposed workers' co-operatives.[59] As Fredrick Engels put it, Proudhon "wants existing society, but without its abuses".[60]

Large income differentials of up to three to one were to be allowed under Proudhon's Mutualist utopia. No welfare payments would be available to the poor. As Hyams, who is very sympathetic to Proudhon, puts it: "Mutualism, excluding welfarism, has to tolerate poverty; but not degrading poverty".[61] Proudhon supported piece work and fee for

---

56. Quoted in Draper 1978, pp.293–94.
57. Hyams 1979, p.281.
58. Brogan 1934, p.27.
59. Hyams pp.281–85.
60. Quoted in Draper 1978, p.295.
61. Hyams 1979, p.280.

service, and saw competition on the market by individuals as very important to ensure that they worked hard. He argued:

> The most deplorable error of socialism is to have considered it [competition] as the disorder of society. There can...be...no question of destroying competition... It is a matter of finding an equilibrium, one could say a policing agent.[62]

Unsurprisingly the Mutualist schema was an abject failure when put to the test of practice. Reflecting his own naivety, and in contradiction to his proclaimed anti-state principles, Proudhon called on the French government to fund his People's Bank.[63] When the government refused his request, he tried to establish a People's Bank on the basis of private financial subscriptions. It quickly collapsed – though it should be noted that this proclaimed libertarian appointed himself "the sole responsible manager" of the bank, registering it as "PJ Proudhon and Company".[64] Indeed he attempted to impose dictatorial control over the entire Mutualist system.[65] The whole project was of course an utter fantasy. As though the capitalist class and its state were ever going to allow themselves to be peacefully forced out of existence by competition from producer-owned enterprises. If Proudhon's Mutualist enterprises had started to pose any serious threat to big business the police and army would have been unleashed to crush them.

The final core element of Proudhon's philosophy was hostility to political organisation and parties, and to politics in a more general sense. For Proudhon, the masses should not look to political solutions to their problems. They should rely instead solely on their own economic strength. It was by economic competition from producer-owned enterprises that the existing order would be undermined. In the 1848 revolution in France no revolutionary working-class party existed to organise the ranks of the rebellious workers of Paris or to provide a socialist political alternative to the bourgeois Republicans.

---

62. Guerin, pp.52–3.
63. Graham, n.d.
64. Woodcock 1987, p.143.
65. Draper 1969.

Proudhon's influential anti-party current opposed any such attempt, which helped contribute to the terrible defeat and mass repression that workers suffered.

## Proudhon's ongoing legacy

Later anarchists like Bakunin and Kropotkin ditched some of the more outlandish and utterly reactionary elements of Proudhon's politics. Anarchists today don't campaign against strikes or oppose divorce or taxes on the rich or want to abolish age pensions. Anarchists, with rare exceptions, no longer champion the idea of a People's Bank as the way forward to freedom. Nonetheless as *An Anarchist FAQ* acknowledges, Proudhon's core principles still profoundly influence anarchism.

Bakunin and other anarchists such as Errico Malatesta saw themselves as revolutionaries and rejected Proudhon's reformist perspective that capitalism and the state could gradually be abolished or fade away in the face of economic competition from producer-owned enterprises. But Proudhon's reformist orientation is embodied in the approach of lifestyle and individualist anarchists, who form easily the largest anarchist current today. Lifestyle anarchists believe that by disavowing the norms of mainstream society and living an alternative lifestyle in communes or squats, by eating ethically, growing their own food, dumpster diving or running soup kitchens they can escape the state, or make it irrelevant and thus lay the basis for freedom. Just like Proudhon they don't see the collective struggle of the working class as the key to liberating humanity.

But it is not just the lifestyle anarchists who don't recognise that it is *only* the collective power of the working class that can liberate human-ity. Various anarchists who would see themselves as revolutionaries look to classes or social layers other than the working class as a revolu-tionary liberating force. Indeed Bakunin viewed the Russian peasant commune as a basis for socialism.[66] He looked to a whole variety of non-proletarian social layers – peasants, criminal elements, students, petty-bourgeois intellectuals – to tear down bourgeois society. Bakunin considered the "world of tramps, thieves, and brigands" to be among

---

66. van der Walt and Schmidt 2009, p.97.

"the best and truest conductors of a people's revolution" as they were gifted with "evil passions" and the "devil in the flesh".[67]

Similarly the Narodniks in Russia saw the peasantry as the revolutionary force and dismissed the workers. Right down to this very day many anarchists, including *An Anarchist FAQ*, hold up Nestor Makhno's peasant army in Russia as a force that could have established an anarchist society. But it is not just *An Anarchist FAQ* that looks to the peasantry as an anarchist force. Even some of the most left-wing anarchists like van der Walt and Schmidt champion Makhno – a reflection of the fact that like Proudhon they don't have a thoroughgoing class analysis of society.[68] They argue that the property-owning peasantry can, by a voluntaristic act of will, create socialism even in a poverty-stricken pre-capitalist society. Material conditions do not matter to them. "It was not necessary to wait for capitalism to create the material basis for freedom, freedom would create its own material basis."[69]

The continuing influence of Proudhon's petty-bourgeois utopian outlook is also reflected in anarchist circles in their opposition to centralised working-class power and support for decentralised, small-scale local communities or collectives linked up only by loose and voluntary federation. It is not simply lifestyle anarchists who adhere to this Proudhon-derived orientation. Bakunin was a strident supporter of federalism, as was Peter Kropotkin, who savaged the 1871 Paris Commune for setting up a system of representative democracy.[70] In their virulent opposition to centralisation *An Anarchist FAQ* and van der Walt and Schmidt are definitely representative of current anarchist opinion.

*An Anarchist FAQ* opposes "any form of organisation based on the delegation of power"[71] and argues that only on the basis of decentralisation "both structurally and territorially can individual liberty be fostered and encouraged".[72] Some modern day anarchists go even further, arguing for an almost total decentralisation of production and

---

67. Mendel 1981, p.346.
68. For a Marxist critique of Makhno see Armstrong 2016.
69. van der Walt and Schmidt 2009, pp.97–8.
70. Blackledge 2010, p.148.
71. "Why do anarchists emphasise liberty?", *An Anarchist FAQ*.
72. "What sort of society do anarchists want?", *An Anarchist FAQ*.

the creation of self-sufficient autonomous local economies. This is an absolute impossibility for any modern society. You can't confine the operations of the internet or the phone system or the roads, railways, airlines or shipping industry or the health system to one local village or even to one large city.

In Proudhon's case, support for decentralisation reflected the hostility of peasants, small shopkeepers and other small business owners to the growth of large-scale industry employing masses of workers. But there is nothing inherently progressive about decentralisation and small scale industry. It is simply looking back to a highly idealised image of an earlier form of class society (and a very brutal one at that) which is long gone. Such a society could only be re-established following some cataclysmic collapse of human civilisation brought on by nuclear war or climate change.

Against this reactionary utopianism, Marxists argue that it is precisely the bringing together of workers on a mass scale in large-scale industry and huge cities that laid the basis for working class power and for genuine democratic control over society. Workers in, for example, large hospitals, supermarkets, schools or warehouses have much greater potential power than the tiny number of staff at your local GP clinic, cafe or corner store. And consequently they have a much greater capacity to establish democratic forms of organisation. It is no accident that workers in large workplaces have been, for well over a hundred years, the key driving force of all the major workers' uprisings and were the initiators of mass democratic organisations such as workers' councils.

Centralism is inherently more democratic than federalism and decentralised localised decision-making. It is impossible to hold governments, party leaders or trade union officials to account simply by passing motions or taking action at the local level. Moreover, centralised decision-making is vital for resolving the key challenges facing working-class people, whether it be climate change, the COVID crisis, living standards, food distribution, the refugee question or imperialist war.

In contrast, federalism, as Proudhon was very explicit about, was aimed at frustrating the popular will and democratic rights of the great mass of workers and the oppressed. Subsequent generations of anarchists endorsed Proudhon's anti-democratic approach. As *An Anarchist FAQ* puts it, "Malatesta speaks for all anarchists when he argued that 'anarchists deny the right of the majority to govern human society in general'".[73]

Consensus decision-making, a fad which most autonomists and anarchists have embraced, can play a similar role in frustrating the democratic rights of the majority. And as for the idea that decentralisation is a means to prevent top-down bureaucratic control and reformist degeneration of working-class organisations, experience has shown that decentralised anarcho-syndicalist trade unions have proven to be just as prone to such degeneration as more centralised unions.

Furthermore, when it comes to the central question for revolutionaries of how to successfully challenge the power of the capitalist class, small decentralised federated groups are simply not fit for the task. The capitalist class and its state are organised centrally; if they are to be defeated they need to be challenged by democratically organised and centralised working-class power.

### Class-blind anti-statism
The continuing influence of Proudhon's ideas, even on anarchists who proclaim themselves to be class-struggle anarchists, is most pronounced around the question of the state. Like Proudhon their theoretical starting point is hostility to all forms of authority and hierarchy. For them the central problem is not the class nature of society and the exploitation of the working class by the capitalist ruling class, but states in general. This leads anarchists to oppose the working class imposing its own rule on society via a workers' state, even the most democratic one imaginable. Their thoroughly abstract anti-statism leads anarchists to make no distinction between the capitalist state and a democratic workers' state. Both are equally bad as far as anarchists are concerned and must be resolutely opposed. This means that in a revolutionary struggle, when the working class is striving for

---

73. "Why are most anarchists in favour of direct democracy?", *An Anarchist FAQ*.

power, anarchists end up either being paralysed politically and hence irrelevant, or it leads them to argue to workers that they should not take power. But as Trotsky famously argued: "To renounce the conquest of power is voluntarily to leave the power with those who wield it, the exploiters".[74]

This is precisely what happened in the course of the 1936 revolution in Spain, when the Spanish anarcho-syndicalists of the CNT (National Confederation of Labour) refused to take power, even though they were the overwhelmingly dominant force in Catalonia and the surrounding region. The Spanish anarchists argued that taking power was corrupting, and against their libertarian principles. But this just strengthened the hand of the counter-revolutionary Stalinist and reformist forces, enabling them to rebuild the crippled bourgeois state and eventually crush the revolution. Even worse, the anarcho-syndicalists, while refusing to support the establishment of a workers' state, then took positions as cabinet ministers in the capitalist republican government. Their refusal to make a distinction between a workers' state and a capitalist state in the context of a revolutionary upheaval ended up leading the anarchist leaders to act simply as reformist politicians propping up the bourgeois state.

A few genuinely revolutionary-inclined anarchists have recognised some of the problems with the whole anarchist approach to the question of workers taking state power. They have seriously tried to confront the question of how society is to be organised in the immediate aftermath of a revolution, and in particular how to defend the revolution from a pro-capitalist counter-revolution. While they still say they are not for a workers' state, proposals from the more honest and level-headed of them look very similar to what Marxists would consider to be a democratic workers' state. But the failure of even these more left-wing anarchists to fully clarify their approach to working-class political power severely limits their ability to play a positive leading role in any revolutionary upheaval.

---

74.  Trotsky 1973, p.316.

## An inability to politically challenge reformism

Well short of a revolutionary situation, the anarchist shibboleth of opposition to all authority undermines their ability to advance working-class interests in immediate day-to-day struggles and to combat the influence of reformism. As Anthony Arblaster wrote: "It is absurdly ahistorical to suggest that at all times and in all places it is the state which is 'the main enemy of the free individual.'"[75] We have seen this very clearly in the COVID crisis. The left could not abstain from placing political demands on governments to provide better state health services; to roll out an effective vaccination program, to safely quarantine infected people, to use control measures to help prevent the spread of the disease, and so on. It was important to demand more state intervention into the economy: to provide support for workers unable to work and stricter state regulation of employers to ensure workplaces were safe.

The same general approach applies on issue after issue. On climate change, the left needs to be campaigning for governments to shut down polluting industries. Socialists should vigorously oppose the privatisation of state-run services that are vital for working-class people. We need state provision of free and safe public transport, public education, major increases in pensions and unemployment benefits, and so on. But the placing of such demands on the state goes very much against the grain of anarchism and autonomism.

Proudhon's abstract anti-statism has had a long-lasting influence on the approach of anarchists. Anarchists opposed to or were at least extremely sceptical about reforms for workers delivered by the state, whether it be legislation for the eight-hour working day, the nationalisation of core public services, a government-run health service or even age pensions or unemployment benefits. Peter Kropotkin argued that all "legislation made within the state has to be repudiated because it has always been made with regard to the interests of the privileged classes".[76] Anarchist opposition to the nationalising of the banks contributed to the defeat of the 1871 Paris Commune and the

75. Arblaster 1971.
76. Kropotkin 1970, p.165.

1936 Spanish revolution. In their heyday prior to World War I, many syndicalists opposed state welfare measures which they believed "inculcated loyalty to the state machinery, sapped the fighting spirit of workers, and were reforms provided from above, rather than won from below".[77] In the 1920s some anarchist unions went as far as organising strikes against the introduction of welfare measures. Even modern day anarchists such as van der Walt and Schmidt argue the absurd proposition that: "Only laws forced on the state from without, by the direct action of the popular masses, could benefit the masses".[78] So a regular pension rise or the building of a new hospital or free child care does not benefit the masses?

Similarly, as noted previously, Proudhon opposed campaigns for the right to vote. This approach was maintained by considerable sections of the anarchist and anarcho-syndicalist movement for many decades after Proudhon's death. Prominent US Industrial Workers of the World (IWW) leaders like Elizabeth Gurley Flynn opposed the campaign for the right for women to vote, arguing that it was absolutely irrelevant for working-class women and a setback to the cause of working class liberation.[79] This approach simply abandoned the leadership of the US women's suffrage movement to bourgeois and middle-class forces who opposed militant working-class action and who sought to limit the campaign to demanding a restricted franchise – banning African Americans and poorer working-class women from voting.

Similarly, anarchist opposition to demanding the expansion of state health and welfare services only served to isolate them from the mass of workers who were vitally dependent on such reforms. This approach severely limited the ability of anarchists to challenge the hold of the reformist parties, which by way of contrast appeared to be delivering for workers.

In practice anarchists and anarcho-syndicalists had no serious operational strategy for undermining the hold of reformism politically. They had no transitional approach. They essentially just

---

77. van der Walt and Schmidt 2009, p.223.
78. van der Walt and Schmidt 2009, p.53.
79. Tax, pp.181–82.

stood on the sidelines denouncing the reformist leaders and were ignored by the bulk of working-class militants. Most anarchists and anarcho-syndicalists, for example, rejected as a point of principle the tactic of placing demands on reformists to deliver major reforms for workers, whereas for Marxists this was an important tactic for putting reformists to the test and exposing their shortcomings, if and when they fail to deliver.

The abstract anarchist shibboleth of opposition to every form of authority and hierarchy and all states ties in with a broader anti-politicism in anarchism. It leads to political abstentionism that abandons the field of struggle on vital political terrains to the liberals, populists and reformists. It just means that the reformist leaders go unchallenged by revolutionaries.

There is a general hostility by anarchists to standing in parliamentary elections, whereas Marxists see this as a vital arena for a mass socialist party to engage in political agitation, recruit to its ranks, gauge the level of support it has among workers and pose an alternative to the reformists. Then there is the anarchist hostility to anything approaching a united front, ie revolutionaries making demands on reformist leaders to engage in joint day-to-day struggle in defence of working-class living standards and democratic rights. For Marxists the united front is a vital means to advance working-class struggle and to show in practice the difference between a reformist and revolutionary approach to the defence of working-class interests and democratic rights. Then there is the example of Occupy Wall Street where the autonomist/anarchist leaders opposed the idea of raising any demands at all, which just let the ruling class off the hook, and led participants instead towards utopian ideas about building prefigurative communes.

Finally there is the hostility of anarchists to the whole idea of workers having their own political party, which for Marxists of course is a central question. The anarchist approach in reality involves a massive historical fudge. The fact that Bakunin formed his own political organisation/party – the Alliance – is conveniently denied by most anarchists. The Alliance was a secret conspiratorial and highly authoritarian organisation subject to Bakunin's personal dictatorial control.[80] As Bakunin put it, the Alliance was a "powerful but always invisible revolutionary association" that will "prepare and direct the revolution", "the invisible pilots guiding the Revolution...the collective dictatorship of all our allies".[81] Bakunin glorified the "secret organisation" that his friend and collaborator, the appalling murderer Nechaev supposedly led in Russia, as "a kind of general staff of the revolutionary army", "strong in the discipline, the passionate dedication, and the self-sacrifice of its members and unconditionally obedient to all the orders and directives of a single Committee that knew everyone, but was known to no one".[82] This is precisely the opposite of the sort of democratic mass working-class revolutionary party that Marxists aspire to build.

## So what is the Marxist alternative?

The starting point for Marxists is a concrete class analysis of society. Marxists recognise that the *only* force that has the power to overthrow capitalist rule and establish a genuinely democratic collective society is the working class. Marxists, unlike anarchists, do not start from some abstract principle of "individual autonomy". Human beings are not isolated discrete individuals but "social individuals" that engage in collective social labour and collective struggle. As Paul Blackledge writes:

> Marx does not deny the concept of human freedom... Indeed, the concept of human freedom is a major theme of both his early and mature work. Thus in the Grundrisse he defined freedom as a process through which "social individuals" come to realise themselves through their labours.[83]

Similarly, in *Capital* Marx argued:

> Freedom...can consist only in this, that socialised man, the

80. Mendel 1981.
81. van der Walt and Schmidt 2009, p.249.
82. Mendel 1981, p.335.
83. Blackledge 2008, p.135.

associated producers, govern the human metabolism with nature in a rational way, bringing it under their common control instead of being dominated by it as a blind power.[84]

To move down that road the working class must utilise its organised collective power to establish its own class rule. So socialists don't aim to "abolish authority" but rather to win the battle for democracy. Socialists fight to smash the undemocratic form of authority that currently exists under capitalism and replace it with a democratic alternative. As Marx and Engels put it:

> The abolition of the state has only one meaning for the Communists: it is the necessary result of the abolition of classes, whereupon of itself the need for the organised power of one class to suppress another ceases to exist.[85]

Socialists recognise that there is no reformist road to genuine democracy and human liberation. A working-class revolution is necessary both to break the power of the capitalist class and its state but also because it is in the course of collective revolutionary struggle that mass consciousness is fundamentally transformed and workers make themselves fit to rule a new socialist society.

Workers need to smash the existing state apparatus and establish their own state power based on their democratic organs of power – workers' councils. To lead that struggle and to have any hope of victory, the most politically advanced and class-conscious workers need to be organised in a disciplined, democratic revolutionary socialist party: a party that argues for a clear political direction, strategy and tactics to take the revolution forward; and that combats the reformist forces that will relentlessly attempt to derail mass revolts that challenge capitalism.

---

84.  Marx 1981, p.959.
85.  Marx and Engels 1978, p.333.

## References

*An Anarchist FAQ*. https://theanarchistlibrary.org/library/the-anarchist-faq-editorial-collective-an-anarchist-faq

Arblaster, Anthony 1971, "The Relevance of Anarchism", *Socialist Register 1971*, Merlin. http://socialistregister.com/index.php/srv/article/view/5336

Armstrong, Mick 2016, "Nestor Makhno: the failure of anarchism", *Marxist Left Review*, 12, Winter. https://marxistleftreview.org/articles/nestor-makhno-the-failure-of-anarchism/

Blackledge, Paul 2008, "Marxism and ethics", *International Socialism*, 120, Autumn. http://isj.org.uk/marxism-and-ethics/

Blackledge, Paul 2010, "Marxism and anarchism", *International Socialism*, 125, Winter. http://isj.org.uk/marxism-and-anarchism/

Brogan, DW 1934, *Proudhon*, Hamish Hamilton.

Carr, EH 1961, *Michael Bakunin*, Vintage.

Carter, April 1971, *The Political Theory of Anarchism*, Routledge & Kegan Paul.

Draper, Hal 1969, "A Note on the Father of Anarchism", *New Politics*, Vol. 8, No. 1, Winter. https://www.marxists.org/archive/draper/1969/father-anarchism.htm

Draper, Hal 1978, *Karl Marx's Theory of Revolution, Vol. II. The politics of social classes,* Monthly Review Press.

Draper, Hal 1990, *Karl Marx's Theory of Revolution, Vol. IV. Critique of other socialisms*, Monthly Review Press.

Garnham, Sarah 2021, "The failure of identity politics: A Marxist analysis", *Marxist Left Review*, 22, Winter. https://marxistleftreview.org/articles/the-failure-of-identity-politics-a-marxist-analysis/

Goldman, Emma et al 1907, "Anarchy and Organization: The Debate at the 1907 International Anarchist Congress". https://theanarchistlibrary.org/library/various-authors-anarchy-and-organization-the-debate-at-the-1907-international-anarchist-congres

Goldman, Emma 2017, *A Nearly Complete Collection of Emma Goldman's Writings*, compiled by DH Lewis. https://anarcho-copy.org/free/emma-goldman-nearly-complete.pdf

Graham, Robert n.d., *The General Idea of Proudhon's Revolution*. https://theanarchistlibrary.org/library/robert-graham-the-general-idea-of-proudhon-s-revolution

Guerin, Daniel 1970, *Anarchism*, Monthly Review Press.

Hyams, Edward 1979, *Pierre-Joseph Proudhon. His Revolutionary Life, Mind and Works*, Taplinger Publishing Company.

Kropotkin, Peter 1970, "Modern Science and Anarchism", *Kropotkin's Revolutionary Pamphlets: A Collection of Writings by Peter Kropotkin*, Roger Baldwin (ed.), Dover.

Marx, Karl 1976, "The Poverty of Philosophy. An Answer to the *Philosophy of Poverty* by M. Proudhon", *Collected Works*, Vol. 6, Lawrence and Wishart. https://www.marxists.org/archive/marx/works/1847/poverty-philosophy/

Marx, Karl and Frederick Engels 1978, *Collected Works*, Vol. 10, International Publishers.

Marx, Karl 1981, *Capital*, Vol. 3, Penguin.

McKay, Iain 2009, *Review: Proudhon's General Idea of the Revolution*. https://theanarchistlibrary.org/library/ anarcho-review-proudhon-s-general-idea-of-the-revolution

Mendel, Arthur P 1981, *Michael Bakunin. Roots of Apocalypse*, Praeger.

Proudhon, Pierre Joseph 1847, *On the Jews*. https://www.marxists.org/ reference/subject/economics/proudhon/1847/jews.htm

Pyziur, Eugene 1955, *The Doctrine of Anarchism of Michael A. Bakunin*, Gateway.

Skirda, Alexandre 2002, *Facing the Enemy. A History of Anarchist Organization from Proudhon to May 1968*, AK Press.

Stirner, Max 1844, *The Ego and His Own*. https://www.marxists.org/reference/ archive/stirner/ego-and-its-own.htm

Tax, Meredith 1980, *The Rising of the Women*, Monthly Review Press.

Trotsky, Leon, 1973, *The Spanish Revolution,* Pathfinder. www.marxists.org/ archive/trotsky/spain/index.htm

Van der Walt, Lucien and Michael Schmidt 2009, *Black Flame – The Revolutionary Class Politics of Anarchism and Syndicalism*, AK Press.

Walter, Nicolas 1969, "About Anarchism", *Anarchy*, Vol. 9, No. 6. https:// theanarchistlibrary.org/library/nicolas-walter-about-anarchism

Woodcock, George 1962, *Anarchism*, Penguin Books.

Woodcock, George 1987, *Proudhon*, Black Rose Books.

JOEL GEIER

# Trotskyism confronts World War II: The origins of the International Socialists

**Joel Geier**, a revolutionary Marxist activist for over six decades, has written extensively on economics, history and Marxist theory. He was a co-founder of the International Socialists (US) and is writing a history of the group, of which this article is one chapter.

THE INTERNATIONAL SOCIALIST TENDENCY came into existence in opposition to imperialist war, which is the acid test for revolutionary socialists. Imperialism and its wars defined twentieth century capitalism; they were the nemesis of the socialist movement, periodically shipwrecking it and forcing it to be rebuilt on stronger foundations.

The Socialist International collapsed in 1914 when its national parties betrayed working class internationalism and supported the imperialist aims of their national ruling classes in World War I. As Karl Kautsky justified it, "the International is for peace time".[1] Social democracy never looked back: from then on it always supported its ruling classes' wars. In the process, it was converted into a counter-revolutionary force that actively opposed every attempt at working-class power.

Anti-war socialists who paid the price in blood for this catastrophe drew the necessary conclusion that opposition to class collaboration and imperialism required the formation of independent revolutionary parties. The Communist International arose from the wreckage of pre-war socialism, grouping together anti-war and anti-imperialist socialists and syndicalists.

---

1. Riddell 1984, p.236.

In October of 1917, the Russian proletariat led by the Bolshevik party carried out the first successful socialist revolution in history. The establishment of the Russian workers' state touched off a world-wide revolutionary upsurge. Workers' councils appeared throughout Europe but eventually capitalist reaction succeeded in drowning socialist revolutions in Germany, Hungary and other countries.

A multinational coalition of imperialist powers invaded Russia to overthrow the workers' state, and to aid the White Russian counter-revolutionaries. They were defeated by the Red Army organised by Trotsky, but in the course of the civil war Russia was devastated; the socialist working class that made the revolution decimated and dispersed. The Bolsheviks, led by Lenin and Trotsky, using desperate, sometimes substitutionist means, struggled to preserve the integrity of the revolution, hoping that a German revolution would come to their aid. But after Lenin's death, a new ruling class emerged from the structure of the state bureaucracy itself, led by Joseph Stalin.

The rise of Stalinism in Russia transformed the new, revolutionary Communist parties into camp-followers of the Russian bureaucracy. During World War II, social democrats and Communists once again united, supporting the Allied camp and its imperialist aims.

The major opponent of social-patriotic support for imperialist war was an international movement founded by Trotsky. Known as the Fourth International, its goals were to overthrow the Stalinist bureaucracy and restore the Russian revolution, redeem or replace the Stalinist Third International, and lead a new world revolution to prevent or end World War II. But just as the outbreak of World War I triggered a profound crisis in the Second International, the outbreak of World War II touched off a crisis in Trotsky's newly formed network.

The Trotskyist movement was forced to confront unexpected political questions posed by a series of shocking, unforeseen events: the Hitler-Stalin Pact as the trigger for the outbreak of the war; the eruption of Stalinist imperialism in Eastern Europe; bureaucratic revolution in the newly conquered Eastern European countries, which destroyed the capitalist class, its private property and capitalist social relations of production, and in their place replicated the production forms and relations of Stalinist Russia, where the working class was exploited by the state bureaucracy.

A dissident section of the Trotskyist movement, responding to these developments, made a radical political re-evaluation that overcame Trotskyism's most profound political crisis with new theoretical breakthroughs. These wartime debates, which culminated in a split in the Fourth International and the formation of the Workers Party (later renamed the Independent Socialist League), laid the basis for the political ideas of the International Socialists (IS) of the United States of the 1960s and 1970s, and eventually to wider layers of the international left. From the Workers Party, the IS inherited the best of the Trotskyist revolutionary tradition, and programmatic continuity with the heritage of classical Marxism, Bolshevism, the Russian Revolution, the early Communist International, the 1920s American Communist Party and the Left Opposition.

With the outbreak of the Cold War – the third imperialist world conflict of the twentieth century – socialist and labour movements around the world were torn apart, weakened, debilitated, declined as independent forces, politically gutted by support for so-called "democratic" Washington or "workers'" Moscow. The most courageous rejectors of this capitulation were Third Camp socialists, who opposed all imperialism and both war camps – the only basis for an emancipatory, revolutionary policy in the imperialist epoch. Their political clarity arose from the fierce ideological struggle within the Trotskyist movement at the start of World War II. That history, largely unexplored, misrepresented or forgotten, continues as a guide to revolutionary resolve against imperialist war – and to socialist policy in general.

## The fork in the road

World War II shattered fundamental aspects of Trotskyism's assumptions by events whose possibility the theory had previously denied. Revolutionary Marxism faced a fork in the road. To remain true to its reason for being as the conscious expression of the unconscious striving of the working class for emancipation, it would have to overcome any weaknesses or errors that contradicted that aim. The new dynamics of class and world politics demanded changes to established but now outworn analysis. Unless Marxists corrected key programmatic and theoretical mistakes, made evident by the rapidly changing international situation, they would be hurled into confusion and error. Worse, traditional theories were now in conflict with Marxism's basic principles and program: the self-emancipation of the working class as the road to revolution, and working-class rule as the essential foundation of socialism.

It was not an accident that the Trotskyist movement was where politics that centred on workers' self-emancipation would reappear. Trotskyism was the living continuation of revolutionary Marxism in the 1920s and 1930s. While the movement was often small, isolated, marginalised, even at times sectarian, it had relentlessly fought for the defence of workers' democracy against the rise of the Stalinist bureaucracy, for world revolution against the nationalist theory of "socialism in one country", and against the destruction of the revolutionary communist parties by their subordination to the foreign policy needs of the Russian bureaucracy.

The Communist International of the 1920s had made important Marxist theoretical breakthroughs and innovations in analysis of world conditions and politics. The conformist authoritarianism of Stalinism wrecked theoretical thought with orders from above. It was in the Trotskyist movement that Marxist theory continued to develop. Trotsky's contributions represented the major Marxist advances of those years: the theory of permanent revolution and independent working-class organisation, applied to the Chinese revolution of 1925–27; the united front against fascism in Germany, counterposed to both social democratic lesser evilism and Stalinist Third Period "social fascism", which together greased the wheels for the Nazi rise to power; opposition to the Popular Front support for liberal capitalists, which reformists and Stalinists used to destroy the workers' revolution in Spain. These theoretical conquests, among others, continued to apply the programmatic ideas and methods of the pre-Stalinist Comintern.

In the United States, Trotskyism's greatest accomplishments were not limited to theory: Trotskyists led two of the three great strikes of 1934 that initiated the upheaval that organised industrial unionism. The merger of the Trotskyists and Musteites[2] – the leaders of the teamsters' and auto-lite general strikes respectively – into one revolutionary organisation was, as *The Militant* proudly headlined, "Minneapolis and Toledo Unite". This capable fusion of theory and practice allowed the Americans to become the largest, most important Trotskyist organisation in the 1930s. Its theoretical journal, *The New International*, became the organising centre for the Fourth International.

But these great achievements were not sufficient to prevent a crisis with the actual outbreak of war. To understand Trotskyism's most important theoretical upheaval, it is necessary to free the narrative from latter-day distortions and self-serving historical myths, by allies as well as opponents, and locate it in its contemporary context, examining the actual events and ideas in a world whose assumptions have long since disappeared, and their impact on the Communist and Trotskyist movements of that time.

## The Hitler-Stalin Pact launches World War II

World War II began on 1 September 1939, when Germany invaded Poland. Britain and France – Germany's rivals and Poland's allies – declared war, challenging Germany's growing domination over Europe. Germany's imperial goals made the Second World War inevitable. Like World War I before it, World War II was a struggle for the redivision of the world; Germany's expansionary aims – for "*Lebensraum*", the conquest of territory of previously independent European countries – were held back by the dominant imperialist powers, Britain in particular.

For months prior to the invasion, Hitler had been manoeuvring to gain Polish territory through diplomatic measures. He hoped to force through a repeat of the Munich appeasement policy, when the Western powers had sold out Czechoslovakia – thus postponing war for a few more years. But after Poland refused to agree to a German takeover of Danzig, Hitler unilaterally revoked the German-Polish Non-Aggression Pact in April 1939. If diplomacy would not gain Polish

---

2. The Communist League of America and the American Workers Party respectively; AJ Muste was the main leader of the latter.

territory, Hitler was prepared to gamble on immediate war. (Russia also had a Soviet-Polish Non-Aggression Pact, reaffirmed in 1938 to last through 1945.)

The central strategic military objective of Germany's war preparation was avoidance of a two-front war, in both Western and Eastern Europe, a major cause of Germany's World War I defeat. Lesson learned, the German foreign office and military high command pressed Hitler for a one-front war, as the plan with the most reasonable chance of success. Stalin came to their aid. The initial fulfilment of the one-front war strategy was made possible by the Stalinist bureaucracy's newly acquired imperialist ambitions. Only after he had the go-ahead from Stalin did Hitler launch the attack on Poland initiating World War II.

Just ten days before the war began, on 22–3 August 1939, Germany and Russia signed what for propaganda purposes was called a "non-aggression pact". In reality, this was a *mutual aggression pact*, which set the stage for the Second World War. The German war machine depended on Russia for critical logistical and material support. Russia supplied the crucial raw materials – oil, strategic minerals, and food – necessary for Germany's battle on the western front. The *quid pro quo* was Nazi support for Russia's invasion of Poland, followed by Estonia, Latvia, Lithuania, a part of Finland, and later Bessarabia and Bukovina from Romania. These Russian takeovers had the logistical advantage for Germany of safeguarding its rear, securing its borders in the east, north and north-east, which would be protected by its Russian ally. Germany was free to fight a one-front war in the west, winning the invasion and occupation of France, Belgium, Holland, Denmark and Norway.

The Hitler-Stalin Pact was indispensable to the initial German conquest of Western Europe. Russian support was a key to the early success of the Nazi war camp, which in return guaranteed the first stage of a new Russian imperialism, the seizure of eastern Poland and other parts of Eastern Europe. The same day that the Russians took Latvia, the Germans conquered Paris, and Molotov extended to the German ambassador "warmest congratulations...on the splendid success of the German armed forces".[3]

---

3.   Schulenburg 1940.

## Stalinist counter-revolution

The shocking eruption of Stalinist imperialism in collaboration with the Nazis caught the international left unprepared. There existed no such thing in the Marxist vocabulary as an imperialist workers' state. Russian imperialism developed rapidly following the bureaucratic consolidation that culminated with the Moscow purge trials of the 1930s. But when the war began, Marxist theory had not yet come to grips with the full implications of the Stalinist counter-revolution.

The Moscow Trials were the final act of the bureaucratic counter-revolution, a process that had been going on for more than a decade. The purges wiped out the entire generation of surviving Bolsheviks, including almost all of the original Stalinist faction. Bourgeois historians argue that it was the Bolshevik Party that created Stalinism, when in reality Stalinism could only triumph by destroying the remains of the Bolshevik Party, already distorted and crippled during the degeneration of the Revolution. The Party, despite its corrosion, was the last vestige of the Russian Revolution, the final remaining political structure of the Russian worker's state. It was the last surviving link to workers' rule.

The destruction of the Bolshevik Party removed the last obstacle to the bureaucracy's consolidation of its class rule, and was the necessary prelude to the bureaucracy's imperialist drive. As usual, consciousness and theory lagged behind these changing conditions. But events would soon fatally undermine the beliefs of millions of Communists, and highlight a basic flaw of Trotsky's analysis of the Stalinist state – in particular, the proposition that nationalised property was enough to determine that the working class continued to be the ruling class.

## "Fascism is a matter of taste"

The Moscow Trials' main allegation was that Lenin's revolutionary associates were agents and spies for Hitler. Communist Party members defended the indefensible: the hallucinatory accusation that those who had made the revolution, including Trotsky, were fascist agents who should be sentenced to death. Communists were forced to parrot a party line that would soon require a total somersault.

Just one year after the last trial of "fascist fifth columnists", it was the Stalinists who were now allies of the Nazis. This collaboration was grotesquely conveyed when swastika flags graced Moscow streets to welcome the Nazi negotiators for the Hitler-Stalin Pact – and Russian foreign minister Vyacheslav Molotov proclaimed at the Pact's signing: "Fascism is a matter of taste",[4] while Stalin toasted Hitler: "I know how much the German nation loves its Fuehrer".[5]

The two years of the Pact witnessed unimaginable crimes of Stalinist treachery and collaboration with fascism. One of its low points was Stalin's turning over to the Gestapo of 800 German Communists, including Jews, who had sought refuge in Russia. In occupied France, the CP originally tried to collaborate with the Vichy puppet government as a loyal opposition. In Germany, the Pact led to the demoralised collapse of the underground Communist resistance.

## Popular Front and collective security

The Hitler-Stalin Pact created unprecedented upheaval in the world Communist movement. In the late 1930s, Communist activity focused on domestic anti-fascist struggle – the Peoples' Front – and the foreign policy of collective security, to protect Russia from the war threat of a rising Germany and its fascist allies. Because of the international prestige of the Communist parties as the heirs of the Russian Revolution these policies dominated the left of the 1930s. The Nazi-Soviet Pact overturned these two pillars of Communist policy.

"Collective security" was Russia's foreign policy strategy of forming military agreements with any capitalist country opposed to Nazi Germany. Local Communist parties were used as one of the bargaining chips for collaboration with domestic ruling classes. Capitalist governments that formed an alliance with Russia could count on domestic support from Moscow's agents, the local Communist Party, as part of a "Popular Front" policy. This collaboration could provide significant protection for bourgeois governments during the 1930s depression years of working-class ferment and revolutionary upheavals. In America, the CP helped channel the radical working-class upsurge into

---

4.   Sheen 1948, p.115.
5.   *The Militant* 1948, p.3.

an alliance with the "progressive" section of the capitalist class, represented by Franklin Delano Roosevelt's Democratic Party. This policy of subordination to liberal capitalist politics continues to corrupt and weaken the American left today.

The worst crimes of the misnamed "popular front against fascism" were those carried out in revolutionary Spain. In the battle that raged behind Republican lines during the Civil War, the Spanish CP provided the political muscle to destroy the ongoing working-class revolution. This betrayal proved Moscow's usefulness to its capitalist allies; in the name of anti-fascism and Western unity, Moscow proved that it could deliver its native agents to put down any attempt at working-class socialist revolution.

## The missed opportunity

The policy eroded the Communist Party's standing among its many left sympathisers, on whom they previously relied to staff their social, cultural and political mass organisations. The CP had previously been successful in convincing these fellow travellers – trade unionists, social democrats and liberals – that progressives had to justify, apologise for, and rationalise away all the crimes of the Russia camp. But an alliance with Hitler was a bridge too far. Never again did the American CP create mass organisations with the same substantial non-Communist popular support.

The Hitler-Stalin Pact also crushed the faith of many Communist militants whose political lives were dedicated to the struggle against fascism. Communist Party membership (including members of the Young Communist League) peaked in 1939, at between 80–100,000. Membership loss after the Pact was greatest among immigrant workers from the countries Russia invaded. Steep losses occurred among Finnish and Latvian workers, two of the most important ethnic groups of the 1920s Communist Party. Among Polish workers, the backbone of the Detroit auto sit-down strikes and factory occupations, losses prevented the CP from ever regaining its pre-Pact strength in the United Auto Workers, the most important CIO union. Large numbers of Jewish workers, for generations the stronghold of the left and the CP, quit as "Jewish Communists in New York City's garment districts were met with derisive greetings of 'Heil Hitler'".[6] But the CP leadership dismissed it all, and continued to demand loyalty to the Moscow leadership.

The Hitler-Stalin Pact presented American Trotskyism with its greatest opportunity to break out of its isolation and to reach these confused radicals. The Communist Party had overwhelming hegemony over the left, through its heroic accomplishments in the industrial union upsurge of the CIO, and in the fight against Jim Crow racism. The CP used this power to impose upon most of the left the political perspective that Trotskyists were "fascists, mad dogs" who had to be isolated; they could not be allowed to participate or collaborate in any left activity, a practice the CP would try to maintain until 1956.

But with the Party's ideological and organisational disarray following the Hitler-Stalin Pact, its membership and periphery were open as never before to the critical arguments of Trotskyism. The Pact confirmed every charge Trotskyists had made about Stalinism: unprincipled, opportunistic, anti-socialist, counter-revolutionary, totalitarian; popular front and collective security policies were incapable of preventing another world war. The Pact verified Trotsky's contention that the world Communist parties – all of whom supported the Pact – were not independent revolutionary workers' parties, but had been transformed from revolutionary working-class vanguards into border guards of the Stalinist bureaucracy.

Tragically, this once-in-a-generation opportunity to overcome Stalinist hegemony, to win over CP militants or sympathisers was absolutely lost. The Trotskyist movement was paralysed, politically incoherent, incapable of action, "asleep at the wheel", as one of its leaders said. It could play no role, and gain no advantage, in the greatest political crisis the CP had until then experienced. The Pact, the invasion of Poland and subsequent events tossed the Trotskyist movement into convulsive shock, its internal disorientation and ideological disarray as deep as that of the Communist Party. Its political positions were as unprepared for these events as those of the CP. Without an effective alternative the momentarily diminished CP was able to maintain its dominance. The greatest opening in radical politics was missed due to

---

6.   Isserman 1982, p.35.

internal confusion, incompetence, paralysis. It wasn't until 1956, when the Hungarian Revolution led to the collapse of the CP, that another opening emerged for the emergence of a new revolutionary left.

## The crisis of Trotskyism

The Pact itself had not come as a complete surprise to the Trotskyist movement. A Russian-German alliance had been predicted by perceptive observers, foreign diplomatic services, newspaper correspondents, and most notably Trotsky, as a logical outcome of Munich. It was clear that after the Western powers abandoned Czechoslovakia that "collective security" was not a believable guarantee, if it ever had been, that the Allies would come to Russia's defence in the event of German attack. Russia could therefore be expected to move to defend itself from attack through some sort of accommodation with Germany.

Such an accommodation had been foreseen and accepted in the movement; revolutionaries did not view a defensive agreement with German imperialism, however repulsive, as being qualitatively different from similar pacts with the bourgeois democratic imperialist powers. Russia had signed a conventional non-aggression pact with Germany in 1926, which Hitler had endorsed after the Nazis took power; strengthening of that pact of 1926 would have been acceptable to the revolutionary left.

What was not foreseen or allowed for in the past, as Trotsky himself acknowledged, was the unprecedented content of, and actions flowing from, the new Pact of 1939, which fatally undermined traditional perspectives on Russia's relationship to the war, imperialism and proletarian revolution. For the Hitler-Stalin agreement, as delineated in its secret protocols, was not a defensive accommodation with Germany to prevent war, but an *imperialist aggression pact*, for the carve-up of Poland, for division of Europe, for conquest, for spheres of influence, for mutual material support and collaboration in World War II.

After the German armies marched into western Poland, the Germans pressed Stalin to move. Sixteen days later, Russia declared war against Poland, and its armies advanced into eastern Poland. The two armies met, celebrated together and divided the country. German generals actually complained bitterly as they were ordered to retreat from areas they had already conquered with casualties, in order to give Stalin his share of the loot.

Poland was conquered and divided by Hitler and Stalin – by the Nazis and by what Trotskyist theory still misguidedly labelled a "workers' state". All class-conscious workers, they declared, had to defend this "workers' state" in its war. This meant they had to defend Russia's imperialist military invasion and conquest of the Polish people, in collaboration with the Nazis. Polish workers were called upon to greet and provide support to the Russian invaders. Those who refused to fight for the invasion while it was going on, charged Trotsky, were "petty bourgeois" – an alien class element, capitulating to the pressure of bourgeois public opinion.

Trotskyism's crisis was that the actual events resulting from the Pact wreaked havoc with its pre-war assumptions. In responding, and in failing to respond, to changing events, official Trotskyism ended up refuting its own fundamental programmatic views on World War II, imperialism, national self-determination, the meaning of proletarian revolution, and ultimately, the question of whether the working class was even necessary for socialist revolution or for working-class rule. Changing objective conditions overwhelmed outworn theory with its unresolvable contradictions. Weak theoretical ideas proved incapable of providing revolutionary guidance for the new questions posed by the war. The traditional theories had been accepted for years because, until then, they had provided the strongest, clearest analysis and revolutionary understanding of the Stalinist bureaucracy, its rise, and the degeneration of the Russian Revolution. Now the altered world situation required overcoming their limitations and contradictions.

## Trotskyists split

The immediate question posed by the Russian invasion of Poland was what position revolutionary internationalists should take on this actual, existing war – and not some hypothetical, future war in which Trotsky and his followers expected all of the capitalist powers, Britain as well as Germany, to unite against the Russian workers' state – a reprise of the invasion of Russia following the 1917 Revolution by a coalition of 14 nations, including the United States. The traditional Trotskyist position called for the unconditional defence of the Soviet Union against an imperialist attack. But in this war, there was no imperialist attack on Russia. Instead, the Soviet Union, as an ally of one of the imperialist camps, initiated the attack, conquest and occupation of other countries, and gave Hitler the ability to start World War II. Russia was collaborating with Nazi Germany for mutual imperialist gain.

As we have seen, Russia's invasion of Poland was quickly followed by attacks on Finland, Lithuania, Latvia, Estonia, Bessarabia and Bukovina. It was opposition to support for Russia in these ongoing imperialist wars – opposition to calling upon workers of these countries to support and give material aid to the Russian invasion – that unleashed the fight inside the Trotskyist movement and gave birth to the origins of the International Socialist viewpoint.

The ideological struggle surrounding that birth was prolonged. It took up all of the immediate theoretical and practical questions, as well as – like most faction fights, unfortunately – extraneous political and personal issues of little lasting substance. Trotsky, with his immense authority, political brilliance, Marxist erudition and outstanding revolutionary practice, dominated the debate. He wrote all the political documents for the majority, while the confused, theoretically inadequate Cannon leadership of the American Socialist Workers Party (SWP) was reduced in practice to being "a mimeographing machine for Trotsky's articles and letters".[7]

But Trotsky's old positions, however brilliantly they had served an earlier period, were now woefully inadequate. Objective events revealed their errors and weaknesses, and demanded that these be corrected. Unfortunately, as Trotsky tried vigorously to defend old orthodoxy, he proved for the most part unable, or unwilling, to immediately rise to the new occasion, and instead became entangled in the contradictions of old tenets. Great people when they make mistakes make great mistakes; smaller minded critics will often use this to try to discredit their much more important great work. Trotsky was murdered by a Stalinist agent a year later, and one only can

---

7.  Shachtman 1954.

speculate and hope that Trotsky would have eventually overcome his initial mistakes – particularly since, under the pressure of the opposition, some of the new theoretical ideas he suggested during the fight might have led him to better future outcomes. The experience of his widow, Natalia Sedova,[8] and others who initially supported him changing their views following the experience of World War II, suggests such a break was at least possible.

But the struggle against wartime support for imperialist Russia was led by the American SWP opposition, which after its eventual expulsion, constituted itself as the Workers Party. Its most well-known founding personalities were Max Shachtman, Hal Draper, CLR James, Martin Abern, Ernest Rice McKinney, Al Glotzer, Joseph Carter, Raya Dunayevskaya, TN Vance, Anne Draper, Ernest Erber, Mary Bell, Carlo, Dwight MacDonald, Nathan Gould, Saul Mendelson, Irving Howe, Saul Bellow, Susan Green, Grace Lee Boggs, Julius Jacobson, Phyllis Jacobson, BJ Widick, Art Fox and more. In a few short years they produced an enormous quantity of remarkable intellectual achievements, creative Marxism, theoretical leaps – an explosion of theoretical advances and innovations that would present a world view that remained intact and relevant for decades. The core political principles and world view of the endeavour would congeal as International Socialism: "Neither Washington nor Moscow"; socialism from below; self-emancipation of the working class as the only road to socialist revolution; workers' economic and political control as the defining core of what constitutes a workers' state; the difference between property forms and property relations; the bureaucratic class nature of Stalinism; its imperialist dynamic; and the contradictions that would eventually lead to social and national revolutions against it.

To develop these views, the Workers Party had to reaffirm revolutionary Marxist theory to a world situation that now included Stalinist imperialism and bureaucratic revolution, and its relationship to previous Marxist theory on questions of war, imperialism and national self-determination.

Many subsequent accounts of the Workers Party's ideological fight

---

8.   See Sedova Trotsky 1951, p.3.

inaccurately present the central issue as *the class nature of Russia* – rather than the true core question, *the war and Russia's role in the war*. This approach is particularly common in those "orthodox Trotskyist" accounts that are retrospectively reluctant or embarrassed to admit to continued defence of Russia's invasion and occupation of Poland and Eastern Europe. They try to airbrush away these politics with the assertion, through ignorance or malice or both, that Trotsky led a heroic fight against deserters who refused to defend the "workers' state" from imperialist attack. Unfortunately, the British Socialist Workers Party has also presented historically inaccurate accounts of this split, distorting the real history to present these questions as only having emerged after World War II – when every literate Trotskyist knows the history of this fight of 1939–40. The British SWP tried to create a *cordon sanitaire* between their international tendency and the innovations of the Workers Party in which so much of their own political views originated; it was a sectarian approach that allowed them to present themselves as the sole source of IS theory.

At the same time, while the debate raged over the central issue of war policy, it could not avoid the new light that Stalinist imperialism shed on the class nature of the Russian state. The opposition was unified on the question of the war and the political conclusions to be drawn from that, but did not start with a unified or fully worked-out position on the class character of Stalinism. It explicitly chose to postpone internal discussions on that question in order to concentrate its fight on the more immediate issue of the war. Nonetheless the war raised questions revealing the inadequacies of the old theory. How could a workers' state play such a reactionary role? Either the new states identical to Russia were workers' states, or Russia was not a workers' state. Could workers' states emerge from invasion, conquest, occupation and bureaucratic social transformation? Was the Russian army the vehicle for working-class liberation? If so, what of basic theories like self-emancipation? What about the counter-revolutionary nature of Stalinism? In the next few years, these questions would lead to two analyses of the nature of Stalinism. The majority, headed up by Shachtman, Carter, Draper and others, argued it was bureaucratic collectivism, neither capitalist nor socialist, but a new form of class society. A minority led by CLR James,

Raya Dunayevskaya and Grace Lee Boggs, argued instead that it was state capitalism.

Trotsky was the greatest fighter against the rise of Stalinism. Many of the contradictions and errors in his positions were political baggage he carried over from the prolonged process of the degeneration of the Russian Revolution – the mindsets, ideas, struggles, frames of reference and tempo developed during the process of the loss of workers' power in the first workers' state. Trotsky had been the main organiser of the fight for workers' democracy against the rising bureaucracy. In doing so, he had always placed events in their moment, in the context of what stage of degeneration had been reached, as the bureaucracy advanced and workers' democracy atrophied, and what remained of the revolution's gains – which eventually were reduced to state nationalisation of the land, the means of production and the monopoly of foreign trade.

But recent events had shown that it was necessary to bring revolutionary Marxist theory up to date, to adapt it to qualitatively different conditions. That Trotsky failed to do so is tragic, but not all of those he educated and trained failed this test.

In regenerating its theory for an entirely new, changed world situation, the Workers Party attempted to draw upon the theoretical heritage of the Bolshevik Party and of the Comintern prior to the rise of Stalinism. One of Lenin's greatest contributions had been to revise Marxism for the era of imperialism, and to cleanse it of the reformist overlay developed in the period of the Second International. Now, the Workers Party saw that its task was to revise Marxism for a period in which imperialist conflict included the new phenomena of Stalinism and bureaucratic revolution, and to cleanse revolutionary theory not only from reformism but also from the overlay distorted by the years of degeneration of the Russian Revolution and the Comintern.

## Russian imperialism

In the real, existing imperialist war confronting the left, Stalinist imperialism, like all imperialism, denied self-determination to the weaker countries it conquered. As Russia occupied the newly conquered countries, the Stalinist bureaucracy nationalised the land, the means of production and the means of exchange. It eliminated the private ownership of capital, destroyed the entire capitalist class and transformed capitalist social relations into those identical to Russia's. It carried out a bureaucratic social revolution in the occupied countries – without the working class, against the working class, and in the face of working-class opposition. Trotsky, in an uncharacteristic mixture of fantasy, ignorance and confusion, proclaimed that workers and peasants in Poland and Finland were welcoming the Russian army, rising up and taking over the land, and with Russian support establishing workers' control in the factories.

These events, and the response of orthodox Trotskyists to them, altered and destroyed many of the theoretical foundations of 1930s Trotskyism. Without fundamental revision of their view of the Soviet state, orthodox Trotskyists were led from blunder to blind error and finally to theoretical shipwreck.

The first casualty was the movement's traditional policy of the unconditional defence of the Soviet Union against imperialist attack. Orthodox Trotskyists of a later period were taught that Russian defence was a fundamental component of the revolutionary program that separated Trotskyists from reformists. Worse, any opposition objecting to defence of Russia constituted an alien class element – with sometimes the added slander that those who didn't defend Russia were traitors, and really supporters of capitalist imperialism: if you didn't support Moscow you must be "objectively" supporting its rival camp, American capitalist imperialism. In actuality, in the 1920s and 1930s, Trotskyism shared Russian defencism with almost the entire left – the official Communist parties, communist dissident groups (Lovestoneites, Brandlerites, etc), and many social democratic and labour parties. Even Norman Thomas' reformist Socialist Party called for the unconditional defence of the Soviet Union. What differentiated social democrats, Communists and Trotskyists prior to World War II were questions of proletarian revolution, internationalism and workers' democracy – not Russian defencism.

The motivation given for the Russian defence slogan was that all workers had an obligation to defend the only surviving victory of the European proletarian revolution of 1917–23, which continued to maintain the gains of the October Revolution. Any war which Russia took part in was therefore, *ipso facto*, a progressive war. Further, in the last analysis, it was argued, the real struggle in the world was between capitalism and "socialist Russia". Whatever temporary divisions existed between the capitalist powers, Trotskyism held, would eventually be overcome by capitalist class unity. At that point, the capitalist powers would all unite to carry out a joint imperialist attack on Russia – just as the US and 13 other nations had done in 1918, when together they had launched an invasion in a failed attempt to overthrow the Bolshevik Revolution.

## Bonapartism and workers' democracy

Theory was further confused by Trotsky's lack of clarity on the relationship of workers' democracy to workers' rule. This weakness was ironic, since Trotskyism had organised the fight for workers' democracy against the rising bureaucracy in Russia. But the Trotskyists' Achilles heel was their belief that Russia remained a workers' state, despite its degeneration, because the bureaucracy was "forced by working class pressure" to defend the remaining gains of the revolution: nationalisation of the means of production, exchange and the land, and the monopoly on foreign trade. Trotsky argued that preservation of nationalised property created by the revolution meant that the working class remained the ruling class.

According to Trotsky, the Stalinist bureaucracy had usurped all of the political power and control of the working class; politically the Russian government was totalitarian, with similarities to fascism. But he continued to hold to the idea that it retained the economic foundations and property relations resulting from the revolution. The economy, however bureaucratically distorted, remained socialistic in character. The bureaucracy, he believed, was a policeman in the process of goods distribution, not locating its primary role in the process of production. Trotsky accepted Stalinist claims that a command economy was a planned economy, and that it escaped the crises of anarchic capitalism; the contradiction between bureaucratic command and real planning took decades to become fully apparent, with the economic stagnation and collapse of the USSR. In the 1930s, its rapid growth seemed to proved that state nationalisation was more efficient and more progressive, and historically superior to, crisis-ridden, stagnant, and decaying capitalism. As such, it had to be protected against possible capitalist restoration.

Trotsky thought that the Stalinist bureaucracy's rule was a form of Bonapartism, analogous to the regime first set up by Napoleon in the conservative reaction that followed the French Revolution. In form, Bonapartist regimes appear to stand above and restrain potentially destructive class struggle, by imposing a dictatorship that dispossesses all classes of political power. Yet in content, the Bonapartist state serves ultimately as an instrument of the dominant, ruling class, because it preserves the latter's property relations, and consequently, its economic and social power. Similarly, Trotsky believed, the Stalinist bureaucracy was not an independent class. Like all other state bureaucracies, it served a ruling class – in his theory, the working class. Since under Stalinism the bureaucracy defends the property form of nationalised property, which proletarian socialism does as well, Trotsky argued that the working class remains the ruling class despite being dispossessed of all political control and power.

The confused Bonapartist analogy had arisen during the prolonged process of degeneration of the Russian Revolution, as Bolsheviks made analogies between the process they were going through and the stages of decline of the French Revolution. As the bureaucracy advanced, and workers' democracy atrophied, it was believed that the gains of the revolution still remained because of the maintenance of nationalised property. But the events of World War II clarified the implications of this historical analogy, revealing it to be an obstacle to understanding the difference between capitalist and working-class rule. Extending it to the bureaucratic revolution in the newly conquered countries could only lead to reactionary conclusions. Bonapartism can exist under capitalism, but not under socialism.

Capitalism can flourish with or without political democracy. Capitalists can be the dominant class despite having no direct political control, so long as capitalist private ownership of the means of production and exchange – capitalist property relations – are defended and can develop as the dominant mode of production. Capital's rule is exercised through its economic power, not political control – desirable as the latter may be from a capitalist point of view. No other class system has had such a sharp separation between politics and economics. Capitalists can and have existed as the ruling class under diverse political systems – absolute monarchy, republic, democracy, military dictatorship, fascism, welfare state – few of which include its direct political power.

The working class, and a workers' state, as the Workers Party came to understand, is entirely different. Because it is not a property-owning class, the working class can come to economic power, and maintain it, *only* by wielding political power. Workers' only method of rule is through collective political control of the economy and a state, which is the repository of nationalised property, through some form of workers' democracy. Democracy is not a desirable addition or optional feature under socialism, as it is under capitalism. Socialism, the class rule of the working class, cannot exist without workers' democracy. Workers' democracy – workers' political rule – is indispensable to workers' power and workers' economic rule. As the *Communist Manifesto* proclaimed, "the first step in the revolution by the working class is to raise the proletariat to the position of ruling class, to win the battle of democracy...to centralise all instruments of production in the hands of the State, i.e., of the proletariat organised as the ruling class".[9]

The working class ruled Russia during the revolution, the civil war and the degeneration of the revolution – through the political institutions of the workers' state, soviets, unions, factory committees, workers' control of production, the armed militia, and the Bolshevik Party – however attenuated its rule became. The loss of all working-class political power and control marked the qualitative class difference between the degenerating revolution of the 1920s and the consolidated class rule of the Stalinist bureaucracy in the 1930s. The loss of working-class political power meant the loss of its economic power, and so the loss of its position as ruling class. Politics and economics are fused in a workers' state, an idea which became confused in the long drawn out process of degeneration and bureaucratic counter-revolution in Russia.

---

9.   Marx and Engels 1969, p.26.

The faulty logic of Trotsky's opposite theory, of working class as ruling class with no economic or political control, identified the dictatorship of the Russian proletariat with the dictatorship of the Stalinist bureaucracy. Dictatorship, in this Marxist use of the term, means class domination, with the interests of all other classes subordinated to the interests of the dominant class. Bourgeois democracy by this definition is one of the forms of the dictatorship of the bourgeoisie. Similarly, the dictatorship of the proletariat simply means workers' democracy, workers' power, a workers' state, the rule of the working class. The fetish of nationalised property separated from who controlled it, the confusion of property forms and property relations, led Trotsky to the dead-end conclusion that "the social content of the dictatorship of the bureaucracy" was determined by

> those productive relations that were created by the proletarian revolution. In that sense we may say with complete justification that the dictatorship of the proletariat found its distorted but indubitable expression in the dictatorship of the bureaucracy.[10]

This incredible theoretical muddle led those who maintained it to destructive conclusions for Marxism – from the repudiation of its fundamental programmatic foundations, the idea that socialism is the self-emancipation of the proletariat, to the conclusion that socialist revolution could be achieved without the working class, through in Trotsky's words, "bureaucratic, military means".

## Stalinist counter-revolution and socialism from below

The Hitler-Stalin Pact fatally undermined yet another fundamental tenet of pre-war Trotskyism: that Stalinism was defined by the policy of "socialism in one country". The original two pillars of the platform of the Left Opposition were *world revolution vs. socialism in one country* and *workers' democracy vs. the bureaucracy*. Russian conquest of much of Eastern Europe, followed by the imposition of what Trotskyists concluded were several "workers' states" within it,

---

10.  Trotsky 1935.

destroyed the pre-war view of Stalinism as characterised by "socialism in one country".

"Socialism in one country" was a policy derived from the 1920s, when Stalin had overturned the perspective on which the October Revolution had been carried out: where Bolshevik leaders insisted that the seizure of state power by the working class in economically backward Russia could only start the process of socialist transition. The future of the Russian Revolution would depend upon the success of a European-wide proletarian socialist revolution. Without revolutionary socialist aid from the industrialised countries, Russia could not survive.

But after the defeat of the German Revolution in 1923, the rising apparatus, the conservative Russian bureaucracy and its leader, Stalin, changed course. Backtracking from the policy of world revolution, they proclaimed that socialism *could* be built in one country – Russia – in the midst of a capitalist world. To justify this new doctrine, Stalin proclaimed that "We desire no foreign land, but we shall not surrender a single inch of our own land to any one.".[11]

In the 1930s, Stalin's betrayal of the Spanish Revolution would convince Trotsky that socialism in one country meant socialism nowhere else, that working class power anywhere was a threat to the Stalinist bureaucracy's continued rule. Trotsky's conclusion then became that the bureaucracy was counter-revolutionary, incapable of carrying out a social revolution. But at the start of World War II, like it or not, the Stalinist bureaucracy carried through in the conquered countries what Marxism had always classified as a social revolution – destruction of the capitalist class by expropriation of its private ownership of the means of production – and established identical social, political and economic relations to those existing in Russia. In class terms, therefore, Trotsky reluctantly concluded that a proletarian socialist revolution had taken place, through " in a military bureaucratic fashion".[12]

The conclusion that there existed a proletarian socialist revolution in Eastern Europe forever destroyed two of Trotsky's

---

11. Litvinov 1933.
12. Trotsky 1939.

fundamental assumptions: that "socialism in one country", touted by the bureaucracy, could not succeed; and that the counter-revolutionary bureaucracy was incapable of carrying through a social revolution. Instead, Trotsky's theory now became mystified into a concept he described as a "counter-revolutionary workers' state",[13] created by a proletarian social revolution carried out from above.

The primary justification Trotsky had given for the creation of a new revolutionary Fourth International – despite its participation by only tiny groups without mass working-class support – was that the mass Communist parties were no longer revolutionary forces but had instead become reformist and counter-revolutionary parties that would always capitulate to capitalism and would never carry through a socialist revolution. Now, the Stalinist occupations and conquests, followed by bureaucratic revolutions establishing property and social relations identical to those of the Russian "workers' state", posed an inescapable contradiction: either these newly conquered countries were also workers' states, or Russia was no longer a workers' state.

If the answer was that the nationalisation of property made Poland, Estonia, Latvia, Lithuania, etc, workers' states, then the inevitable conclusion was that workers' states could arise without a working-class revolution, without the self-emancipation of the working class. To hold to the old theory of Russia as a degenerated workers' state meant that *the working class was not necessary for socialist revolution* – that the bureaucracy could, however poorly, do the job. Working-class revolution, the raising of the working class to the position of ruling class, could be accomplished without the working class – indeed, even against it – and likewise, of course, without a revolutionary party or International.

Holding to the concept that nationalised property alone was sufficient to constitute a workers' state, Trotsky concluded that in Poland, the bureaucracy gave "an impulse to the socialist revolution through bureaucratic methods".[14] Shachtman, speaking for the opposition,

---

13.  Trotsky 1973, p.25.
14.  Trotsky 1973, p.56.

counterposed what Hal Draper was later to define and develop as "socialism from below":

> Here again, I find myself compelled to disagree with you. The bureaucratic bourgeois revolution – that I know of. I know of Napoleon's "revolution from above" in Poland over a hundred years ago. I know of Alexander's emancipation of the serfs "from above" – out of fear of peasant uprisings. I know of Bismarck's "revolution from above"... But the bureaucratic proletarian revolution – that I do not know and I do not believe in it. I do not believe that it took place in Poland even for a day – or that it is taking place or is about to take place in Finland...
>
> I find even less for your...astonishing remarks about Finland... that "the Red Army in Finland...introduces workers' control"...
>
> There is no trace of workers' control in the Soviet Union itself, there is even less than that in Finland...
>
> I repeat, I do not believe in the bureaucratic proletarian (socialist) revolution... I do not consider it possible. I reject the concept not out of "sentimental" reasons or a Tolstoyan "faith in the people" but because I believe it is to be scientifically correct to repeat with Marx that the emancipation of the working class is the task of the working class itself. The bourgeois revolution, for a series of historical and social reasons, can be made and was made by other social classes and social strata; the bourgeoisie could be liberated from feudal rule and establish its social dictatorship under the aegis of other social groups. But the proletarian revolution cannot be made by other than the proletariat acting as a mass; therein, among other things, it is distinguished from all preceding revolutions. No one else can free it – not even for a day.[15]

It was this reframing of the self-emancipation of the working class as the key to socialism that is the core of International Socialist politics.

---

15.  Shachtman 1940a.

## Marxism and war

In rigorously confronting the nature of the war, and the questions which arose as the war developed, the Workers Party produced a rich body of Marxist theory on war, imperialism, resistance movements and self-determination. It revived and built upon its point of departure – the body of revolutionary theory developed in World War I by Lenin, Zinoviev, Luxemburg, Trotsky and other revolutionary internationalists. Marxism argues that no single abstract, ahistorical position can encompass all wars – some wars are reactionary, others are progressive. Each has to be analysed separately and concretely, on its political dynamics – which include its economic, social and class attributes.

The starting point for Marxist approach to war is Clausewitz's famous proposition: "War is the continuation of politics by other, forcible means". A revolutionary socialist's attitude to any war is determined by our assessment of the politics of that war, particularly the policies of the ruling classes carrying out those wars, who attempt to identify their class interests as national interests. Revolutionary Marxists determine our position based upon the politics, as Lenin repeatedly emphasised, of *all* the belligerents, not just the politics of one of them. If, before the outbreak of war, we support the politics of any of the belligerents as just and progressive, and those politics subsequently lead to the use of forcible means, then – not being pacifists – we continue our support when the question becomes armed conflict, a war for those politics. If, by contrast, we are opposed to those politics, then – not being social patriots – we do not change our views when those politics lead to war. This is the key to developing a Marxist position on each concrete war, particularly in the era of imperialism.

World War II began not with an imperialist attack against Russia, but with Russia collaborating with Nazi Germany in an imperialist attack on Poland, followed by Russia's further imperialist conquest of Eastern Europe. At a minimum, this Russian expansionism required an examination by the left of how these new conditions fit, and what changes were needed in, the traditional socialist slogan of unconditional defence of the Soviet Union against imperialist attack. The untenable contradiction between defence *against* imperialism, and the defence of Russia as it *engaged in* imperialism, led Trotsky to shift the grounds for support – from defence against imperialist attack to support based, quite simply, on the nature of the Russian state.

Trotsky was opposed to the Russian invasions. But since he clung to the view that Russia was a workers' state, he concluded that the nature of the state required support for Russia in the war, *whether or not* Russia was being attacked. This retreat from Marxist war methodology rendered irrelevant any political analysis of any particular war in which Russia engaged; it dispensed with the traditional concrete Marxist determination of whether any given war is just or unjust, progressive or reactionary – and therefore worthy of support or opposition. If the nature of the state, as Trotsky maintained, is the sole criterion for determining support or opposition, then it is not necessary to examine the politics of the actual war, because the nature of the state usually stays the same for whole historic epochs. (The nature of the state, of course, reveals some of the politics – in particular, who is the ruling class and what are their class interests and policy.)

Marxist analysis should have led to the conclusion that Soviet workers had no class interest in attacking Poland, or in taking over Lithuania and the other Eastern European countries. The war had been organised by the Stalinist bureaucracy for its own interests, its own power and privileges – not for the interests of the working class. Instead, argued the opposition, by clinging to Russian defencism, Trotsky's position was a retreat from a materialist, Marxist attitude to war. "The conception that since nationalized property is 'progressive by its very nature' a regime based upon it must automatically be fighting a progressive war…is nothing but a variety of immanent idealism."[16]

The confusion of the Trotskyist movement extended to other war questions. For example, the American SWP correctly opposed America's entry into World War II, but on grounds that "[n]o imperialist regime can conduct a just war". That assertion is generally, but

---

16.  Shachtman 1940b.

not always, true. The Spanish Republic in the 1930s was an imperialist state. It had colonies in Morocco and Northern Africa. One reason it lost the war to Franco's fascists was that it refused to grant self-determination to Morocco, from where many of Franco's troops were recruited; had the Republic granted Moroccan independence, Franco's army could have disintegrated. Nonetheless, revolutionaries critically supported the imperialist Republic in the Spanish Civil War, because the decisive politics of that war was democracy vs. fascism. Trotsky strongly rejected ultra-leftists who raised the capitalist, imperialist nature of the Spanish state as the decisive criterion. It was the education of the movement that Trotsky provided during the then recent conflict of the Spanish Civil War that set the stage for the rejection of the nature of the Stalinist state as the decisive determinant in the debate that erupted over World War II. In our own time, there are echoes of this approach in the "tankist campism" of parts of the left, who find progressive features in any state, no matter how reactionary, authoritarian and anti-working class, so long as that state is opposed by American imperialism.

The first question raised by the opposition that would become the Workers Party was: *What exactly is your position on this war?* The position of the Socialist Workers Party, and much of the Fourth International, was: *We're against the invasion, however, we're for the Red Army and we think that the people of Poland, Finland, Estonia, Latvia, etc should support the Russian army as it invades.* As Max Shachtman stated for the opposition during the debate:

> They condemn the invasion but support the invaders. They're against seizures of new territories by the Kremlin... but support those who are seizing them. They are against the invasion before it takes place, they are against them after it has succeeded, but they are for the invasion for the victory of the Red Army while it is taking place. This is what their war position had become.[17]

---

17. Shachtman 1940b.

## Russian imperialism

Traditional Marxist principles and theory demanded support for the right of national self-determination against imperialist attack from whatever quarter. But support for Russia in the war meant opposing the national right of self-determination for Poland, the Baltic States, Finland, etc. Trotsky's followers tried desperately to invent some other category or terminology – "seizure", "expansionism", or some other formulation – to deny imperialist reality and to cover up national imprisonment through forcible conquest. As it became impossible to deny that this was a war for conquest, Trotskyists did mental gymnastics, trying somehow to separate conquest from imperialism. Both the official Communist parties and the orthodox Trotskyists rejected the very idea that Russia *could be* imperialist.

The attempt to deny reality by verbal gymnastics, maintaining that only advanced monopoly, finance capitalism is imperialist – and therefore that no other society, no matter what its actual actions are, is imperialist – had nothing in common with Marxism or Lenin's position on imperialism and imperialist wars. The opposition countered by attempting to re-establish the Leninist norms of imperialism, by going back to Lenin's writings on the question. Here is one of many similar programmatic policies formulated by Lenin, this one from his revision of the party program in October 1917 on the eve of the revolution: "Imperialist wars also occurred in the period of slavery (the war between Rome and Carthage was on both sides an imperialist war), as well as in the Middle Ages and in the epoch of mercantile capitalism...".[18] According to Lenin, the Spanish conquest of the Americas at the *dawn* of capitalism – not at its highest, final stage – was imperialist. One of the reasons why this was so clear to Lenin, if not to future generations of confused revolutionists, was that the tsarist empire – which was a backward, semi-feudal state, the prison house of nations – was imperialist. It hardly represented the highest stage of monopoly finance capitalism. Its imperialism was of a semi-feudal, dynastic character. During World War I, Lenin wrote that even in peacetime, tsarist "Russia set a world record for the oppression of nations with an

---

18.   Lenin 1972, p.162.

imperialism that is more crude, medieval, economically backward and militarily bureaucratic".[19]

Lenin summed up what determines whether a war is an inter-imperialist one:

> A war is certainly imperialist if both warring sides oppress foreign countries or nationalities, and are fighting for their share of the loot and for the right to "oppress and rob" more than the others.[20]

His words provide an apt description of the decisive crux of World War II, from its inception with the invasion of Poland, through its conclusion with the imperialist victors carving up Europe and Asia at the Yalta and Potsdam conferences. It was this basic Leninist principle that Trotskyism moved away from – disastrously, to accommodate support for a Russia engaged in an imperialist attack – and that the Workers Party reasserted.

In his depiction of "both warring sides...fighting for their share of the loot and for the right to 'oppress and rob'", Lenin boiled down the essence of imperialism. His description in no way undermines our understanding of the dynamics of modern, advanced capitalism and its drives to imperialism; neither does it deny the imperialism of other social systems, no matter what their stage of economic development, no matter what the dynamics of their imperialism are. Marxists have to oppose *all* imperialist wars, *all* foreign conquests – no matter with whatever rationale the conquerors cloak their actions, no matter what precise dynamic drives those countries to foreign conquest.

Every nation has the democratic right to self-determination, to run itself without the "guidance" of the foreign conqueror, the forcible occupier, who denies these rights to the peoples it defeats. The Workers Party reasserted the theoretical basis for what in today's parlance is called "knee-jerk anti-imperialism". The WP opposed *all* imperialism and championed the right of every nation to resist foreign invasion. Foreign conquest, no matter who is carrying it out, no matter what reasons and justifications are given, is always in the interests of one

---

19. Lenin 1974, p.359.
20. Lenin 1972, p.162.

group only – the ruling classes who decide upon and carry out the wars, in which the masses of working people who do the fighting never have any say. Oppressed nations are oppressed precisely because they are conquered, annexed and denied the right to determine their own fate.

## Neither Washington nor Moscow

The Workers Party was the only revolutionary organisation in the United States to oppose all sides in World War II. Upon their expulsion from the Socialist Workers Party, in the first issues of their newspaper *Labor Action* and their theoretical magazine the *New International*, they raised as their defining political banner the slogan "Neither Berlin/Moscow, nor London/Paris, but for the Third Camp of international socialism!" Later, when Russia switched sides and the US entered the war, the slogan was updated to: "Neither Berlin/Rome/Tokyo, nor London/Washington/Moscow". When the war ended with the two major victors unleashing a new stage of imperialist struggle for world domination in 1946, the slogan was revised to "Neither Washington nor Moscow, but for the Third Camp of international socialism". The evolving slogan channelled the changes in imperialist struggle, while the basic idea originating it at the start of World War II remained the core of international socialist politics.

> The only party in the country committed to a program of consistent struggle against imperialist war found itself tongue-tied, because when the war finally broke out it did not take precisely the form that had been envisaged. The imperialist world did not launch an attack on Russia; Russia and Germany joined, instead, in an imperialist assault for the division of the booty named Poland, and later on of other countries of Eastern Europe... [T]he Minority rejected the slogan of "unconditional defense" of Stalinist Russia in this war and raised instead the slogan of victory of the Third Camp – not the camp of the imperialist Axis or the camp of the imperialist democracies (plus their more than one totalitarian ally!), but the independent camp of the working class of the world and the oppressed colonial peoples. We pointed out, and it has yet to be refuted, that it was impossible to do anything

in the "defense of the Soviet Union" that did not mean aid and support of the imperialist camp of which it was an integral and subordinate part.[21]

The Workers Party shared with the orthodox Trotskyists the belief that the war would end with revolution. It held that World War II would end the way that World War I did – with an international revolution in many countries, in which those who had opposed the war with a correct program would be able to play an outsized role, similar to what the Bolsheviks did in Russia in 1917, or to what the Spartacist League with only a few thousand members did in Germany in 1919. However wrong this turned out to be, this perspective gave central importance to attitudes to war, which increased the heat of the internal Trotskyist struggle.

## China in World War II

The rigorous fight in which the Workers Party freed itself from outworn doctrine, forced its members to devote serious effort to developing Marxist theory – more so than any previous American revolutionary organisation. As the war unfolded, the Workers Party made further significant contributions to the Marxist understanding of war politics. Among its most important was its analysis of China's role in World War II, and of the national resistance movements more broadly.

Allied camp war propaganda defined its side as the "four great democracies" (or what President Roosevelt named the "Four Policemen"), led by the "four great democrats". The great democratic policemen were the US, Britain, Russia and China; the four great democrats were Roosevelt, Churchill, Stalin and Chiang Kai-Shek. Two of these, Roosevelt and Churchill, were the world's greatest imperialists; the other two were ruthless dictators. China had become one of the four major powers in the Allied war camp.

War in China began with the Japanese invasion of Manchuria in 1931, followed by full invasion of China in 1937. Revolutionary socialists

---

21. Shachtman 1943.

opposed the Japanese attack to conquer colonial China. So for China, this was a just war of national liberation – even though the country and its war effort was led by Chiang Kai-Shek, a corrupt warlord, dictator, and the butcher of the Chinese revolution of 1925–27, a man who spent much of the war fighting the Chinese Communists rather than the Japanese invaders. Nonetheless, the decisive characteristic of the war was Japanese imperialism against national independence of the Chinese. The entire radical movement supported China in that war.

After Pearl Harbor and the US entrance into the war, China joined the Allied war camp in the Pacific theatre of World War II. But this was a war fought for the imperialist division of the world – not for the independence of China. War is the continuation of politics by forcible means, but as the Workers Party maintained, politics also continues during war. Shifts in the politics of the actors can and have altered the character of wars *during their course*, as Marx and Engels analysed for the Franco-Prussian war of 1870–71. So it was in the case of China's involvement in the broader conflict. China evolved from a country fighting a progressive war for its national liberation, to a constituent part of an imperialist camp in an inter-imperialist war.

Despite this, China continued to receive political support from the SWP and much of the Fourth International. By contrast, the Workers Party dropped its previous support for China, as it came to the conclusion that Chinese integration into the Allied war bloc made its position analogous to that of Serbia in World War I. In that conflict, Lenin, Luxemburg, and Trotsky had all argued that socialists would have been obliged to support Serbian national independence against Austrian imperialism, had the conflict been an isolated one. But the conflict was not an isolated one: World War I was not a war for Serbian independence. The *decisive* dynamic of a war must determine the attitude of revolutionary Marxists, not its subsidiary dynamics. So despite the national element of Serbian independence, revolutionaries did not support Serbia in a war whose overwhelming, decisive politics were imperialist division of global spoils.

Similarly, when China became a part of the Allied camp in World War II, its war was no longer simply the war of China against Japanese imperialism, but a part of the global conflict of the imperialist powers.

The latter determined the decisive, overriding character of the war. Most Chinese Trotskyists, and almost all Asian Trotskyists, supported this Workers Party position or took similar stances. (The Workers Party considered itself a part of the Fourth International until 1948, and significant groups of Trotskyists from other countries supported its views first on the invasion of Poland and Finland, and then on the role of China in the war.)

With the majority Trotskyists supporting the war waged by Russia and China – two of the four members of the Allied war camp – there was a drift by some of them to adapt politically to the other two allied powers, America and Britain. The Socialist Workers Party, influencing others, blurred some distinction of opposition to the Allied camp, through a policy they called the "proletarian military policy". Its central idea was a muddled, utopian call affirming a desire to fight Germany with the existing imperialist army, as long as it was under "trade union control". In a further adaptation, as the Roosevelt government prepared and mobilised for war, the American SWP came out for conscription, denouncing opposition to the draft as pacifist. They supported the draft for the existing imperialist army as it prepared for imperialist war, *even if not* controlled by the unions. In similar fashion, they dropped their support for what had probably been their most popular slogan in the late 1930s – "Let the people vote on war" – which called for a referendum on the war prior to its declaration. These decisions explain why the Workers Party insisted that it was their opponents who were adapting to "petty-bourgeois pressures" and patriotism.

## National resistance

Another important question of the war was posed by the national liberation struggles that developed in Europe, when the conquest and occupation of the Balkans, Poland, and Eastern and Western Europe by the Axis led to the rise of mass resistance movements in France, Greece, Poland, Yugoslavia, Norway, Holland, Belgium and elsewhere.

The German occupation of Europe was different from past imperialist conquest. The Nazis were colonising previously independent countries of the advanced industrial world, not economically underdeveloped states. Some of these countries were themselves imperialist countries. Now they were conquered, occupied, colonised – reviving again in Europe the national question: the right to self-determination, national independence and national liberation.

To fight against foreign occupation, national resistance movements were organised throughout Europe. Yet many were not supported by the SWP and by some European Trotskyist organisations. The so-called "orthodox Trotskyist" arguments for not supporting the resistance movements were static and abstract: the right of self-determination, they said, was a democratic demand for oppressed colonial countries, not applicable to advanced capitalist, previously imperialist countries. In these countries, they argued, the agenda should be socialist revolution, not national independence; the resistance movements were bourgeois, raising bourgeois democratic demands relevant to a past era, not applicable to contemporary Europe.

The Workers Party refuted these sectarian traps. Now that various countries had been conquered and occupied or incorporated into Germany, Italy, Hungary, a version of the colonial question existed in Europe. To maintain otherwise was to hide from reality behind a conservative sectarian screen. National oppression exists wherever any nation is conquered and occupied by force against its will. Any conquered country – no matter what its political or economic system – has the right to resist foreign occupation, the democratic right to national self-determination, and the right to fight for its national liberation, including the right to separate from its occupiers. "Orthodox politics" were leading to opposite, reactionary conclusions. Likewise, some Trotskyists told their members not to join the Resistance because the movement was fighting for national independence and not socialist revolution.

The contrasting Workers Party analysis championed the resistance movement as the only mass movement in Europe at that time. Although it drew from all classes under the Nazi oppression, it consisted overwhelmingly of workers who had been trained in the social democratic, communist and trade union movements. The Workers Party maintained support for the national resistance movements so long as they were not controlled and dominated by, or subordinated to, the Allies with their imperialist goals. Under traditional Marxist principles, the independence of movements such as these is the decisive determinant. They can take aid, they can even collaborate – the way Irish revolutionaries received arms from Germany during World War I; the way Palestinians and other national liberation movements in our own day did from Russia; the way Hamas may take aid from Iran. The decisive question is not whether resistance movements take aid from whatever source they can. So long as they are under their own control, their war remains a just one for national liberation.

Moreover, the WP argued, it was in the resistance movements that the socialist movement would be able to reorganise itself, by fighting for working-class politics, interests and demands, and for working-class leadership – by linking the struggle for democratic demands with socialist demands. While many Fourth Internationalist groups counter-posed socialist revolution to democratic demands in the advanced countries, it was the Communist parties who led and who played an enormous role in the resistance movement, overcoming the legacy of popular hostility toward the Communist collaboration with the Nazis at the beginning of the occupation. In France, Greece, Italy, Vietnam, the Philippines and elsewhere, the Communist parties emerged as a dominant force within the working class as a result of the role they played in the wartime resistance movements. This dominance was to shape the politics of the left for the next generation.

## War policy then and now

On the critical wartime questions that confronted Trotskyism – Russia, China, national resistance movements, accommodation to social patriotism – the Workers Party approach to war and imperialism was proven to be right. To move forward it was necessary to break with frozen, outmoded theories, and to use Marxism as a guide to develop a new revolutionary program for revolutionary action. The positions of the Trotskyist majority and the Workers Party minority were tested in practice again at the end of the war, when the two main victors, the United States and Russia, divided the world between themselves at Yalta and then went on to a new struggle for imperialist domination in the Cold War. The Fourth International was to claim that the Cold War struggle was an international class struggle; it would demand support for the Russian camp in that period, including for the "workers' [nuclear] bomb". The Workers Party position of "Neither Washington nor Moscow" would find support during the Cold War among other Trotskyists, particularly in Britain where the *Socialist Review* group (predecessor of the International Socialists and the Socialist Workers Party) opposed both camps in the Korean War and adopted the Workers Party's position. "Neither Washington nor Moscow, but International Socialism" became the central slogan of the International Socialist tendency.

Today these ideas have a much broader acceptance throughout the international left, including in today's Fourth International, than they did in the 1940s. The collapse of Russian and Eastern European Stalinism opened sections of the left to rethink many questions. Yet the political heritage of the Workers Party remains underappreciated and underexplored. Those who today insist on the centrality of working-class struggle for a classless society as the basis for the ending of all oppression, war and exploitation, can learn much from this era of creative application of Marxist principles to a complex and changing world.

## References

Isserman, Maurice 1982, *Which Side Were You On? The American Communist Party During the Second World War*, Wesleyan University Press.

Lenin, VI 1972 [1917], "Revision of the Party Programme", *Collected Works*, Progress Publishers, Vol. 26. https://www.marxists.org/archive/lenin/works/1917/oct/06.htm

Lenin, VI 1974 [1916], "The Discussion of Self Determination Summed Up", *Collected Works*, Progress Publishers, Vol. 22. https://www.marxists.org/archive/lenin/works/1916/jul/x01.htm

Litvinov, Maksim 1933, "Address before the Central Executive Committee of the USSR", 29 December. http://soviethistory.msu.edu/1936–2/popular-front/popular-front-texts/litvinov-before-the-central-executive-committee/

Marx, Karl and Frederick Engels 1969 [1848], *Manifesto of the Communist Party*, *Selected Works*, Vol. 1, Progress Publishers, Moscow, 1969. https://www.marxists.org/archive/marx/works/download/pdf/Manifesto.pdf

*The Militant* 1948, "Nazi Documents Disclose Details of Stalin-Hitler Secret Deals", Vol. 12, No. 5, 2 February. https://www.marxists.org/history/etol/newspape/themilitant/1948/v12n05/stal-hitl.htm

Riddell, John 1984, *Lenin's struggle for a revolutionary international*, Pathfinder.

Sedova Trotsky, Natalia 1951, "Resignation from the Fourth International", *The Militant*, Vol. 15, No. 23, 4 June. https://www.marxists.org/archive/sedova-natalia/1951/05/09.htm

Shachtman, Max 1940a, "The Crisis in the American Party", *New International*, Vol. 6, No. 2, March. https://www.marxists.org/archive/shachtma/1940/03/crisis.htm

Shachtman, Max 1940b, "The Soviet Union and The World War", *New International*, Vol. 6, No. 3, April. https://www.marxists.org/archive/shachtma/1940/04/ussrwar.htm

Shachtman, Max 1943, "Three Years of the Workers Party", *Labor Action*, Vol. 7, No. 17, 26 April. https://www.marxists.org/archive/shachtma/1943/04/3years.html

Shachtman, Max 1954, "Twenty Five Years of American Trotskyism", *New International*, Vol. 20, No. 1, January–February. https://www.marxists.org/archive/shachtma/1953/11/25years.html

Sheen, Fulton John 1948, *Communism and the Conscience of the West*, Bobbs-Merrill.

Schulenburg, Friedrich-Werner (German Ambassador to the Soviet Union) 1940, Telegram to the German Foreign Office, 18 June. https://avalon.law.yale.edu/20th_century/ns145.asp

Trotsky, Leon 1935, "The Soviet Union Today", *New International*, Vol. 2, No. 4, July. https://www.marxists.org/archive/trotsky/1935/02/ws-therm-bon.htm

Trotsky, Leon 1939, "The USSR in War", *New International*, Vol. 5, No. 11, November. https://www.marxists.org/archive/trotsky/1939/09/ussr-war.htm

Trotsky, Leon 1973 [1939–40], *In Defense of Marxism*, Pathfinder. https://www.marxists.org/archive/trotsky/idom/dm/index.htm

APRIL HOLCOMBE

# Analysing China's COVID response

**April Holcombe** is a transgender woman and contributor to *Red Flag* newspaper. She was a leading activist in the successful campaign for marriage equality.

Chuang, *Social Contagion and other material on microbiological class war in China*, Charles H Kerr Publishing Company, 2021

T THE BEGINNING OF THE PANDEMIC, China was ground zero. Yet today, according to its government, China is very close to COVID-zero. How has the country at the heart of the crisis so far avoided the worst of it? The most common answer points to China's centralised, authoritarian state, and its apparent advantages over Western states – the latter rich but hampered by democratic rule and special interest groups.

A new book published by the communist collective Chuang challenges this narrative. *Social Contagion and other material on microbiological class war in China* is a collection of essays, reports and interviews dealing with the emergence of the pandemic, the experience of lockdown in China, and the ramifications for the future of Chinese capitalism and its state. Although at times a scattered grab-bag of ideas and information, *Social Contagion* is worthwhile reading for left-wing observers of Chinese politics.

## Capitalism and pandemics

Most commentary on COVID-19 is fixated on how states have responded. Chuang argues that Marxists ought to begin their analysis of the pandemic with capitalism, and not the state or its policies.

> The rule is to speak of the plague without speaking of its origins, to speak of the pandemic as a purely administrative matter conducted by those at the helm of the state. In short, the most common way that the pandemic is spoken of today is not to discuss it at all and to discuss the state in its place. (p.110)

With this in mind, the first essay – *Social Contagion* – contains a useful analysis of how capitalist dynamics produce pandemics in general, and COVID-19 in particular.

While pandemics have their origin in pre-capitalist urban civilisations, capitalism drives their potential to new extremes. Industrialisation, urbanisation and globalisation provide pathogens with constant potential to mutate in animals, jump from animal to human (zoonosis), and spread rapidly between humans. Historically, the centre of gravity in the world capitalist system – where the above processes are occurring most rapidly – has been the seedbed of new and devastating pandemics.

This centre was once colonial Europe – with its bovine-borne rinderpest that ravaged much of Africa – before shifting to the United States. The misnamed Spanish flu is now widely believed to have originated amongst Kansas livestock before spreading through the US meatworks industry and cramped, dirty working-class slums.

More recently it is China that has been ground zero for many viruses. The first known case of H5N1 "bird flu" was traced to Hong Kong in 1997, followed in 2002 by the original SARS coronavirus, first identified in the southern province of Guangdong. Yet contrary to popular imagination, this has nothing to do with Chinese people eating "weird" animals or having dirty habits. Rather, as Chuang points out, it follows from China's rapid transformation into the world's major manufacturing hub. Adam Tooze makes the same point elsewhere: "There has been much debate in economics about the 'China shock' – the impact on

Western labor markets of globalisation and the sudden rise in imports from China in the early 2000s. SARS-CoV-2 was a 'China shock' with a vengeance".[1]

China has completely changed since the state opened its capitalist economy to foreign investment in the 1980s. Hundreds of millions of rural migrants – after millennia of labouring on private plots – moved to urban centres to become wage labourers. The urban population has leapt from 20 percent in 1970 to 60 percent today. It is an unparalleled transformation in world history. The driving force has not been an abstract progress, developmentalism or consumerism, but capital's insatiable need to accumulate profits and expand production.

Not only has urbanisation massively increased population density and factory farming; it has also led to a complete encroachment into wilderness. Capitalism no longer has a "natural periphery", only "a subordinated hinterland...plugged into global value chains". (p.31) Deforestation and the trade of wild animal products increases humanity's chances of interacting with novel pathogens, and ever-growing cities shrink the space between them. As Wallace explains, this also destroys "the kind of environmental complexity with which the forest disrupts transmission chains".[2] While investigations into the origins of COVID-19 are ongoing, the most likely scenario is that the virus originated in bats and was transmitted to humans by an intermediary wild animal.

Globalisation has dramatically increased the risk and speed of pathogen spread. Production chains have fanned out across countries and trade between them has deepened. China, the world's largest exporter, is a nexus of globalisation, and Wuhan, a transport hub of China, doubly so. "Who knew that there were regular direct flights from Wuhan, China, to America?" Thomas Friedman asked in the *New York Times* on 30 May 2020.[3]

Lastly, as in so many parts of the world, the dire state of Chinese healthcare – privatised, managerialised, and "rationalised" – has massively aggravated the lethality of the pandemic. The system has

---

1. Tooze 2021, p.21.
2. Wallace 2020.
3. Friedman 2020.

been left to decay for decades. Collapsing expenditure has been "obscured behind the splendor of glittering cities and massive factories" with "most public spending directed toward brick-and-mortar infrastructure – bridges, roads, and cheap electricity for production". (p.25) The average citizen saves very large portions of their income for the inevitable medical bills that accumulate as they age. Hundreds of millions of migrant workers living outside their registered locality are ineligible for any kind of social benefit except through the insurance funds of their employers, who frequently refuse to pay into them. Ordinary Chinese people have had a lifetime of experience with the dilapidated, user-pays healthcare system to learn that they should do everything they can to avoid a new virus.

## The myth of authoritarian efficiency

From this point, Chuang sets out to answer the key question: so how did China manage to suppress the virus? The mainstream perception is that China's centralised, authoritarian – even totalitarian – state was the secret to its rapid suppression of the virus. According to this narrative, the West succumbed to the virus due to the inexpediency of democratic governance, but the all-seeing Chinese state could track the virus through CCTV and issue demands down its well-greased chains of command.

The democracy-as-obstacle argument has been made from many corners, including, unsurprisingly, the Chinese Communist Party itself. "Why has the West still failed to prevent the epidemic?", its newspaper *Global Times* asked on 15 March 2020. "In the West, politics is subjected to other forces. To win votes, politicians have to please the powers that control both the public and capital."[4]

While attempting to argue *against* authoritarianism, Fabienne Peter puts a near-identical case in a 27 August 2021 piece for the *New Statesman*:

> The Covid-19 case shows that authoritarian regimes can work
> for the people... A combination of top-down decision-making

---

4.   Song 2020.

mechanisms and the institutional power to ruthlessly enforce those decisions led to a set of policies that have been described as "brutal but effective".[5]

A report for the Lowy Institute concluded that "The power of the communist party, once applied in full, is akin to 'war powers' in a democracy and has proved highly effective in containing the virus within China".[6]

The book stridently and convincingly challenges this talking point. Chuang compares it to the old reactionary adage that "Mussolini at least made the trains run on time". (p.4) In both cases, the statement is not only politically suspicious, but factually untrue.

Around the world, there appears to be no useful correlation between dictatorship, democracy, and pandemic outcomes. Many Western states had little, even less, difficulty in applying "war powers" once the need became clear.

## The Wuhan lockdown

China's political system actually *undermined* suppression efforts, as described in an interview between Chuang and three Wuhan residents in the book's third chapter. Authoritarianism was better suited to suppressing news of the virus than suppressing cases of it. Censorship of social media, denial and lies from municipal government in the news, and the arrest of whistle-blower doctors and journalists – these much more exemplified the initial state response. As activist and Trotskyist Au Loong Yu explained in an interview in February, 2020: "We have a government which is so effective at cracking down on dissidence and civil society, but it is absolutely incompetent in fighting the virus, or just warning the people".[7]

Interviewees first heard of the virus from friends living in Hong Kong and Japan. A visit in mid-January by a Shanghai friend wearing a face mask made a deep impression. "That was the first time we really became aware of the danger. He spoke of Wuhan as if it were a war zone,

---

5. Peter 2021.
6. MacGregor 2020.
7. Denvir 2020.

whereas most people here didn't take it seriously". (p.68) At this time, the Wuhan government was still denying that it was SARS and that it was transmissible. Four days later, on 23 January 2020, a lockdown was finally announced at 2 o'clock in the morning. Effective from eight hours hence, all public transport was cancelled and no one was allowed to leave the city.

But aside from these measures, the lockdown was a disorganised, shambolic affair. Hundreds of thousands of residents had already left Wuhan for Chinese New Year. No preparations whatsoever had been made to bolster the healthcare system or ensure supply of provisions to people sheltering in place. There were not even arrangements for alternative transport once tens of thousands of health workers could no longer take the bus to work.

In the early days of the lockdown, public feeling ran hot in Wuhan. Social media erupted in anger at the death of whistle-blower doctor Li Wenliang. The city mayor was forced to admit on television that they had delayed the release of critical information. One interviewee describes the sentiment right after the lockdown was announced:

> The government's behaviour felt like a joke, when they suddenly decided to close down the city after weeks of inaction, without providing any information about the virus or how to deal with the crisis – and worse, propagating misinformation. At that time, people were wondering whether the government was giving up on Wuhan, and our trust in the authorities was shattered, so we felt we could only rely on ourselves to get whatever we would need to survive. (p.95)

Despite this, the virus was suppressed. Chuang identifies three factors that worked very fortuitously in the government's favour.

First was the extraordinarily opportune timing for an emergency shutdown. People had been buying large amounts of food in the lead-up to festivities, and most shops and workplaces already planned to shut or reduce operations for weeks of the holiday period. The Chinese state would have had a far bigger crisis on its hands if it had

had to solve the issue of food supply and business shutdown almost any other time of year.

Secondly, the worst of the initial outbreak was centred on one locality. "The central government only had the capacity to provide effective coordination in the Hubei epicenter. Its responses in other provinces – even wealthy and well-regarded places like Hangzhou – remained largely uncoordinated and desperate." (pp.42–3)

The last factor was the mass mobilisation of millions to bolster the COVID relief effort, and the willing compliance of the vast majority who were rightly afraid of infection. The videos – quickly suppressed – of patients dying in hospital corridors and waiting rooms were a sign of the total incapacity of the state to protect or provide. In those first few weeks of lockdown, tens of millions strictly adhered to staying home; not because the government could make them, but because the government would not help them if they got sick.

But voluntary efforts went well beyond choosing to stay home. At the outset, the government faced such a resources and personnel crisis that all residents were effectively deputised to commandeer vehicles, create roadblocks, and quarantine people at their discretion. Images of village entrances defended by "big uncles" with weapons give a sense of both the seriousness with which people took the virus, and who was left to plug the gaps in the state's response.

In those initial weeks and months, Chinese state had little capacity to truly enforce compliance nor to provide for people's basic needs. Xi Jinping's call for a "people's war" on the virus was a nationalist way of admitting that the Communist Party did not have the personnel or resources to manage a lockdown in even one city. Or as the *New York Times* described it, "entrusting front line epidemic prevention to a supercharged version of a neighborhood watch".[8]

There is a lot of information in the book about the mutual aid efforts of Wuhan citizens in those early weeks. Networks of volunteers providing face masks to citizens, as well as food, PPE and sanitary products for intensely overworked health workers, are a testament to

---

8.    Zhong and Mozur 2020.

the cooperative spirit that can take hold in a crisis. Some selfless volunteers even lost their lives to COVID-19 by carpooling health workers after public transport was cancelled.

However, as Chuang points out in the fourth essay, these volunteer efforts did not cast themselves as political or radical in any way. This was not merely tactical discretion; it reflects a deep depoliticisation across Chinese society that presents serious challenges for radicals organising illegally. Authority was not challenged, but merely supplemented. "The presumption that mutual aid is politically empowering [does] not carry if this empowerment not only fails to oppose the state but, in fact, keeps it afloat." (p.122)

Although the writer provides a sharp critique of their deficiencies, the "mutual aid" efforts are studied in microscopic detail. This is informed by the "workers' inquiry" tendency that the author describes as "the most fruitful left-wing current in contemporary China today". (p.45) I am more sceptical that ultra-fine empirical studies on production processes and workers' daily routines – or charity networks in this case – are the most illuminating area of study for Chinese radicals today. Certainly, for those reading from afar, this kind of radical sociology detracts from their broader interrogation essential to understanding the key dynamics at play in China today: of capital accumulation, state power, party rule and class struggle.

Despite the initial debacle, the virus has been very strongly suppressed – and at times eliminated – in China. This has undoubtedly increased the legitimacy of the Communist Party dictatorship; the great frustration and anger at the initial coverups have abated. Yet COVID-zero was a common feature across many Asian Pacific countries, "democratic" or not. The region's experience of the first SARS outbreak from 2002–4 ingrained much stronger health norms such as mask wearing and some preparedness in health policy and institutions. This – not uniquely authoritarian capacities – led to China's initial success in the first wave.

Since then, the more infectious Delta strain of the virus has changed the game in the Asia Pacific, with only Taiwan and China left standing as near-COVID-free. Yet the Chinese Communist Party's determination to maintain COVID-zero, a worthy goal for humanity, is not pursued for its sake. The party fears political destabilisation if the virus is allowed to circulate, since Chinese citizens have maintained very high expectations that the country remain COVID-free. Strength and fragility characterise the Chinese state in equal measure.

## China's state-building project

The pandemic is shaping the future of the Chinese state. In the final essay – as long as the other three chapters combined – the writer deals with the nature of the dictatorship and its possible trajectory. Despite a very scattered approach that jumps between topics, themes and arguments, a strong defence and application of the Marxist conception of the state shines through:

> Market and state are neither separate nor opposed in a capitalist society. This is a basic, irreducible component of the communist critique of the present world. (p.134)

The state is not an independent body, but integrated into the more fundamental economic relations of capitalist production. The key functions of the state are the "maintenance of baseline conditions for accumulation and management of conflicts within the ruling class". (p.202) In liberal-democratic states, there is a division of labour between politicians in the state who "represent" the people and the capitalist class they really serve. No such illusion of separation exists in Chinese capitalism: "the Chinese state is direct administration of society by the organised capitalist class". (p.135)

The writer describes at length how aspects of China's social formation are drawn from its pre-capitalist past. Or, in their academic language, the Chinese ruling class "incorporates incidental institutional logics from its own indigenous genealogy of statecraft". (pp.202–3) There is more than a grain of truth to this: Chinese capitalism was not built on virgin soil but out of the ruins of a very old civilisation.

Yet much more decisive were developments in the twentieth century. In the Mao era, capitalist accumulation began from an extremely low base. The mass of capital required to industrialise demanded its extreme concentration. The intensity of global competition – both military and economic – meant this capital had to be forcefully directed to specific ends. This compelled the ruling Communist Party to nationalise the entire economy. This case is made very convincingly in Robert K Schaeffer's book *Red Inc: Dictatorship and the Development of Capitalism in China, 1949 to the Present*: "From the outset, the regime worked furiously to accumulate the capital it needed to finance rapid industrialisation and provide wealth for the ruling class...a goal shared in common with many other developmentalist dictatorships during the postwar period".[9]

Unfortunately, the Chuang collective argue that China in the Mao era was a socialist developmental regime before turning to capitalism under Deng Xiaoping. While this is not a central thesis of this book, it influences its arguments. Continuities of state power between the "socialist" era and the modern one are attributed to deeper ancestral roots, "incidental institutional logics", rather than to the fact that China was capitalist throughout. Nonetheless, Chuang's analysis of contemporary Chinese society has many strengths since they firmly insist that it is completely run by and for capitalist interests.

The writers argue that this state is a work-in-progress and not some totalitarian Leviathan. China's first lockdown, from January to March 2020, demonstrates that its political apparatus remains a highly decentralised one – much to the chagrin of the central authorities. The Wuhan municipal government did not act until the latter intervened decisively one month after it knew of the virus. Once the virus spread outside the province, Beijing authorities were quickly overwhelmed, with local authorities applying a patchwork of lockdown rules.

It took a whole month – from December 2019 to January 2020 – for the central authorities to step in and try to overcome the bureaucratic inertia of the municipal government. As Chuang notes, there was a far-sighted capitalist logic to this: protecting the health of the workers it exploits and preventing an even deeper crisis of political legitimacy. Yet ruling class foresight is limited and disciplined by the fundamentally

---

9.  Schaeffer 2012, p.viii.

short-term logic of wealth expansion. The state – even in state capitalism – cannot hold out indefinitely against the urgent drive for capital accumulation imposed on it by global competition. Within a few weeks, pressure was mounting. Beijing pushed Foxconn to rapidly implement certain health measures in order to restart production.[10] On 23 February 2020, Xi Jinping told 170,000 party cadres it was time to reopen. The *South China Morning Post* reported on the meeting under the headline: "Xi Jinping rings alarm on China economy as country shifts priority to maintaining growth".[11]

By this time, however, the example set in Wuhan compelled local governments all across China to take very stringent measures, for fear of being held responsible for losing control of the virus. Just as the initial sluggish response of the Wuhan municipal government demonstrated the decentralised disconnect between central and local authority, so too did the overzealous response of local governments thereafter. "What worried the centre now was no longer Hubei-style malfeasance and foot-dragging but the centrifugal tendencies unleashed by overzealous local action", Tooze writes.[12] Once the central government tried to rein them in to restart the economy, they again faced local inertia, but of the opposite kind.

Chuang also puts in perspective another widely discussed aspect of the Chinese state: its surveillance powers. Does China have "the most expansive and sophisticated surveillance system in the world", as the press commonly argue?[13] The United States and China have roughly the same number of CCTV cameras per person[14] and the former's database for fingerprint and criminal history is far more sophisticated, streamlined and centralised. The same kind of facial recognition technology used in China is in operation in many Australian states, even before legislation has passed to allow it.[15] Chuang compares China's Orwellian "social credit scheme" – subject of much media commentary – with "the much more systematic and thoroughly enforced influence of

---

10. Tooze, p.79.
11. Tang 2020.
12. Tooze, p.77.
13. Yuan 2020.
14. Ivanova 2019.
15. Goldenfein 2020.

one's combined credit history and criminal record in any Western country". (p.186)

There is no question that political repression is more severe in China than in capitalist "democracies". This is especially true in Xinjiang, Hong Kong and Tibet, where much surveillance technology is pioneered. Yet in terms of technical and organisational capacity to spy on, track and trace each member of the population, China still lags behind the advanced capitalist countries. There are clear efforts to narrow this gap and come out ahead: the grid management system – which delegates officials to collect information suburb by suburb, street by street – has expanded to hundreds of thousands of people in some cities and provinces. Yet such grand schemes require able bureaucrats and functioning chains of command. COVID-19 has shown that China does not have these.

Crises have exposed the state's weaknesses and accelerated attempts to overcome them. Whereas the Global Financial Crisis propelled forward a greater centralisation of financial and industrial policy, the pandemic has forced the state to consider the nature of its local power and the networks that constitute it. At a moment of national crisis, the Chinese Communist Party – incompetent at the local level, overstretched at the central – depended on mass voluntary compliance and mobilisation. Whilst this exposed the government's weaknesses, the response has bolstered it. A lack of faith in state *capacity* was not a rejection of state *legitimacy*.

The mass volunteer efforts during the lockdowns flooded previously hollow and defunct village and neighbourhood committees and gave them new life. Once the state eventually intervened, it shut volunteer groups and slotted this informal activity into its structures of command to create what Chuang calls "paraformal" relationships. Lacking any political critique of the state, these "grassroots" networks have simply knitted a tighter fabric of authority that has traditionally frayed as it approaches the ground.

On this basis, the writer predicts greater trends towards "new, seemingly democratic evolutions of local 'autonomy' that are nonetheless designed to bulwark the official bureaucracy". This faux-democratic engagement will be "that of the social media platform.

In other words, a tyrannical form of constant participation that offers little genuine autonomy and instead increases surveillance, snitching and self-censorship". (p.186)

Another dimension of modern Chinese state-building touched on, but not explored by the writer, is the development of a more robust rule of law. Not only popular nationalist mobilisation, but more impersonal, regularised courts and contract law can strengthen the dictatorship's rule by *consent* as it navigates through the crisis potentials of the 2020s. This concept is usefully elaborated by Elaine Hui in an interview about her new book *Hegemonic Transformations*:

> The Chinese labour law system has produced a double hegemony, which deflects workers' radical opposition against both the market economy and the Party-state, and thus pre-empts their rebellion... The abundance of labour laws has convinced some workers that the Party-state protects workers, and that the political regime is "autonomous" from the market economy and is willing to curb economic misdeeds. Furthermore, owing to the decentralised politics of China, local governments are delegated the task of capital accumulation, while the central government is preoccupied with maintaining political legitimacy and social harmony. Some workers perceive government corruption and its pro-business bias as being the fault of local governments and do not criticise the central government or the Party-state as a whole. This shifts the target of workers' contempt from systemic state-capital collusion to individual officials and/or local governments.[16]

## Workers in the pandemic

As described in the book's second chapter – a translated essay from the *Worker Study Room* blog – the effect of economic shutdown was severe for workers. During the Global Financial Crisis of 2008–9, millions of workers lost their jobs in the manufacturing hubs of southern China,

---

16. Franceschini and Hui 2018.

many others suffered wage cuts, and class struggle declined. But the central government's massive stimulus package led to a rapid recovery and significant labour shortages. By 2010, a strike wave was gripping China, starting in manufacturing but spreading to various regions and industries. The movement sharply declined from 2015, through a combination of harsh state repression and stronger "rule of law" mediation measures.

The impact of COVID-19 crisis was much greater than this. Under the initial lockdown, unemployment in the Pearl River Delta reached 20 percent, with 70 million jobs lost. Although recovering within months from this lowest point, the staggered return to work kept unemployment high. Governments and businesses used this to their advantage, with the former creating new legal categories to allow for "flexible employment" and "shared employment" in which workers must divide the hours and income of one job among two or more. Pay was cut for hundreds of millions of workers through this period and, despite a relatively strong recovery from the low point of the lockdown, wages growth is slower than ever.

During the GFC, the price of consumer goods actually fell. However in this crisis the cost of living has continued to rise sharply. As well, there is no boom coming at the end of COVID-19 for Chinese capitalism. While wage stagnation, inflation and labour insecurity may foster greater bitterness in the long-term, they make unlikely a strike-wave in the immediate aftermath, unlike what took place post-GFC. The essay mentions only one reported case of a strike or workers' protest during the first half of 2020. For now, Chinese workers face worse job prospects and feel more hesitant to risk struggle. As the dead-end of arbitration courts becomes more apparent, radical workers may turn to more thoughtful and determined resistance.

## A few criticisms

*Social Contagion*'s order of argumentation at times feels disjointed and repetitive. Rather than developing its arguments chapter by chapter, it jumps from point to point: now the healthcare system of China, now an interview with illustrators about their experience in lockdown, now a digression on academic trends in Chinese political philosophy. This was somewhat unavoidable as a collection of essays from different contributors and periods during the pandemic. Yet especially the last essay could have argued much more concisely the conclusions it draws from previous chapters.

Lastly, while the writing does not count among the worst of modern academic writing on the left – obscure cultural references, indecipherable jargon, novel formulations for their own sake – there is definitely an overwritten style. A few claims – for example, that the "suspension of quotidian life" under lockdown acted on mass psychology like a "strike hollowed of its communal character" (p.10) – would be more compelling if they were more thoroughly argued, rather than simply dropped in as intellectual appetisers.

## Conclusion

*Social Contagion* is a useful contribution to the Marxist left that may challenge preconceived notions about the pandemic and Chinese society. It provides an excellent analysis of the capitalist system behind the COVID-19 crisis, and a strong case for the traditional Marxist critique and antagonism to the state. Sometimes its central theses are obscured behind excessive detail, detours and flourishes. Yet this book is a worthwhile read for English-speaking observers of Chinese politics and ought to stimulate more debate and discussion.

## References

Denvir, Daniel 2020, "Hong Kong with Au Loong Yu", *DigRadio Podcast*, 7 February. https://www.thedigradio.com/podcast/hong-kong-with-au-loong-yu/

Franceschini, Ivan and Elaine Hui 2018, "Hegemonic Transformation: A Conversation with Elaine Sio-Ieng Hui", *Made in China*, 7 July. https://madeinchinajournal.com/2018/07/07/hegemonic-transformation-elaine-sio-ieng-hui/

Friedman, Thomas 2020, "How we broke the world: Greed and globalisation set us up for disaster", *The New York Times*, 30 May. https://www.nytimes.com/2020/05/30/opinion/sunday/coronavirus-globalization.html

Goldenfein, Jake 2020, "Australian police are using the Clearview AI facial recognition system with no accountability", *The Conversation*, 4 March. https://theconversation.com/australian-police-are-using-the-clearview-ai-facial-recognition-system-with-no-accountability-132667

Ivanova, Irina, 2019, "Video surveillance in US described as on par with China", *CBS News*, 10 December. https://www.cbsnews.com/news/the-u-s-uses-surveillance-cameras-just-as-much-as-china/

MacGregor, Richard 2020, "China's Deep State: The Communist Party and the Coronavirus", The Lowy Institute, 23 July. https://www.lowyinstitute.org/publications/china-s-deep-state-communist-party-and-coronavirus

Peter, Fabienne 2021, "Can authoritarianism ever be justified?", *The New Statesman*, 27 August. https://www.newstatesman.com/ideas/agora/2021/08/can-authoritarianism-ever-be-justified

Schaeffer, RK 2012, *Red Inc.: Dictatorship and the Development of Capitalism in China, 1949 to the present*, Paradigm Publishers.

Song, Luzheng 2020, "Many Western governments ill-equipped to handle coronavirus", *Global Times*, 15 March. https://www.globaltimes.cn/content/1182661.shtml

Tang, Frank 2020, "Xi Jinping rings alarm on China economy as country shifts priority to maintaining growth", *South China Morning Post*, 24 February. https://www.scmp.com/economy/china-economy/article/3052131/coronavirus-xi-jinping-rings-alarm-china-economy-country

Tooze, A 2021, *Shutdown: How COVID shook the world's economy*, Allen Lane Publishers.

Wallace, Robert 2020, "Notes on a novel coronavirus", *Monthly Review*, 29 January. https://mronline.org/2020/01/29/notes-on-a-novel-coronavirus/

Yuan, Shawn 2020, "How China is using AI and big data to fight Coronavirus", *Al Jazeera*, 1 March. https://www.aljazeera.com/news/2020/3/1/how-china-is-using-ai-and-big-data-to-fight-the-coronavirus

Zhong, Raymond and Paul Mozur 2020, "To Tame Coronavirus, Mao-Style Social Control Blankets China", *The New York Times*, 15 February. https://www.nytimes.com/2020/02/15/business/china-coronavirus-lockdown.html

DUNCAN HART

# Eric Blanc's Kautsky revivalism

**Duncan Hart** is a socialist activist in Brisbane.

Eric Blanc, *Revolutionary Social Democracy: Working-Class Politics Across the Russian Empire (1882–1917)*, Brill, 2021

OR MOST MARXISTS, Karl Kautsky is a name forever associated with betrayal: both in his failure to steadfastly oppose the first World War and then his subsequent renunciation of the Russian Revolution. The extent of Kautsky's influence and the form this took among the international socialist movement prior to 1914 is generally unexplored, likely because of the shame that Kautsky cast upon himself. Eric Blanc's new book goes some way in rectifying this substantial historical deficit. While Blanc's book helps to flesh out a political tradition and socialist movements little known to English readers, it is marred by questionable conclusions that seek to vindicate Kautskyism as a revolutionary theory.

Blanc's case is that Kautsky's politics provided the political framework for the workers' revolutions in the territories of the Russian empire from 1917–19. This applies both to the revolution in central Russia as well as the still relatively unexplored (and more temporary) working-class revolutionary regimes in Finland, the Baltic states, Azerbaijan and Ukraine. Blanc makes this argument by outlining the politics of what he terms "revolutionary social democracy" (p.46) inspired by Kautsky. Blanc also performs an important historical service by broadening the scope of his study beyond just central Russia and the major urban centres of Petrograd and Moscow. In so doing he shows how Kautsky's politics inspired a broader tradition than the Bolsheviks in the Russian empire, which in some cases led revolutionary struggles. Blanc's aim is to demonstrate that, when the Russian Revolution is understood in its "All-Russian" context, the struggles took place in drastically different contexts, but each revolutionary party held to some form of Kautskyism. Blanc concludes from his study that the Russian Revolution fails to vindicate the politics of "Leninism", ie, the politics expressed by the Third International (Comintern) which sought to generalise the experience of the Russian Revolution to facilitate international workers' revolution. Rather, the genuine expression of the revolutionary period is Kautsky's "revolutionary social democracy".

Blanc's book covers a lot of terrain, impossible to assess fully in a short review. So my focus will be on his central thesis, which calls for rejecting the Comintern in favour of Kautskyism. I will examine the politics of revolutionary social democracy prior to 1917, examine Blanc's account of the revolutions of 1917–19, and wrap up by addressing head-on his critique of the Comintern.

## Revolutionary social democracy prior to 1917

Blanc advocates very well for the politics of Kautskyism as expressed in the *Erfurt Programme*, and corrects a number of historical falsehoods. Firstly, he shows that Kautsky was most influential in the territory of the Russian empire and Eastern Europe, and not in the big parties of the Second International such as those in France, Italy or even Germany. For this reason, Blanc argues, it is wrong to see the Second International's failings as the inevitable result of Kautsky's political limitations (p.40). Interestingly, Blanc does not explore adequately the impact of Kautsky's views. Nor does he assess those of other theoreticians with quite similar politics, broadly categorised as centrist, that were dominant in the wider Second International. Putting aside Kautsky's personal relevance, it is clear that his brand of centrism could not prevent right-wing degeneration in those parties.

Having said that, Blanc is persuasive in arguing that it was in imperial Russia where socialists were most influenced by Kautsky. In the Russian empire Kautsky's commentary on the *Erfurt Programme*[1] was more popular than the *Communist Manifesto* or any other item by leading Marxists (p.39). Other publications by Kautsky, including *The Social Revolution* and *The Road to Power* were also bestsellers in the Russian socialist movement. In this context, Kautsky was seen as the leading radical and opponent of the revisionist trend internationally, not as the conservative he would later become.

For reasons of space and emphasis I cannot fully respond to Blanc's political outline of Kautskyism, which certainly has its problems, including the view that Kautsky did not adhere to an "evolutionist and economic determinist conception of Marxism" (p.50). Readers interested in exploring the relative strengths and weaknesses of Kautsky's politics prior to 1909 should read an article by Darren Roso in an earlier edition of this journal.[2] Instead I will try to distil the elements of Kautskyism which Blanc leans on in his account of the Russian revolutionary movement.

Crucially for Blanc, he identifies that revolutionary social democrats made "a sharp distinction...between countries with or without political freedom".

> In countries with civil liberties and parliaments, revolutionary Marxists argued that social democratic parties should focus on patient and peaceful activities such as promoting socialist ideas through the press, building strong party organisations, running in elections to further spread the message, and building trade unions.

Kautsky argued that such a strategy was revolutionary "as long as it was consistently linked to the assertion of the party's final goals" (pp.55–6).

This argument did not hold in countries where open socialist organising was not possible, such as those in the Russian empire. A strategy of patiently accumulating forces was impossible when "the state so

---

1.　Kautsky 1910.
2.　Roso 2017.

frequently smashed attempts to independently organise workers". This led socialists there "to rely more on mass action tactics than their counterparts abroad" (p.56). In a state like Russia, the immediate priority was to establish a bourgeois democratic regime – the "democratic revolution" which was universally seen as the goal of all wings of social democracy prior to 1917.

It also meant that Kautsky advocated armed struggle in Russia to establish democracy, while renouncing it in "Western European democracies", where workers "would generally seek to use existing democratic channels and freedoms to advance their interests" (p.58).

Another of Kautsky's principles was that of class independence. This was manifested in the Second International in debates about forming coalition governments with bourgeois parties, which Kautsky led the charge in opposing. In the Russian context, this played out as a debate about how the working class would lead the democratic revolution, ie, the necessity for "proletarian hegemony" for the revolution to be successfully prosecuted to the fullest extent. This argument is laid out well in Lenin's *Two Tactics of Social Democracy in the Democratic Revolution* (1905) and revolves around the necessity for proletarian leadership in an alliance with the peasantry for such a revolution to succeed.

Regardless of whether Blanc is right to claim that practically all social democrats in Russia agreed with this strategy prior to the defeat of the 1905 Revolution, it is significant that in its aftermath many began to turn towards class collaboration. This included the Mensheviks, the Bund, the Polish Socialist Party (Revolutionary Fraction) and the Ukrainian Social Democratic Party. Those parties that held true to class independence were the Polish Socialist Party (Left), the Social Democracy of the Kingdom of Poland and Lithuania (SDKPIL), the Social Democracy of the Latvian Territory (LSDSP), the Finnish Social Democratic Party (SDP), and the Bolsheviks. All these latter parties subsequently became Communist parties and founding members of the Comintern.

In the chapter titled "Organisation, Mass Action, and Electoral Work", Blanc explores in some depth the significance of mass action for the Russian revolutionary parties aside from Finland. Yet he fundamentally underestimates the significance that engagement with this strategy had for the revolutionary social democrats in Russia. Those parties which maintained a position of class independence increasingly came to centre strikes and protests, while the class-collaborationist parties, seeking to work with the bourgeoisie, increasingly turned against them. Parties like the Mensheviks which made this turn justified their new approach on the basis that the "Western" methods that Kautsky argued for in "democratic" states had become relevant in Russia after the creation of the Duma (p.129). Blanc quotes Krupskaya in her memoirs on the significance of this issue:

> The method of agitation based on the workers' everyday needs struck deep root in our Party work. I did not fully appreciate how efficacious this method was until years later, when, living in France as a political emigrant, I observed how, during the great strike of the postal workers in Paris, the French Socialist Party stood completely aloof from it. It was the business of the trade unions, they said. In their opinion the business of a party was only political struggle. *They had no clear idea whatever about the necessity of combining the economic with the political struggle* [my emphasis] (p.95).

Yet Blanc passes over this observation without comment. Later in the chapter, Blanc discusses the broader strategic commitment of the revolutionary social democrats in Russia to mass action, highlighting that this was not a personal invention of Lenin's: "Bolsheviks as well as their non-Russian allies consistently promoted bottom-up action in all regions, stressing that collective disruption and the creativity of the working people was the motor driving the revolution forward, as well as the basis for building a new state of and for working people". Blanc quotes Lithuanian socialist leader Peteris Stucka only days after the February Revolution, stating that "six months in the life of a revolution equals the same as decades of peaceful development" (pp.135–6). This evidence makes clear that social democrats in Russia who maintained a class struggle approach, again with the exception of Finland, developed a practical and theoretical reliance on mass action. Instead of admitting that this strategic reliance on mass action *distinguished in practice* the revolutionary social democrats in the Russian empire from many other social democratic parties elsewhere, and from the Russian social democrats' own theoretical starting point in Kautskyism, Blanc instead argues that a strength of Kautskyism was its ability to apply different tactics in different contexts.

This downplays the significance of the practical merger of economic and political action which the revolutionary social democrats' reliance on mass action pioneered. In Kautsky's debate with Rosa Luxemburg on the mass strike in 1905, it was abundantly clear that he had no grasp on the transformative and revolutionary dynamics of mass action on workers' consciousness. Instead, he understood it as a tool of political struggle, which could be utilised only when constitutional methods were blocked (which was, after all, his basis for supporting revolutionary methods in Russia). This is crucial because it bears on the entire premise for how revolutionary change can occur. Is it a process of working-class self-emancipation, where the revolutionary workers organised in factory committees, workers' councils and unions learn through their own experience their ability to reshape society, and ultimately to rule it themselves? Or is workers' activity just subsidiary to, and in service of, the efforts of reformers in the capitalist state?

Blanc agrees with Kautsky that mass action is an optional extra, an at times useful tool that is not necessary in forging a revolutionary party and revolutionary working class (p.183). This is demonstrated most of all in his account of Finland 1917–18, which he sees as a vindication of Kautsky's strategy of "patient and peaceful" activities.

### Re-litigating the Finnish Revolution

In an earlier article in the *Marxist Left Review*,[3] I went through earlier writings by Blanc on the Finnish revolution and addressed his primary contention that the SDP should serve as a model for socialists today. Readers interested in an over-arching revolutionary socialist narrative of the revolution should read that piece alongside John Newsinger's excellent contribution in *International Socialism*.[4]

---

3.   Hart 2018.
4.   Newsinger 2018.

In general, Blanc outlines quite accurately the perspective of the Finnish SDP leadership, including its left wing. This left held to Kautskyist politics, described by one of its leaders as "1) peaceful, continuous but not revolutionary class war, and at the same time 2) an independent class-war, seeking no alliance with the bourgeoisie".[5] As Blanc eloquently says of this current, it

> focused its efforts on the parliamentary and trade union arena, [and] it saw the mass movement as useful for generating pressure to push through a platform of radical reforms... [C]oncerned not to lose their influence over the increasingly militant wings of Finnish workers, Finland's leading revolutionary SDs supported – or at least went along with – the surge from below (pp.141–2).

Blanc argues that this approach was vindicated because the Finnish SDP leaders eventually launched an armed struggle which, in defeat, led to the deaths of approximately 30,000 working-class people, the majority due to massacres and starvation in concentration camps. He criticises the views of myself and other historians who have labelled the Kautskyist leadership as fatalistic and forced by the rising tide of reaction into seizing power without adequate preparation. He argues that such views are themselves ironically fatalistic, as we "problematically assume that certain objective circumstances on their own are sufficient to compel socialists to lead a workers' revolution" (p.313).

This misunderstands a revolutionary critique of the Kautskyists. It is not that their commitment to independent working-class organisation and principled refusal to capitulate to the bourgeoisie did not contribute to the development of the Finnish Revolution. Rather, the argument is that to actually *lead* a victorious insurrection and civil war, the Finnish SDP needed a perspective which actually aimed at seizing power and furthering workers' self-activity. In Russia the Bolsheviks and other revolutionaries actually *led* the soviets, factory committees, and unions in the struggle. It is abundantly

---

5.    Kuusinen 1919, p.7.

clear, and admitted openly by Blanc, that the Finnish SDP tailed equivalent bodies during their own revolution, such as the Trade Union Federation (SAJ), the Helsinki Workers' Council, and the Red Guard. For instance, the Helsinki Workers' Council called on the SDP to organise the Red Guard nationally 44 days before the SDP did so. The SAJ sent an ultimatum on food supply to the newly elected bourgeois Finnish government and threatened an insurrectionary general strike well before the SDP took action. Finally, the Red Guard acted as a pressure group on the SDP leaders, demanding that they lead an insurrection.

It bears repeating that the failure of the SDP to take power during the November general strike was not just a fair enough decision to make in fraught circumstances as Blanc portrays it (p.144). The congress of the SAJ which met to declare the strike on 14 November is described in Anthony Upton's history of the revolution as *unanimous* in deciding to launch a struggle "for the ruling power in the land [to be] suppressed... the battle for victory or death". Not only was the general strike a total victory for the spontaneous activity of the workers against a weak Finnish bourgeoisie, but a majority of the Revolutionary Council set up by the SDP, Red Guards and SAJ voted 14–11 for the seizure of power. The Kautskyist faction of SDP leaders, including Kuusinen, Sirola and Manner, totally betrayed this movement of the class-conscious proletariat by refusing power despite the *clear and unambiguous will of the workers*. This stab in the back by the Kautskyists sapped the courage of the union leaders and Red Guardists, who, faced with unanimous opposition by every SDP representative on the Revolutionary Council, abandoned their plans for insurrection.[6]

It is scandalous for Blanc to compare this clear-cut betrayal of the workers to the decision of the Bolsheviks in Petrograd or other cities throughout the empire not to seize power when they were in an isolated minority, such as the July Days of 1917. A more genuine comparison would have been if Zinoviev and Kamenev had won the argument after the Second Congress of the Soviets in October for the Bolsheviks to accept a minority stake in a combined socialist government led

---

6. The best account of these events can be found in Upton 1980, pp.149–62.

by Mensheviks and Socialist-Revolutionaries, despite the clearly expressed will of the millions of workers and peasants who backed a Bolshevik government.

There are clear differences between the revolutionary social democrats in the broader Russian empire and the Finnish social democrats in Blanc's own account. The former emphasised mass action and working-class self-activity, whereas the latter subordinated the mass struggle of the workers to the parliamentary struggle. Blanc clearly shows that the SDP argued for the parliament as the arena in which social change could take place, despite the contradiction *in practice* of the SDP leading an uprising after *losing an election*. By insisting that the revolution was not about which class would rule, but instead about "restoring democracy", the SDP restrained workers' consciousness even when they did rise up.[7]

## The Russian Revolution

Blanc's account of the revolution in Russia is an attempt, like the entirety of his book, to separate the revolutionary movement from its own self-assessments. Whereas books and pamphlets written by members of the Bolsheviks and the Third International during and after the revolution in order to explain the significance of the first workers' revolution to take state power are dismissed, we are told that the ideas that Kautsky himself had already abandoned by 1917 were of greater significance. With this marvellous method, Blanc blithely insists that *State and Revolution*, written by Lenin in September 1917, is an unimportant text for the revolution. Blanc doesn't go through every piece of writing written by the Bolsheviks or early Third International he disagrees with, instead favourably citing a 1985 article by James White which suggests that Trotsky's *History of the Russian Revolution* (1918) and John Reed's *Ten Days that Shook the World* were self-justifying propaganda and therefore unreliable histories of the revolution (p.392). Blanc justifies his own dismissal of the Third International's politics by saying that "the real strategic break among revolutionary social democrats...came well after October, when the Bolsheviks began

---

7.    Kuusinen 1919, pp.18–19.

to theoretically justify their ad hoc domestic decisions and when they started to export abroad a soviet model of revolution" (p.391). According to this view, Lenin was able to produce a theoretical justification of "ad hoc domestic decisions" for the first successful workers' revolution before that revolution had even succeeded! Far-sighted indeed.

To show that the Bolsheviks were fighting for a democratic revolution rather than socialism in 1917, Blanc illustrates quite well the continuities between the position of the Bolsheviks prior to Lenin's return in April and afterwards. Blanc shows that there was already widespread support for a soviet government among the Bolsheviks and hostility to the Provisional Government prior to April. This makes perfect sense, since out of the 1905 revolution the Bolsheviks had already concluded that the soviets were the embryo of the "democratic dictatorship" of workers and peasants and were hostile to any government with bourgeois parties (pp.373–5). Instead, Blanc argues that this continuity means that the Bolsheviks were not "arguing for socialism" prior to taking power in October, but for a straight democratic revolution. The point here is to show that the Russian Revolution has limited international application, especially in countries that already possess democratic institutions.

It could be said that it was a measure of the strength of Bolshevik implantation in the working class that they largely posed their propaganda concretely, even in a revolution. But this is very different from Blanc's claim that "it is not factually accurate to claim that the Bolsheviks or their allies saw [the revolution as socialist] for most of 1917" (p.390). Let's see what the Bolsheviks saw in the revolution of 1917.

In May 1917, Bukharin wrote:

> [T]he conquest of political power by the proletariat will, under the existing circumstances, no longer mean a bourgeois revolution, in which the proletariat plays the role of the broom of history. The proletariat must henceforth lay a dictatorial hand upon production, and that is the beginning of the end of the capitalist system.[8]

---

8.   Bukharin 1917.

At the Sixth Congress of the RSDLP (Bolsheviks) on 30 July in Petrograd, Stalin said:

> Some comrades say that since capitalism is poorly developed in our country, it would be utopian to raise the question of the socialist revolution... [T]he workers could not, without committing political suicide, abstain from actively interfering in the economic life of the country in favour of socialist changes. It would be rank pedantry to say that Russia should "wait" with socialist changes until Europe begins".[9]

In September 1917, Trotsky wrote in *Pravda*:

> [T]hose who are of like mind with Comrade Martov, in opposition to us, deny the social-revolutionary character of the political task. Russia, they declare in their platform, is not yet ready for Socialism, and our function is necessarily limited to the founding of a democratic bourgeois republic. The whole attitude is based on a complete rejection of the international problems of the proletariat. If Russia were alone in the world, Martov's reasoning would be correct. But we are engaged in carrying out a world revolution, in a struggle with world imperialism, with the tasks of the world proletariat, which includes the Russian proletariat.[10]

In May 1917, Lenin wrote in the newspaper *Volna* that the Bolsheviks were "for socialism. The Soviets must immediately take all possible practicable steps for its realisation."[11]

In *The Impending Catastrophe and How to Combat it* (October 1917), Lenin wrote:

> Either we have to be revolutionary democrats in fact, in which case we must not fear to take steps towards socialism. Or we fear to take steps towards socialism, condemn them in the Plekhanov,

---

9. Stalin 1954a.
10. Trotsky 1917.
11. Lenin 1964.

> Dan or Chernov way, by arguing that our revolution is a bourgeois revolution, that socialism cannot be "introduced", etc., in which case we inevitably sink to the level of Kerensky, Milyukov and Kornilov, i.e., we in a reactionary-bureaucratic way suppress the "revolutionary-democratic" aspirations of the workers and peasants.[12]

While the Bolsheviks clearly saw the viability of the workers' revolution in Russia as bound up with the international revolution, they clearly assessed that socialism was on the agenda. Blanc is flatly and bizarrely wrong on this score. Given that Blanc also understands that the Bolsheviks and their allies conceived "of socialist revolution as a single international process" (p.338), it is even more confusing that he attempts to draw a line between the "democratic" and "socialist" revolution in Russia.

The most class-conscious workers in Russia understood that their ability to pass over into a socialist society was conditioned on the success of the international revolution. The resolution adopted by the Petrograd Soviet of Workers' and Soldiers' Deputies that met immediately after the overthrow of the Provisional Government, for instance, spoke of their "unshakeable conviction" that the "workers' and peasants' government...will firmly advance towards socialism, the only means of saving the country". Furthermore "the Soviet is convinced that the proletariat of the West European countries will help us to achieve a complete and lasting victory for the cause of socialism".[13] Speaking at a public meeting in Moscow in April 1918, just after the defeat inflicted by the Brest-Litovsk treaty, Trotsky reminded his audience that

> to establish at last, for the first time, such an order upon this earth as would do away, on the one hand, with the man bent and oppressed and on the other, with he who rides on the back of his fellow-men... All this we can and shall realise completely only when the European working class support us.[14]

---

12.  Lenin 1977.
13.  Lenin 1972.
14.  Trotsky 1918, p.18.

The second pillar of Blanc's argument for Kautsky's "orthodox" Marxism over the interpretation of the revolution offered by the Third international is that

> the major socialist debates on revolutionary power in 1917 did not revolve around the question of whether the Russian Revolution was "democratic" or "socialist" in nature, nor whether a soviet government was a higher form of democratic rule than a parliamentary regime... [T]he fundamental political question facing socialists in 1917 was: Was it necessary to ally with or break from the bourgeoisie? (p.379).

Again, this amounts to a denial by Blanc that revolutionary social democratic, and even general working-class consciousness, was impacted by the experience of the revolution and the World War. True, the argument for "all power to the soviets" was an argument for a government of workers and peasants that excluded the bourgeoisie. But clearly the conclusion drawn by the Bolsheviks was that this amounted to a new form of state – a workers' state, a transitional institution on the path towards communism. This latter point is basically ignored by Blanc. This was the significance of *State and Revolution* and a point never made in Kautsky's writings. Blanc makes out that *only Lenin* understood the significance of the soviets as *new form of state* (p.380). This is clearly wrong and ignores what other leading Bolsheviks wrote before the October Revolution.

In 1973 Stephen Cohen showed that Lenin drew much of his analysis in *State and Revolution* from arguments with Bukharin on the Marxist theory of the state in 1916.[15] Bukharin was the leading Bolshevik active in Moscow during 1917. Stalin wrote in *Rabochy Put* on 13 October that "all power to the soviets" did not just imply a change in "the composition of the Provisional Government" and adding "'socialist' ministers" to it. The Provisional Government was powerless to carry out even the most basic reforms because it had not conducted "a thorough purge of every government institution

---

15. Cohen 1980, pp.39–43.

in the rear and at the front, from top to bottom". For the soviets to take power,

> all "persons in authority" in town and country, in the army and navy, in "departments" and "establishments", on the railways and in post and telegraph offices must be elected and subject to recall... Power to the Soviets means the dictatorship of the proletariat and revolutionary peasantry...an open, mass dictatorship, exercised in sight of all, without plots and underhand dealings.[16]

This is all pretty clear, but I think it is also fair to say that the politics of the Bolsheviks in 1917 were in the process of evolution. The unbelievable flaw in Blanc's account is not that many Bolsheviks and other revolutionary social democrats in the empire did not entirely grasp the significance of their actions during the revolution. Rather, it is that their subsequent attempts to generalise from the revolution were wrong, even in terms of their own ideas. It is axiomatic for Marxists that mass consciousness lags behind mass action, that the theoretical exposition of events generally follows from the events themselves. Lenin made this point at the first Congress of the Comintern in March 1919, when he said:

> [D]uring the first eight months of the Russian Revolution the question of soviet organisation was very much discussed, and the workers did not understand what the new system was and whether the soviets could be transformed into a state machine. *In our revolution we advanced along the path of practice and not of theory.* [my emphasis][17]

The point is that the politics of the Third International represented a theoretical development upon the existing politics of the Bolsheviks and other revolutionary social democrats. It built on the practical experience of the working-class revolutions of 1917–19, an experience

16.   Stalin 1954b.
17.   Quoted in Riddell 1987, p.162.

in which the orthodox social democracy of Karl Kautsky exposed itself to be fundamentally counter-revolutionary.

## The Third International and its relevance

Blanc refuses to ascribe any significance to the fact that all of the parties which he argues held true to Kautskyist revolutionary social democracy during the 1917 revolution became founding members of the Third International. The Latvian social democrats, the Polish Socialist Party (Left), the SDKPIL, the Finns – all formed communist parties and assisted the Bolsheviks in forming the Comintern. Blanc highlights the diversity of revolutionary parties during the revolution itself, as a way of arguing that the course of events was not a vindication of "Leninism", but rather the property of a larger revolutionary social democracy. However, he is curiously silent when it comes to attributing similar agency to those self-same parties in forming the Comintern, the politics of which he ascribes purely to "Leninism".

A reasonable conclusion to draw from the evidence Blanc presents is that the social democrats in the Russian empire who stayed true to a class-struggle programme following the 1905 revolution increasingly developed as a distinct political current, despite their origins in Kautskyism. This current emerged fully and developed more clearly as the Comintern was established, arguing that workers' revolutions everywhere had to smash the state through workers' collective action, up to and including insurrection, and replace it with a workers' state, the dictatorship of the proletariat.

The only exception to this rule was the Finnish social democrats. Yet their experience validates this argument, not Blanc's. For when their exiled leaders formed the Finnish Communist Party, they made clear that they did so after having learned painful lessons from their experience in the revolution.[18]

## Conclusions

Blanc sums up by arguing that the politics of "revolutionary social democracy", i.e. classic pre-1909 Kautskyism, were vindicated by the

---

18.  The most thought-out reflection is Kuusinen 1919.

experience of the Russian Revolution. As Blanc offers no clear advice to modern socialists based on Kautskyism for today, in fact at times denying its relevance at all, it is clear his primary agenda is tearing down revolutionary socialists. To do so he must deny the political conclusions drawn by the very people he is studying.

It is ironic that in trying to develop a "revolutionary" Kautskyism against Lenin, Blanc ends up regurgitating Kautsky's most counter-revolutionary arguments. In 1918, in *The Dictatorship of the Proletariat*, Kautsky argued, like Blanc, that the most heinous crime committed by the Bolsheviks was arguing for a revolutionary strategy internationally.[19] Kautsky, like Blanc, refused to acknowledge the momentous breakthrough represented by the workers' state, and like Blanc, blindly defended the bourgeois system of parliamentary "democracy".

Rather than accepting Blanc's narrative that the revolutionary social democrats of the Russian empire successfully utilised Kautskyism, but then abruptly discarded it after the October Revolution for some apparently self-justifying reason, the evidence Blanc presents makes more sense if the autocratic conditions of the Russian empire are used to explain the development of the revolutionary tradition that became the Third International, ie, revolutionary socialism.

This evolution was marked by several ruptures that led to the cohering of a new revolutionary politics, in particular the First World War, which created conditions for international revolution, and a schism in the international workers' movement. It was out of this experience of anti-war organising that an international current clearly began to be organised which distinguished itself both from the revisionist right wing as well as the Kautskyist centrist wing.

There is much of interest in Blanc's book, but it will be difficult to parse it through his many dubious conclusions. Extending the frame of analysis of the course of the Russian Revolution and the empire's socialist movement beyond central Russia is important and something which should be continued. Identifying the generalised interest and theoretical background of Russia's social democrats in Kautskyism should also help establish the tendencies that explain the later

---

19.   Kautsky 1919.

emergence of the Third International with more precision. Hopefully Blanc's study can motivate revolutionaries to apply themselves to understand the Russian revolutionary movement more deeply in all its geographic richness and political diversity.

## References

Bukharin, Nikolai 1917, "The Russian Revolution and Its Significance", in *The Class Struggle*, Vol. 1, No. 1, May-June. https://www.marxists.org/archive/bukharin/works/1917/rev.htm

Cohen, Stephen 1980, *Bukharin and the Bolshevik Revolution*, Oxford University Press.

Hart, Duncan 2018, "The Lost Workers' Revolution: Finland 1917–1918", *Marxist Left Review*, 15, Summer. https://marxistleftreview.org/articles/the-lost-workers-revolution-finland-1917–18/

Kautsky, Karl 1910 [1892], *The Class Struggle [Erfurt Programme]*, Charles H. Kerr and Co. https://www.marxists.org/archive/kautsky/1892/erfurt/index.htm

Kautsky, Karl 1919 [1918], *The Dictatorship of the Proletariat*, National Labour Press. https://www.marxists.org/archive/kautsky/1918/dictprole/index.htm

Kuusinen, Otto Wille 1919 [1918], *The Finnish Revolution: a Self-Criticism*, Workers' Socialist Federation.

Lenin, VI 1964 [1917], "Political Parties in Russia and the Tasks of the Proletariat", *Collected Works*, Vol. 24, pp.93–106, Progress Publishers. https://www.marxists.org/archive/lenin/works/1917/apr/x02.htm

Lenin, VI 1972 [1917], "Meeting of the Petrograd Soviet of Workers' and Soldiers' Deputies", *Collected Works*, Vol. 26, pp.239–41, Progress Publishers. https://www.marxists.org/archive/lenin/works/1917/oct/25a.htm

Lenin, VI 1977 [1917], "The Impending Catastrophe and How to Combat It", *Collected Works*, Vol. 25, pp.323–69, Progress Publishers. https://www.marxists.org/archive/lenin/works/1917/ichtci/index.htm

Newsinger, John 2018, "'The axe without an edge': social democracy and the Finnish Revolution of 1918", in *International Socialism*, 159, Summer. http://isj.org.uk/the-axe-without-an-edge/

Riddell, John [ed.] 1987, *Founding the Communist International*, Anchor Foundation.

Roso, Darren 2017, "Kautsky: the abyss beyond parliament", *Marxist Left Review*, 14, Winter. https://marxistleftreview.org/articles/kautsky-the-abyss-beyond-parliament/

Stalin, Josef 1954a [1917], "Report of the Political Situation", *Works*, Vol. 3, Foreign Languages Publishing House. https://www.marxists.org/reference/archive/stalin/works/1917/07/26_2.htm

Stalin, Josef 1954b [1917], "Soviet Power" in *Works*, Vol. 3, Foreign Languages Publishing House. https://www.marxists.org/reference/archive/stalin/works/1917/10/13.htm

Trotsky, Leon 1917, "International Tactics" in *What Next? After the July days*. https://www.marxists.org/archive/trotsky/1917/next/index.htm

Trotsky, Leon 1918, *A Paradise in this World*, British Socialist Party.

Upton, Anthony 1980, *The Finnish Revolution 1917–1918*, University of Minnesota.

BEN REID

# The PT, Bolsonaro and Lula's comeback

**Ben Reid**, a long-term socialist activist, has researched and written extensively on Southeast Asian politics. He is the author of *Philippine Left: Political crisis and social change* (2000, Manila and Sydney: Journal of Contemporary Asia).

Perry Anderson, *Brazil Apart, 1964–2019*, Verso, 2021.

Richard Lapper, *Beef, Bible and Bullets: Brazil in the Age of Bolsonaro*, Manchester University Press, 2021.

A S AUTHOR PERRY ANDERSON NOTES, Brazil has often been a country "apart" in many senses. With a population of over 200 million, the eighth largest economy globally, but with a (very unequally divided) per capita income of $9,270, it is a large but still impoverished capitalist state. Somewhat insular and separated from most of Latin America by language, its political life emerged as a major topic of international interest since the election of "right populist" Jair Bolsonaro as president in 2018. Bolsonaro's election also came after a decade and a half of Partido dos Trabalhadores [Workers' Party] (PT) rule.

The PT was considered by many to be the archetype "broad party" of the left that other countries should emulate. Yet as Mick Armstrong pointed out in this journal, its rule ended in the "disaster" of Jair Bolsonaro,[1] which has subsequently become defined by its appalling management of the COVID-19 pandemic. Bolsonaro's approval ratings

---

1. Armstrong 2019.

have collapsed in the polls. In March 2021, the country's supreme court quashed the corruption convictions against the principal historical leader of the PT and ex-President Luiz Inácio "Lula" da Silva. Lula announced he will run against Bolsonaro for President in 2022 and is currently the most popular challenger.

It remains to be seen what will occur. Bolsonaro's rule was the result, arguably, of combined economic and political crises that broke apart the main political blocs in Brazil that had emerged after military rule. The problem was that the left – through the PT – allowed itself to get embroiled in the system. These two books give important insights into these problems, and why many will be rightly sceptical of another Lula presidency.

### "Beef, bible and bullets"

Both texts provide a wealth of information. While Anderson, long-time editor of *New Left Review*, continues his aristocratic disdain for economical sentences, the analysis is sharper. Lapper's prose is crisper, though as an "ex-lefty" *Financial Times* journalist, he too often falls into lazy cliches.

The authors have a long history of engagement with Brazil's culture and history. The title of Lapper's book is an often-used phrase that describes much of the established political class. Oligarchic in character, the political and electoral systems owe much to the country's poorer and more remote north and east. A combination of violence and resource-intensive development keep much of the poor dependent on big landowners and other elite patrons, while appeals to religion consummate the system.

These political machines persist by doling out favours to a poor and fragmented electorate. As Anderson explains, although class had long emerged as a major theme in Brazilian politics,

> conflict between them was always overdetermined by a vast sub-proletariat, urban and rural, living in pre-modern conditions whose existence skewed the system away from a class confrontation to a populist opposition between the rich and poor, in which the poor were as available for demagogic or clientelist

capture by politicians of conservative as they were of radical stamp. (p.145)[2]

The PT originally emerged as a break from this system during a mass upturn in social and political struggles that marked the end of a long period of military rule between 1964 and 1988. Founded in 1980 by trade union militants, the PT initially advanced independent class politics. Its election results were modest, but it increasingly became clear that Lula's huge popularity was one of its biggest assets.

The military eventually negotiated a return to civilian rule after mass protests erupted in 1984 demanding direct elections. With a new constitution adopted in 1988, the first direct election for president occurred the following year. Lula came second, though the winner – the "playboy demagogue from one of the country's oldest and richest political families" Fernando Collor de Melo – quickly floundered. With the PT leading large popular mobilisations, Brazil's Congress impeached Collor for corruption in 1992.

However, it set the scene for the consolidation of a new regime for managing Brazil's society and economy, under the neoliberal presidency of Fernando Henrique Cardoso. While Lula and Collor came from marginal political organisations, Cordosso headed the Partido da Social Democracia Brasileira [Brazilian Social Democratic Party] (PSDB). The PSDB, founded in 1988, was a break from the main bourgeois party, the Partido do Movimento Democrático Brasileiro (PMDB).[3]

The PMDB and the PSDB emerged as the two main players in bourgeois politics, gathering the largest share of congressional seats and governorships. Brazil's party system, however, had little discipline or coherence, with many smaller (mostly right-wing) parties represented.

Cardoso resoundingly won the presidency in 1994 in the wake of his key role in introducing the new currency, the *Real*, slashing inflation

---

2. Unless otherwise indicated, page numbers in the text refer to Anderson 2019.
3. Originally just the MDB, it was the main "big tent" opposition party to the military regime. It added "party" to its name in 1980, before dropping it again in 2017.

and temporarily boosting the income of Brazilians. Still fearful of a Lula presidency, most of the country's business class embraced Cardoso. The cost of the immediate gain was a long period of neoliberal restructuring. By 1998 growing indebtedness resulted in another economic crisis.

## PT in government

By 2002, it was Lula's turn to govern. The PT, however, had long evolved into an electoral machine and it ran in alliance with a minor bourgeois party.

In the wake of Lula's election, he appointed an "unblinkingly orthodox economic team at the Central Bank and Finance Ministry" that implemented even more extreme austerity. The resulting "weak reformism" was based upon an "entente with financial capital and a pact with clientelism". (p.145)

Anderson explains that – much like Italy – Brazil's political system is "serpentine". There are undercurrents of corruption in all facets of political life. The PT lacked a majority in the Congress, so Lula stitched together an alliance with a patchwork of smaller parties through a *mensalão,* a monthly payment to secure votes from these deputies.

By 2005, a scandal broke over these payments. The PT had already undergone a small split, with the Partido Socialismo e Liberdade [Party of Socialism and Liberation] (PSOL) breaking away. Lula survived, however, despite the alienation of some of the PT's better-off voters in the country's south. Lula and the PT even scored a second term in 2006 with an increased share of the vote.

Two factors helped to ensure this. First, "a super-cycle of commodity prices" started in 2005. Demand for Brazil's raw materials increased export income and tax revenue. Second and accordingly, there was a massive expansion in domestic consumption. (p.103)

The PT boosted consumption further through mild social reforms. Increases to minimum wages and pensions, combined with the expansion of cash transfers to the poor through the Bolsa Família program, further lifted incomes. With a cost equivalent to less than 0.5 percent of gross domestic product, the latter resulted in the country's Gini index (measure of inequality) falling from the astronomical 0.58 to the merely catastrophically high 0.538 in a few years. As Jennings notes, there was an enormous expansion of formal sector jobs. Spending on travel and education expanded, with increased access for poorer Brazilians. (Lapper 2021, pp.62–64)

Perhaps the strongest aspect of Anderson's book are his discussions of Portuguese-language sources analysing the Lula years. Daniel Singer argued that Brazil's "sub-proletariat, comprising nearly half – 48 percent – of the population, [was] moved by two principal emotions: hope that the state might moderate inequality, and fear that social movements might create disorder". (p.69) Lula provided stability and passive increases in living standards for the countries' poor that allowed the PT to break through and win the support of the country's more impoverished north and east.

However, Chico de Oliveira provides a darker analysis. Olivera is a veteran Marxist sociologist and was among the founders of the PT, who broke with the party in 2003. He was linked to the current phase of global capitalism and the forestalling of any "meaningful national development project". There was, instead, "a regression, taking Brazil back to earlier cycles of reliance on primary commodities for growth". (p.78) These temporary boom conditions hastened the transformation in the character of the PT:

> [T]he party and the trade-unions…became the apparatus of power on which it rested. The leadership of the CUT (Central Única dos Trabalhadores [Unified Workers' Centre]), …was put in charge of the country's largest pension fund. The cadres of the PT colonised the federal administration, where a Brazilian president has the right of nomination to over 20,000 well-paid jobs… (p.79)

As Anderson notes, the PT "achieved the consent of the dominant to their leadership of society, only to ratify the structures of their own exploitation".

Eventually, Lula's handover of the reins of power to Dilma Rousseff corresponded with the end of the economic boom and a new round of corruption scandals. Upon election, Rousseff made matters worse by introducing austerity measures that "plunged the country into a full-blown recession"[4] and her popularity collapsed.

Yet, the seeds of her political demise had already been laid in 2013. An investigation into suspicious foreign exchange transactions at the *Lava Jato* (car wash) in Brasilia revealed a massive scale of political corruption. The resulting scandal revealed a systematic system of bribery that involved the PMDB, PSDB, the PT and a host of business sector entities.

Utilising a model of judicial activism derived from Italy in the early 1990s, a team of investigators prosecuted a selective anti-corruption campaign. They drip-fed a series of leaks to the media. In the aftermath of the elections, a narrative emerged that Rousseff had relied on corrupt sources to finance her election campaign. By early 2015, 80 percent of the population supported her removal. A right wing-led mass movement emerged on the streets. The base of these groups was among the growing numbers of evangelical protestant followers among Brazil's middle classes. (p.120)

Rousseff's running mate for vice-president in 2014 was Michel Temer – the former PMDB Congress speaker. In early 2016, the *Lava Jato* investigators began to implicate Lula in their investigation, and he was taken into custody. The PMDB abandoned any support for Rousseff's government. On 17 April the Congress voted to impeach her.

Temer easily stitched together a coalition with the PSDB and assumed power that immediately unleashed a torrent of austerity measures. Anderson explains:

> [T]he new regime passed three classical pieces of neo-liberal statecraft in short order (with) legislation freezing social expenditures for twenty years... No sooner was it passed with a two-thirds majority than the country's labour code was comprehensively scrapped... The new rules gave a generalised green light to outsourcing of employment and zero-hour contracts... Next up was radical pension reform, increasing contributions and raising retirement ages, to bring down the

---

4.   World Bank 2021.

costs of constitutionally mandated social security in the name of reducing the national debt. (p.164)

The PT was out of power. The party's membership and base of support had also become demoralised and atomised. Lula had long rejected using popular mobilisation to back up his government's measures in favour of a "pact" with the traditional parties. (p.194) The base that the PT developed amongst the country's poor, moreover, remained "passive beneficiaries of PT rule, which had never educated or organised, let alone mobilised...as a collective force". (p.105)

However, Temer and other PMDB and PSDB leaders could not hide their role in the corruption scandals for long. By 2017 Brazil's Supreme Court issued a wider indictment against Temer and other PMDB leaders. They set the scene for the emergence of Jair Bolsonaro as president.

## Bolsonaro

Bolsonaro had previously been a marginal political player in Brazil's Congress. Circumstances, however, created an unprecedented political opening for him.

An ex-military officer, he had built an electoral base in Rio de Janeiro, among current and former military members. He developed a reputation for controversial speeches, often glorifying the country's dictatorship years. He boosted his evangelical credibility by being baptised in Israel. Like Donald Trump, his family – especially his four sons – were the core of his political machine.

He took over the largely moribund Partido Social Liberal and crafted a campaign harnessing fear of insecurity. As the long-running recession ate away at the PT's support base, Bolsonaro deployed a moralistic rhetoric. The sharper end of Bolsonaro's message focused on "law and order". The deterioration of economic conditions corresponded with an epidemic of crime and violence in the northeast costing some 60,000 lives a year. This was fertile ground for political demagoguery.

The PT attempted to run Lula as its presidential candidate in 2018, pretending until the last moment that he could win. Despite still appealing his convictions, the country's senior judges eventually voted to bar him from running. The PT's new candidate Fernando Haddad lost to Bolsonaro, with the latter winning 55 percent of the vote.

The PMDB and PSDB also lost out. By 2018 they were even more mired in the same catastrophe. The PSDB's candidate (along with a plethora of smaller parties) attracted less than 5 percent support. The PMDB candidate scored barely above 1 percent. In Congress, both parties lost many seats.

Anderson only provides some initial analysis on the likely character of the regime. There is more discussion in Lapper's book, but it too only covers part of 2020.

## What happened next?

Overall, for all Bolsonaro's bluster, his regime quickly deteriorated into farce.

While Bolsonaro may well be characterised as a fascist, his regime quickly became mired in crisis and possessed little ability to implement his full program. That is not to say Bolsonaro was and is no threat at all. The government's policies continued Temer's regressive changes, with large cuts to education spending and pensions in 2019. Although there was considerable mass resistance, the PT and other left and centre-left parties often played an ambivalent role.

However, the regime's defining issue has been its chaotic mismanagement of the COVID-19 epidemic, with Bolsonaro famously dismissing it as a "little flu". In November 2020, he claimed that "All of us are going to die one day... There is no point in escaping from that, in escaping from reality. We have to stop being a country of sissies".[5]

Brazilians did die, with 21 million cases and 519,518 fatalities at the time of writing.[6] Brazil ranks number three among countries with COVID case numbers and second overall for deaths, amounting to a "campaign of terror against black and Indigenous people".[7]

However, Brazil's elites would not overlook the fiasco for long. Anderson warned gravely, in 2019, that Bolsonaro enacted a "return of the Armed Forces to the front of the political stage". (p.181) However,

---

5. Quoted in Stone 2021.
6. Worldometer 2021.
7. Belano 2020.

faced with the COVID fiasco, much of the armed forces hierarchy remained aloof from the regime.

By August 2021, 54 percent of Brazilians rated Bolsonaro as "bad or terrible" compared to just 23 percent as "good or great".[8] Bolsonaro turned to desperate remedies to hold on to power. Despite previously scaling back Bolsa Familia, he recently proposed increasing them by 50 percent.

Then, in April 2021, Brazil's supreme court effectively overturned Lula's convictions for corruption, suddenly sweeping away the basis for the "judicial coup" that helped bring Bolsonaro to power. Two factors enabled the reversal. First, it was clear that Lula and the PT were minor players in the affair compared to the traditional parties in Congress. The press now published thousands of leaked messages, also revealing the extensive and illegal involvement of the United States through the FBI.[9] Second, the growing social crisis meant that sectors of the elite now wanted "anybody but Bolsonaro".

Bolsonaro has hit back, staging a mass rally of 120,000 in São Paulo on 7 September. He has increased his defiant rhetoric, declaring: "I have only three possible fates: arrest, death, or victory. And tell the bastards I'll never be arrested".[10]

It is not clear what direction the struggle will take. Many are now passively waiting for Lula's re-election.

### Where is Brazil going?

Both books are valuable English-language contributions to understanding recent political events. Understandably though, they focus more on how Bolsonaro's regime emerged than what comes next.

With Brazil possibly heading for another Lula presidency, the books make for sobering reading. Compromises with bourgeois political forces dominated the PT's decade and a half in executive power and it only implemented modest social reforms. Moreover, the PT did not organise its hard-won support base among the country's poor. Alongside two waves of corruption scandals, these factors opened an

---

8.   Rosati 2021.
9.   Bourcier and Estrada 2021.
10.  Harris and Pooler 2021.

opportunity for the elite opposition to depose Lula and his successor, at the cost of discrediting much of the political class. While the country's supreme court has now acknowledged that the legal campaign against Lula was flawed, the hard right will not be so easily settled.

On the other hand, evidence suggests that contemporary "right-wing populism" in developed and developing capitalist democracies alike seems unable to implement its more ambitious goals. Once in power, it reverts to the standard neoliberal formula for governing, except even more incompetently.

Where does this leave Brazil's class-struggle left and the worker-peasant masses? Neither book mentions much about the left opposition within and (now largely) outside the PT. More of a federation of factions than a party, it is unclear how much PSOL can play cohering an extra-parliamentary opposition. The party, however, has grown, with its congressional vote increasing to over 2 million, and it has recruited mass movement leaders. Yet even its success has appeared to come at a cost with some elements appearing to want to give free rein to supporting Lula in 2022.

It is with the struggle on the streets that hope for a left solution to Brazil's interminable political and economic crisis resides.

## References

Anderson, Perry 2019, *Brazil Apart: 1964–2019*, Verso.

Armstrong, Mick 2019, "Learning from disaster: The Workers' Party and the left in Brazil", *Marxist Left Review*, 18, Winter. https://marxistleftreview.org/articles/learning-from-disaster-the-workers-party-and-the-left-in-brazil/

Belano, Robert 2020, "Bolsonaro's Coronavirus Response is a Campaign of Terror Against Black and Indigenous People", *Left Voice*, 3 June. https://www.leftvoice.org/bolsonaros-coronavirus-response-is-a-campaign-of-terror-against-black-and-indigenous-people/

Bourcier, Nicolas and Gaspard Estrada 2021, "'Lava Jato', the Brazilian trap", *Le Monde*, 3 November. https://www.lemonde.fr/international/article/2021/04/11/lava-jato-the-brazilian-trap_6076361_3210.html

Harris, B and M Pooler 2021, "Bolsonaro tests Brazilian democracy: 'Only God can take me from presidency'", *Financial Times*, 27 September. https://www.ft.com/content/1770b0f8–3740–45db-a032-eedfdb0f8920

Lapper, Richard 2021, *Beef, Bible and Bullets: Brazil in the age of Bolsonaro*, Manchester University Press.

Rosati, Andrew 2021, "Bolsonaro's Disapproval Reaches Record With Lula Gaining Ground", *Bloomberg*, 18 August. https://www.bloomberg.com/news/articles/2021–08-17/ more-than-half-of-brazilians-disapprove-of-bolsonaro-poll-shows

Stone, Judy 2021, "Covid-19, Brazil's Bolsonaro, And Herd Immunity", *Forbes*, 6 November. https://www.forbes.com/sites/judystone/2021/11/06/ covid-19-brazils-bolsonaro-and-herd-immunity/?sh=42c1f06a5af6

World Bank 2021, "World Development Indicators". https://databank. worldbank.org/source/world-development-indicators (accessed 15 September 2021)

Worldometer 2021, "COVID Live Update: 230,362,559 Cases and 4,723,957 Deaths from the Coronavirus". https://www.worldometers.info/coronavirus/ (accessed 22 September 2021)